Around the Outsider

Essays Presented to Colin Wilson
on the Occasion of his 80th Birthday

Around the Outsider

Essays Presented to Colin Wilson
on the Occasion of his 80th Birthday

Edited by Colin Stanley

BOOKS

Winchester, UK
Washington, USA

First published by O-Books, 2011
O-Books is an imprint of John Hunt Publishing Ltd., Laurel House, Station Approach,
Alresford, Hants, SO24 9JH, UK
office1@o-books.net
www.o-books.com

For distributor details and how to order please visit the 'Ordering' section on our website.

Text copyright: Various contributors 2010

ISBN: 978 1 84694 668 4

A CIP catalogue record for this book is available from the British Library.

Design: Stuart Davies

Printed in the UK by CPI Antony Rowe
Printed in the USA by Offset Paperback Mfrs, Inc

We operate a distinctive and ethical publishing philosophy in all
areas of our business, from our global network of authors to
production and worldwide distribution.

CONTENTS

Preface

Colin Stanley

In the mid 1980s I set about collecting essays from Wilson fans/scholars/friends in order to compile a volume, *Around the Outsider*, to celebrate the thirtieth anniversary of *The Outsider*. This was belatedly published by Cecil Woolf Publishers in 1988 under the title *Colin Wilson, a Celebration: Essays and Recollections*.

It was a book of two halves: the first, a series of essays by friends who had known Wilson back in those early Soho days; and the second, a number of critical assessments of his work to date.

I was fortunate indeed to receive recollections from the two 'Angry Young Men' closest to Wilson: Bill Hopkins and Stuart Holroyd. Also from Tom Greenwell who, during the 1950s and early 1960s, working as a gossip-columnist for the *Evening Standard*, shared a house with them all at no. 25 Chepstow Road, London W2. Another resident at Chepstow Road was novelist John Braine who promised me an essay when I spoke to him in 1986 but, unfortunately, and sadly, died before setting to work. The recently deceased poet John Rety, editor of the 1950s coffee bar magazine *The Intimate Review* (Wilson's first publisher), provided a very evocative piece describing those early days and I also received a memoir from the writer, photographer and broadcaster Daniel Farson. Angus Wilson wrote a short Introduction from his home in France, remembering the Colin Wilson he befriended when Superintendent of the British Museum reading room in the mid-1950s. Laura Del Rivo's contribution came too late to be included in that volume and has been appended to this. From across the Atlantic came contributions from Joyce Carol Oates, Marilyn Ferguson, A. E. van Vogt and Allen Ginsberg.

The current volume does not boast such famous names. It is intended mainly as an academic *festschrift* and, to this end, invitations were sent to known scholars of Wilson's work worldwide. Just two names from the contents list of *Colin Wilson, a Celebration* remain: Nicolas Tredell and myself. Since 1988 Nicolas has maintained his interest in Wilson's work, updating his original book *The Novels of Colin Wilson* (London: Vision Press, 1982) as *Existence and Evolution: the novels of Colin Wilson* (Berkeley CA: Maurice Bassett) and produced a series of penetrating essays on Wilson's fiction for the University of East Anglia's online *Literary Encyclopedia* (www.litencyc.com). As the editor of *Colin Wilson Studies* (ISSN 0959-180-X. Nottingham: Paupers' Press), now into its sixteenth volume, I was obviously in a good position to instigate and coordinate the *festschrift*. Would-be contributors listed their three favourite Wilson titles (or the ones they considered to be the most important) and were then asked to write a 3000-5000 word essay about one of them. As a result, most, but not all of Wilson's interests are covered: in the present volume you will find illuminating essays on Wilson's fiction and non-fiction, including his writings on philosophy, psychology, criminology, literature, and the occult.

My collection of Colin Wilson's work now forms the basis of an archive at Nottingham University, here in the United Kingdom, known as *The Colin Wilson Collection*. It is hoped that this will be opened for the use of scholars and researchers, concurrently with the publication of this celebratory volume, and the author's significant 80th birthday, in June 2011.

The Fiction

Ritual in the Dark (1960)

An Acceptance of Complexity: Ritual in the Dark

Nicolas Tredell

Ritual in the Dark (1960) is an unsung achievement of postwar British fiction. A favourite with Wilson *aficionados* and with the author himself,[1] and probably enjoyed by many readers who find it casually in a bookshop or library knowing little or nothing of Wilson's other work,[2] *Ritual* has never entered the literary canon in the way that Kingsley Amis's *Lucky Jim* (1954) or Alan Sillitoe's *Saturday Night and Sunday Morning* (1958) have. While Wilson's *The Outsider* (1956) usually gets a brief if often dismissive mention in surveys of postwar British culture, *Ritual* hardly ever figures in accounts of British fiction since 1945.[3] But *Ritual* is of considerable value both in its own right and as a harbinger of new developments in the novel. Published in 1960, on the cusp of cultural change, it exemplifies the English novel expanding, taking on larger themes, after the contracted ambitions which seemed to dominate English fiction in 1950s Britain. In that sense *Ritual* anticipates the enlargement of the thematic and formal scope of English fiction which would occur in the 1960s, in the work of, say, Doris Lessing or John Fowles. But it points as well to a road not taken; for while much subsequent British fiction after Lessing or Fowles has been stylistically and formally ambitious – the work, for example, of Martin Amis or Ian McEwan – it has not been, so to speak, existentially ambitious, preferring to avoid explicit engagement with philosophical themes of meaning and being and, insofar as it seeks wider significance, to do so by latching on to large historical events (for instance, the Holocaust, the Gulag, 9/11, the Iraq war). *Ritual* does, implicitly, have something to say about such events (including those which had not happened when it was

3

first published); and it does explicitly deal with themes which remain urgently topical, such as serial killing. But it aims to do so within a wider philosophical perspective. *Ritual* achieves such a perspective, not only by its explicit engagements with ideas, but also by means of its style and narrative technique. These latter aspects of *Ritual* have hitherto been little explored; this essay aims to open them up for further exploration, and in that way to celebrate Wilson's currently undervalued skills as a novelist.

When writing *Ritual*, Wilson was still closely in touch with the work of those Modernist authors who made such an impact on twentieth-century prose style, such as Joyce and Hemingway. His own prose in *Ritual* provides both precision and poetic effect. The quest for precision is evident in this description of Sorme's reporter friend, Bill Payne: '[w]hen he was tired, his skin took on the greenish tint of the albumen of a boiled duck egg' (54). The combination of precise delineation and poetic resonance appears in the evocation of Austin Nunne's 'brown eyes as soft as an animal's and as sardonic and caressing as a heathen god' (248). A different kind of poetic effect – more Audenesque, perhaps – occurs in the simile which captures Sorme's response when Father Carruthers tells Sorme that Franz Stein has received information which suggests Nunne could be the Whitechapel killer: the 'questions piled up in him, obstructing one another like a cumulative accident on an arterial highway' (253). This is an analytical rather than atmospheric image and the phrase 'arterial highway' has an Audenesque quality, calling to mind 1930s poetry. A further kind of poetic effect, surreal and potent, features in the powerful visual correlative for Sorme's sense of the driving force of the Whitechapel murderer. This emerges as he lies on his bed on the afternoon on which he has heard of the Greenwich murder:

[H]e began to see it: in the half darkness, in a warehouse,

an animal like a crab; something flat with prehensile claws. He was aware of nothing else; only the crablike creature, moving silently into the half light; moving strangely, obliquely, but with intention, entirely itself, possessed by an urge that was its identity, entire unification of its being in one desire, one lust, a certainty. It was not a man; it was what was inside a man as he waited. (198)

The most sustained prose flights in *Ritual* are its two major visionary moments – when Sorme is on the roof of his Camden Town boarding house (137-9) and when he is in a bedroom at the Balalaika Club (179-80). Here is an example of one paragraph (the twelfth) from the first moment when Sorme, 'physically tired but curiously excited' (137), is sitting on the slates, 'feet braced against the parapet' (138):

To change. But no physical change. Only a constant intensity of imagination that would require no cathedral symbol to sustain and remind. Isobel Gowdie, big-breasted farmer's wife, sweating and curving to the indrive of an abstract darkness, the warm secretions flowing to abet the entry of a formless evil. To escape the dullness of a Scottish farm by daylight, the time trap. Symbol of the unseen. The unseen being all you cannot see at the moment. Until the consciousness stretches to embrace all space and history. Osiris openeth the storm cloud in the body of heaven, and is unfettered himself; Horus is made strong happily each day. Why the time trap? Why the enclosure? Invisible bonds, non-existent bonds, bonds that cannot be broken because they are non-existent. Human beings like blinkered horses. (139)

The passage starts with an infinitive which takes on something

5

of the force of an imperative. 'To change', coming at the start of this paragraph, set apart by the full stop which follows it, and repeating a phrase which has occurred twice in the previous paragraph but one, implies that change is both a possibility and a necessity (it could be linked with the concluding imperative of Rilke's poem, 'Archaiser Torso Apollos' ('Archaic Torso of Apollo'), 'Du mußt dein Leben ändern' ('You must change your life'). But the next sentence stresses that it is not a question of physical change. The following sentence provides a statement, in rhythmic prose, of Sorme's – and Wilson's – ultimate aspiration: 'Only a constant intensity of imagination that would require no cathedral symbol to sustain and remind'. Here the sibilants in 'constant', 'intensity', 'symbol' and 'sustain' help to bind the sentence together, while the repeated 're' of 'require' and 'remind' provide some stiffening which prevents the sentence from sinking into a mere susurration. The 'cathedral' image here refers back to an earlier paragraph (the tenth) in this section, when Sorme's thoughts 'moved towards an image of gratitude, of reverence, of affirmation' which 'became a cathedral, bigger than any known cathedral, symbol of the unseen' (138). But the passage now expresses the aspiration to transcend that image, to transcend any image, to attain an ongoing imaginative intensity that would be independent of imagery.

This abstract, general statement of Sorme's aspiration is followed by the specific reference to Isobel Gowdie. It is characteristic of the careful planning of *Ritual* that Isobel has been mentioned earlier in the novel and acquires added significance when she recurs in the context of Sorme's vision. Sorme initially refers to her in his first conversation with Father Carruthers when he describes his sexual failure with Kay, the Slade School student:

I thought about something I'd read that day in a book on witchcraft. About a woman called Isobel Gowdie, who claimed she had sexual intercourse with demons while her husband was asleep beside her [...] At least sex *meant* something to her [in contrast to Kay]. She wanted to be possessed by the devil. She was probably bored stiff on a Scottish farm in the middle of nowhere. So she invented demons and devils. (67, Wilson's italics).

Now Isobel Gowdie returns in Sorme's thoughts on the rooftop, vividly rendered in her physicality ('big-breasted', 'sweating and curving', 'warm secretions'). But this physicality is, in a seeming paradox, powered by the imagination, the physically non-existent, the 'indrive' of an 'abstract darkness' ('indrive' is an unusual term, not in the current online Oxford English Dictionary). The sentence achieves a remarkable amalgam of the physical and the imaginative, the concrete and the abstract.

The start of the next sentence, like the first sentence of the paragraph, is an infinitive – 'To escape' – which, in the context, seems to assume some of the force of an imperative. 'To escape' appears to contain an incipient insistence on the necessity of escape. The sentence stays with the example of Isobel Gowdie and with her desire to escape from a specific situation, 'the dullness of a Scottish farm by daylight'; but the phrase at the end of the sentence, 'the time trap', generalizes the situation of entrapment and defines it in terms, not of space, but of *time*. Gowdie's diabolic lovers are also redefined in the next sentence as a 'symbol of the unseen', repeating the phrase used in the tenth paragraph of this section. The following sentence suggests that the 'unseen' is 'all you cannot see at the moment' – implying that the unseen does exist even if it cannot be perceived – and the next sentence goes on to posit that it may become possible at a certain stage of consciousness to see the unseen: 'Until the consciousness stretches to embrace all time and history'. Ancient Egyptian gods are invoked in the subsequent sentence, which has a hieratic quality, like a priestly chant, enhanced by the alliteration of 'Osiris openeth', and 'Horus happily'. The passage then shifts into the interrogative mode to convey a sense of urgent questioning: 'Why the time trap? Why the enclosure?' The repetition of 'bonds' (three times) and of 'non-existent' (twice) in the penultimate paragraph increases the sense of urgency. In the final sentence, the paragraph comes down to earth with the simile of 'blinkered horses', still an everyday sight in the streets of 1950s England.

This is only one paragraph in a more extended section which consists of fifteen paragraphs in all and runs to over two pages in the original edition of *Ritual*. It demonstrates Wilson's control, range and versatility as a prose stylist in fiction. An even more impressive demonstration is provided by the passage evoking Sorme's vision of Nunne as Nijinsky. This could certainly feature in an anthology of high-quality twentieth-century English prose but its effectiveness is compounded when it is read in the context of *Ritual* as a whole. Like the account of Sorme's rooftop vision, it is an extended section, this time consisting of ten paragraphs in all and covering about a page and a half in the original edition of the novel. The following passage starts at the third paragraph and runs through to the end of chapter 8 (which is also the end of Part 1 of the novel):

[Austin] was standing by the window, staring out. In the faint dawnlight, the big naked body looked like a marble statue. The shoulders were broad: rounded muscle, a dancer's shoulders.

Sorme could not see his eyes. They would be stone eyes, not closed, immobile in the half light, nor like the eyes of the priest, grey in the ugly gargoyle's face. When he closed his own eyes he saw the dancer, the big body, moving without effort through the air, slowly, unresisted, then coming to earth, as silent as a shadow. It was very clear. The face, slim and muscular, bending over him, a chaplet of rose leaves woven into the hair, a faun's face, the brown animal eyes smiling at him, beyond good and evil.

Cold the dawnlight on marble roofs, more real than the jazz. You're gonna miss me, honey. Glass corridors leading nowhere.

And then the leap, violent as the sun on ice, beyond the bed, floating without noise, on, through the open window.

The excitement rose in him like a fire. The rose, blood-black in the silver light, now reddening in the dawn that blows over Paddington's roof-tops. Ending. A rose from an open window, curving high over London's waking roof-tops, then falling, its petals loosening, into the grey soiled waters of the Thames.

He wanted to say it, with the full shock of amazement: So that's who you are!

Certain now, as never before, the identification complete.

It was still there as he woke up, the joy and surprise of the discovery, fading as he looked around the lightening room. He said aloud: Vaslav. (179-80)

Like the description of Isobel Gowdie in Sorme's rooftop vision, the above passage starts by stressing the physicality of 'Nunjinsky' (as this composite figure will hereafter be called); but in contrast to Isobel's sweaty, sinuous fleshiness, this is cool and classical, with the quality of a stone sculpture and a sense of poised athletic strength at rest but ready for action. In one of the many internal echoes in *Ritual* which deepen the resonance of the novel, the phrase 'the eyes of the priest, in the ugly grey gargoyle's face', refers back to Sorme's first impression of Father Carruthers's face as having 'the strong lines of a gargoyle' and 'small, almost colourless eyes' (61). This echo serves to point up

9

a contrast with the petrifaction and inferred immobility of Nunjinsky's eyes. Then Sorme's own eyes close and the sense of statuesque immobility, in the body and eyes of Nunjinsky, gives way, in Sorme's dream-vision, to movement. The rhythm and arrangement of the prose contribute to conveying the quality of this movement. Using present participles ('moving', 'coming') rather than finite verbs ('moved', 'came') enhances the impression of motion, while placing the adverbs 'slowly' and 'unresisted' in between the two phrases which employ those present participles slows down the sentence, holding it suspended momentarily in a way that is analogous to the suspension of the dancer during his leap. The sense of silence, of softness in his coming to earth is reinforced by the sibilants in 'slowly', 'unresisted', 'silent' and 'shadow'. Then a short, simple declarative sentence follows – 'It was very clear' – which encapsulates the clarity of Sorme's dream-vision. Despite the sense of silence and softness, there is nothing vague about it. The next sentence moves into close-up mode, linking Nunjinsky with the Spectre of the Rose, the faun of Debussy's and Mallarmé's afternoon, and Nietzsche's *Beyond Good and Evil*.

From this point, the paragraphs get shorter, as the scene moves towards its climax. The next paragraph starts by reemphasizing the impending dawn and is followed by another reference back, to the jazz Sorme heard in the Balalaika Club earlier that night (173) and to a demotic line from a song lyric. Then there is the image, both surreal and cinematic of '[g]lass corridors leading nowhere', suggesting a kind of entrapment in a transparent maze. The following paragraph starts with an act whose definitive nature is brought home more sharply by being presented as a noun preceded by a definite article ('the leap') rather than a pronoun and finite verb ('he leapt'). The simile of 'the sun on ice' conveys the primal force of the act. The sense of answering motion in Sorme is reinforced by the verb 'rose' and there is a play on words as 'rose' recurs in the next section as a noun. The chromatic connotations of 'rose' as a flower are developed in a vivid palette of related colours ('bloodblack', 'silver', 'reddening'). Then present participles comes to the fore here to enhance the sense of parabolic motion and of a dying fall into the river ('curving', 'falling', 'loosening'). The passage climaxes in a recognition scene which unfolds in Sorme's dream-vision and is confirmed verbally on waking, the actual name withheld until the last, clinching word: 'Vaslav' (in a further internal echo, this recalls the toast 'To Vaslav' proposed by Sorme and endorsed by Nunne earlier in the evening (167)). This identification is the culmination of the process that began with Sorme's encounter with Nunne in the queue for the Diaghilev exhibition at the start of the novel.

The disciplined and evocative prose of *Ritual* is matched by a skilful narrative technique which may show the influence of another writer whom Wilson had discussed in *The Outsider*: Henry James. In an article published in *The Twentieth Century* in December 1959, written while he was marking up the proofs of *Ritual*, Wilson acknowledges his 'admiration' for James which in his teens, when he was drafting the early versions of his first novel, 'amounted to adoration' (493). The published version of *Ritual* employs an approach like that of James's scenic method. The scenes in Wilson's first novel – particularly those which show Sorme with Nunne, with Gertrude and with Glasp – are closely attentive to the subtle changes of mood and perception which occur in interpersonal encounters.

In *Ritual* Wilson adopts another technique associated with James: the use of a narrator who eschews an omniscient perspective and presents the actions through the point of view of a protagonist. *Ritual* is told in the third person but from Sorme's viewpoint – or, to put it another way, the action and themes of the novel are focalized through Sorme. In *Ritual*, Sorme is a young heterosexual man of twenty-six, 'slightly over six feet tall' (8), fair-complexioned (83) and 'very good-looking'

(21), according to Carl Castering, whom Sorme meets briefly in the French pub (the York Minster) in Soho and who compares Sorme's looks to those of Arthur Rimbaud (Castering, whom Nunne calls 'one of the best photographers in London' (21), is a cameo of the real-life photographer John Deakin [4]). It perhaps befits Sorme's Rimbaudian good looks that he is, in his own words, 'scruffy' (12) – baggy trousers (99), frayed turnups, leather strips sewn on to his jacket cuffs (14), hair in need of cutting (99).

Through Sorme's memories and some of his remarks we gain a fragmentary picture of his past. His family comes from, and still live in, Yorkshire (12, 340). When he was a child, his parents used to say he was 'born lucky' and he 'always felt lucky, fundamentally' (134). He is vague about his religious upbringing but supposes it was Church of England (26). He took instruction as a Catholic but did not pursue it, partly because he found his instructor, Father Grey, a hearty priest with no sympathy for mysticism, off-putting (62). He did National Service in the RAF (97, 134). He worked for a year as a clerk in a city office with a belligerent, anti-Semitic Scot as a colleague. He left that job without notice five years ago, after receiving a solicitor's letter informing him that he had been left a legacy which would provide him with a small private income (140-1). Since then, he has lived in boarding houses (in Whitechapel (145) and in a basement in the Marylebone Road (207) before *Ritual* starts, in Colindale when it begins (19), and then in Camden Town for the rest of the novel). Free of the need to work, he has occupied himself by reading 'mystical theology' (158) – 'Plotinus and St. Francis de Sales and the rest' (149) – in his room or in the British Museum Reading Room, writing or trying to write, and striving to achieve a vision of power, meaning and purpose.

It is interesting to consider what we are *not* told, at least not directly, about Sorme, since this helps to highlight Wilson's thematic priorities in *Ritual*. Despite his Yorkshire provenance, there is no indication that he speaks with a Northern accent (unlike Glasp, who has what Sorme thinks at first is a faint Yorkshire accent (146) which sometimes becomes more marked (152, 202), though Nunne tells Sorme that Glasp is Liverpool Irish, from Lancashire (170)). Apart from Sorme's remark that his parents told him he was 'born lucky', nothing else is disclosed about his childhood (certainly nothing resembling the fraught childhood and adolescence that Wilson himself had, despite Sorme's closeness in many respects to his creator). There is no direct indication of Sorme's class background, though his gastronomic gaucheness suggests he is unused to the high life; he needs instruction in how to eat escargots from Caroline (116) and how to eat asparagus from Nunne (167) and he drinks brandy from a brandy glass for the first time at Gertrude Quincey's (80-1). We are also told nothing directly about Sorme's educational background, but there is no indication that he attended university; it does not come up anywhere in the novel, even on the occasion on which he might most naturally talk about it, when Nunne is speaking of the premature death of Nigel Barker, a fellow-student at Oxford (132-3). Other than his job in a city office, we learn nothing of Sorme's previous employment history. His dislike of 'the memories aroused by the scaffolding' supporting the entrance tent wall at the Diaghilev exhibition (8) suggests that he may have worked at some point on a building site, but no further information is given about these 'memories'. Sorme is not provided with a comprehensive backstory and there is a sense that, like F. Scott Fitzgerald's Jay Gatsby, he springs 'from his Platonic conception of himself' (77).

Ritual is not a self-consciously symbolic novel, but it does have recurrent motifs and concerns which help to bind it together and to enhance its significance. As the protagonist and sole viewpoint character, these motifs are focused through Sorme. One key motif is that of violence. In the opening paragraph of the novel, we learn that the London crowds affront Sorme and that if 'he allowed himself to notice them, he found himself thinking: Too many people in this bloody city; we need a massacre to thin their numbers' (7). When he goes to see his eccentric fellow-tenant Mr Hamilton, he feels 'suddenly violently angry, and would have enjoyed snatching up the gramophone and smashing it on the perspiring bald head' (38). When Glasp's landlady shuts the door on him, Sorme feels 'an irritable rage at her rudeness, and had to restrain a desire to kick the door' (401). But Sorme never commits an act of violence and has no real wish to cross the line from aggressive fantasy to brutal reality. Indeed, this is also established in the first paragraph of *Ritual*, when we are told that Sorme's thoughts of massacre make him feel sick: 'he had no desire to kill anyone' (7).

Sorme's sick feeling after his thoughts of massacre exemplifies a further recurrent feature of *Ritual*: the way in which responses are registered viscerally, in the digestive system, the stomach and bowels. After talking about the Whitechapel murders with Bill Payne and Martin Mason, Sorme's 'stomach felt watery and rebellious' (58). As Sorme prepares to explore Nunne's basement flat further, excitement produces 'a watery sensation in the bowels' (106). When he turns over a book on criminology, he sees a photograph of a woman with her throat cut which makes him feel sick. A little later, he makes himself look through the photographs of murder victims in the book and experiences 'a heaviness of continual disgust in his stomach' (108-9). On reading of the murder of Doris Elizabeth Marr in Greenwich, a 'peculiarly unpleasant sensation touched him with disgust' – a 'hot, sticky feeling in the area of his stomach' (197). At the scene of the double murder in Whitechapel, 'fear and excitement stirred his intestines' (214). A little later, the thought that, 'somewhere in London', the murderer was still free produced 'a lurching sensation of the stomach' (222). The most vivid digestive reaction occurs in the scene at the Balalaika Club, where Sorme, after eating chicken, mayonnaise and asparagus and drinking champagne and whisky, feels 'as if something flat and alive, something with legs, turned itself slowly in the pit of his stomach' (176) and vomits violently three times. This is a kind of purgation which helps to prepare him, physically and psychologically, for his vision of Nunne as Nijinsky.

A further recurrent motif in *Ritual* is fire. At the end of the first paragraph, the half-clothed forms in the advertisements on London tube escalators for women's corsets and stockings give Sorme 'an instantaneous shock, like throwing a match against a petrol-soaked rag' (7). This is an experience which combines pain and power, but fire is also associated with power and pleasure when, in a room at the Diaghilev exhibition, Sorme hears the final dance from Stravinsky's *The Firebird* and again sustains a shock, but this time an agreeable one. 'It sent a warm shock of pleasure through the muscles of his back and shoulders, and stirred the surface of his scalp' (9). Metaphorical fire becomes literal on two major occasions in *Ritual*. On Sorme's third day in his new boarding house, in a vividly realized scene, he puts out a dangerous fire started by Mr Hamilton, the tenant of the room above his (43-5). The fire here provides Sorme with a means of self-definition; he shows that he can be a man of action as well as an intellectual. The second major literal fire in *Ritual* offers Sorme a further occasion for self-definition, this time of a verbal kind: it is the one which students light on a London bomb site where they intend to have a party (119-21). When Sorme goes to this fire with Caroline, he is disgusted by what he sees as the adolescent antics of the students, especially of a former boyfriend of Caroline's, Ivor Fenner, who leaps back and forth across a tree trunk at the centre of the flames; but when the fire brigade extinguishes the blaze, he 'revolts automatically at the idea of the authority that could put an end to the party' (120). He sums up his contradictory attitude by describing himself, to Caroline, as an 'authoritarian anarchist' (121).

As an image, fire figures in the account of Sorme's dream-vision of 'Nunjinsky' from which we have already quoted. As Sorme sees the dancer leap through the open window, '[t]he 'excitement rose in him like a fire' (180). Fire provides a memorable simile when Nunne, speaking frankly of his sadism, though not yet of sadistic murder, says: 'You feel like a carpet when a lighted coal's fallen on it – just a hole where the heart should be, with burn round the edges' (128). Stein later tells Sorme that Nunne may have been responsible for setting fire to a haystack when he entered an Alsace monastery after (possibly) killing a male prostitute, and links Nunne with Peter Kürten, who 'liked setting fire to things – especially haystacks. The sight of fire acts as a stimulant to many sadists' (395). But it is the sight of a woman who has suffered death by fire which stimulates Sorme in a different way, making him finally reject Nunne. When Stein takes Sorme to the mortuary to view the Whitechapel killer's latest victim, Sorme cannot connect the gashed corpse with a living being, finding it 'impersonal', 'too dead', 'meaningless'; it is only when he looks at a neighbouring corpse, a woman killed when her husband threw a paraffin lamp at her, that he experiences 'a recognition of humanity'. 'Where the charred flesh came to an end, the skin was burnt and raw. Fragments of clothing still adhered to her legs and arms. The fascination was one of pity and kinship' (398). Here the powerful destructive force of fire is written on the body; and it brings Sorme to a new comprehension of 'death by violence' as 'a complete negation of all our impulses' (411).

References to water and washing also feature in *Ritual*. At several significant moments, Sorme washes himself and while this has an obvious practical function – particularly in view of the limited ablutionary facilities at his boarding house – it is reiterated to such an extent that it becomes more than a mere realistic detail and takes on a slightly ritualistic quality. In the midst of the hectic activity of the novel, it provides occasions for solitude and self-collection. On his first visit to Gertrude Quincey's, Sorme 'washed his hands at the basin, humming quietly' (27). At the British Museum, he goes to the 'downstairs lavatory' where he 'washed his hands and face in hot water, and returned to the Reading Room feeling cooler.' (158). When he is in Gertrude Quincey's house with Caroline Denbigh, he goes to the bathroom where 'he stripped off his pullover and shirt, and washed his chest and neck with warm water' (162). Awaking from sleep and recalling he has a lunch appointment, he goes to the bathroom where 'he plunged his face into a bowl of cold water and blew vigorously, to clear his head. He stripped to the waist and washed' (183). Back in his room with Glasp after leaving a pub, he 'filled the washbowl with hot water, then plunged his hands into it and leaned forward on them, suddenly tired' (276-7). Waking up around 2 am after dreaming of the old man in the room above, Sorme 'went downstairs to the bathroom, and washed his hands and face in water' (298). Sorme's washing is, unsurprisingly, particularly elaborate after his close encounter with fire and smoke when he puts out the blaze in Hamilton's room. He goes up to the kitchen, where 'he turned the tap on full, and held his head underneath it. He pulled off the pyjama jacket and rubbed his body with a wet sponge, which soothed his hot flesh with a luxurious coolness' (44-5). Sorme's most complete immersion, however, occurs at Gertrude Quincey's, where he takes a bath, a kind of vicarious intimacy with Gertrude which anticipates his later lovemaking with her and provides an opportunity for more extended reflection on his situation (191).

Sleepiness is a fifth recurrent feature of the novel. After an hour in the Diaghilev exhibition, the 'heat was making [Sorme] sleepy' (9). When he finally gets to bed after his first meeting with Nunne, '[s]leep came quickly and easily' (33). After unpacking in his new room the next day, he falls into a doze from which the whistle of the kettle awakens him (34) and, later, he finds that the 'heat was making him drowsy' (35). Two days later, he is again in his room and, as he drinks a cup of tea, 'he began to feel sleepy', despite the fact that, as he thinks to himself, he did not get up until eleven o'clock. When he resists the impulse to lie down and close his eyes, he feels 'immediately overwhelmed by the desire to sleep' (71). He forces himself to do more unpacking, restraining the sleepiness which returns, but he finally lies on the bed and falls asleep (73). After emerging from his exploration of Nunne's basement flat, he finds that '[s]ilence and the sense of uncertainty had left him tired' (109). In an Underground train on his way back from a meeting with Father Carruthers, he comes close to falling asleep, wipes 'the tears out of his eyes with his handkerchief', and 'immediately' yawns again (115). In the British Museum Reading Room, he finds that 'the warmth was making him sleepy' (159). The morning after his exhausting visit to the Balalaika Club, he falls asleep in his room while thinking about Oliver Glasp's impending visit that evening, and his head is still 'thick with sleep' when he wakes up (183). After lunch with Gertrude Quincey on the same day, he falls asleep in front of the electric fire while she is making coffee (185). When Bill Payne rings him late that night to ask if he wants to go out with them to do a news story on the Greenwich murder, Sorme says 'I'm deadly sleepy' (211). At Gertrude Quincey's again, Sorme finds that the 'wine he had drunk with Glasp had made him feel sleepy' (329). Sleep and sleepiness tend to be negative terms in Wilson's total oeuvre – one of his main emphases is that human beings are not fully awake and should be conducting a more vigorous 'war against sleep' (the subtitle of his 1980 book about Gurdjieff). But the narcoleptic moments in *Ritual* have a more positive effect, seeming to form part of Wilson's concern with those states of consciousness in which the pressure of everyday reality recedes and possibilities of richer perceptions emerge. In *Ritual,* sleep is sometimes the gateway to hypnagogic images (like that of the force that drives the Whitechapel killer) and to dreams and to visions (like that of Nunne as Nijinsky).

Ritual is also a novel about writing. As well as being a homosexual, a sadist and a serial killer, Nunne is a writer, who has, according to Gertrude Quincey, published three books – Sorme has read two of them (11) – and is starting to build a reputation as a journalist (82). Father Carruthers has written a book on Chekhov (31) and Franz Stein one on Kürten (375). Sorme calls himself a writer and the reader is invited to take him seriously in that role, but as yet he has published little – only 'a few poems in magazines' (25). Despite this incipient poetic career, Sorme's focus seems to be on the novel rather than poetry. When he first meets Nunne, he tells him he is writing a novel about 'Nijinsky's state of mind' – that of someone who, unlike most people, 'believed in himself' (16). Later, in an uneasy encounter with two American beat writers, Cal Teschmeyer and Rudi James, he tells them his novel is about a 'sexual killer' (249), which impresses them, though when Nunne asks Sorme, after Cal and Rudi have left, whether he meant this seriously, Sorme says he 'invented it on the spur of the moment' because it is impossible 'to talk about [one's] work like that, at five seconds notice' (251). Whatever the precise subject of his novel, Sorme seems to be suffering from extended writer's block, or at least from an inability to bring his work to completion; he tells Glasp he has been 'stuck on the same book for five years' and cannot finish it because there is 'something missing' – he suggests it might be 'the inspiration' but this hardly seems intended as a serious diagnosis of the difficulty (205). What is missing, perhaps, is precisely the experiences that Sorme undergoes in the course of *Ritual.* It may be that, in reading *Ritual,* we are reading the novel that Sorme is writing – or that he will write, once those experiences are over and he has achieved a state of interior clarity and 'an acceptance of complexity' (416). *Ritual* in fact tackles both the topics which Sorme specifies for his novel, even if the second topic is a spur-of-the-moment invention: *Ritual* is about both Nijinsky and a sexual killer, figures who come together in the shape of Austin Nunne.

Sorme's search for potency as a writer can be related to his quest for sexual potency. The Sorme who, in *Ritual*, deflowers two virgins within a week may seem like a sexual athlete; but the erotic history which emerges from his own remarks and recollections is more complex. Certainly he is strongly aware of sexual desire; after taking out Caroline for the first time, it strikes him that 'he was hardly ever free of desire; at any hour of the day or night, the thought of a woman could disturb him and arouse the dissatisfaction of lust without an object' (125). He also seems to have been capable in the past of athletic sexual performance. In a conversation with Oliver Glasp, Sorme recalls a girlfriend he had when he 'lived in a basement off the Marylebone Road' and how, one Sunday, he 'made love to her until I felt like a wet dish-rag' and thought he had exhausted desire until he went out to get the milk and saw the legs and thighs of a girl walking overhead in a wide skirt – and felt that he 'could have carried her off to bed whooping!' (207, 239-40). In a later conversation with Glasp, Sorme asks 'Have you ever been in a room with two women who have been your mistress?' (276), implying that this is a situation which he, Sorme, has personally experienced. But these sexual triumphs seem to have been some time ago. On his first date with Caroline he tells her that he hasn't 'taken a girl out for the past five years' (117) and when he takes a bath at Gertrude Quincey's, he reflects on '[f]ive years of celibacy, of partial boredom, of the unsuccessful attempt to harvest his own solitude' (191). He tells Glasp that, after reading 'Plotinus and St Francis de Sales and the rest' (presumably during his five years of solitude), he 'got involved with a couple of a girls for a very short time' (149), but he does not expand on these brief liaisons. The two specific past sexual encounters he recalls in *Ritual* have been failures. Five years ago, three days before leaving his job in a City office, he took out a girl who worked there, Marilyn, and ended up with her in a park where she clearly indicated her willingness to make love; but Sorme 'gently pull[ed] down her skirt after she had raised it' (141). Two months prior to the main action of the novel, he picked up a Slade School student, Kay, in a cafe, went back to her place, and made love to her; but when he returned the next night, he felt 'a complete lack of desire for her' (66, 138). It is not surprising that, before he has made love to either Caroline or Gertrude, he twice describes himself, first in the privacy of his own thoughts, and then to Nunne, as 'sex-starved' (40, 134).

In the course of *Ritual*, Sorme does overcome sex-starvation and achieves both sexual potency and 'the state of creativity that had eluded him for the past year' (233). By the end of the novel, he has acquired a new self-definition and a new relationship to existence. He arrives at 'an acceptance of complexity' (416) and that phrase might serve to summarize the aesthetic of *Ritual* itself. Wilson's first novel does indeed enact and demonstrate 'an acceptance of complexity', not only in its themes but also in its style and narrative technique, and these three elements interact to produce the richness of *Ritual*. In his article in *The Twentieth Century* which was quoted earlier in this essay, Wilson considers starting an 'academy for novelists and philosophers' which would have 'a neon sign' over its door that states, as the starting-point of the kind of education it would offer: 'ACCEPT THE COMPLEXITY' (494). If *Ritual* ends with the 'curious elation' produced by an experiential realization of this injunction (416), that end is also a beginning; the beginning of the after-image, the assemblage of after-images, which a good novel leaves in the mind, on the body, and which prompts further discussion, analysis and re-reading. This essay has aimed to show that *Ritual* can sustain and reward close attention but it is also the case that such attention can never exhaust an object as fertile as Wilson's first novel. *Ritual in the Dark* has that capacity to generate fruitful re-reading and reinterpretation which is the distinctive feature of a classic literary work.

Works Cited:

Deakin, John, *John Deakin: Photographs*, selected and with an essay by Robin Muir (Munich, Paris, London: Schirmer/Mosel, 1996).

Fitzgerald, F. Scott, *The Great Gatsby*, ed. Matthew J. Bruccoli (Cambridge: Cambridge University Press, 1995).

Gindin, James, *Postwar British Fiction: New Accents and Attitudes* (Berkeley, California: University of California Press, 1962), esp. pp. 223-4.

Moore-Gilbert, Bart, 'The Return of the Repressed: Gothic and the 1960s Novel', in Bart Moore-Gilbert and John Seed (eds), *Cultural Revolution: The challenge of the arts in the 1960s* (London and New York: Routledge, 1992), pp. 181-99.

Muir, Robin, *The Maverick Eye: The Street Photography of John Deakin With 192 photographs in duotone and colour* (London: Thames & Hudson, 2002).

Stanley, Colin, 'The Reluctant Librarian' (1990), collected in *'The Nature of Freedom' and Other Essays*, Colin Wilson Studies, no. 2. (Nottingham: Paupers' Press, 1990), pp. 8-18.

West, Paul, *The Modern Novel* (London: Hutchinson, 1963), esp. pp. 143-4.

Wilson, Colin, 'Introduction', *Ritual in the Dark* (Berkeley, California: Ronin, 1993), pp. 1-6.

- - - 'The Month', *The Twentieth Century*, vol. 164, no. 994 (December 1959), pp. 492-8.

- - - *Ritual in the Dark* (London: Victor Gollancz, 1960).

Notes:

1. See Wilson's concluding sentence in his introduction to the 1993 Ronin edition of *Ritual*: 'But I think that there can be no doubt that the sheer amount of time and effort that went into *Ritual* has made it my most solidly constructed and satisfactory novel. It is, at all events, my own favourite' (6).

2. Of course, those who discover *Ritual* by chance and enjoy it may go on to explore Wilson's work further. In 'The Reluctant Librarian' (1990), Colin Stanley recalls how, at the age of 18, he came across *Ritual* in an Exeter bookshop; he knew nothing then of its author but it was the start of a lifelong interest in Wilson's work (9).

3. *Ritual* is briefly discussed in James Gindin's *Postwar British Fiction: New Accents and Attitudes* (1962), pp. 222-5, and Paul West's *The Modern Novel* (1963), pp. 143-4. Perhaps the potentially most interesting reference is in Bart Moore-Gilbert's essay 'The return of the repressed: Gothic and the 1960s novel' (183) which focuses on the fiction of Iris Murdoch, John Fowles and Muriel Spark but points to 'the wider range of work centrally influenced by Gothic in the decade', including Colin Wilson's *Ritual in the Dark* and *Adrift in Soho* (1961), David Storey's *Radcliffe* (1963), and Jean Rhys's *Wide Sargasso Sea* (1966) (183). The claim that *Adrift in Soho* is 'centrally influenced by the Gothic' seems questionable – *Man Without a Shadow/The Sex Diary of Gerard Sorme* (1963) would be a better candidate – but a reading of *Ritual* as a modern Gothic novel could prove fruitful.

4. See *John Deakin: Photographs*, selected and with an essay by Robin Muir (1996), p. 28; and Robin Muir, *The Maverick Eye: The Street Photography of John Deakin With 192 photographs in duotone and colour* (2002), p. 32.

Necessary Doubt (1964)

Fighting against Sleep: *Necessary Doubt* as a
Phenomenological Thriller.

Thomas F. Bertonneau

Appearing roughly five years after *Ritual in the Dark* (1960) and
roughly five years before *The Philosopher's Stone* (1969), Colin
Wilson's ambitious novel *Necessary Doubt* (1964), originally
written in the form of a play for television (Wilson 2008, p.19),
represents its author in the moment when, beginning to appropriate genre formulas (murder mystery, science fiction,
espionage novel) he simultaneously began to foreground philosophical themes and to exploit a version of Platonic dialogue for
the dramatic exposition of ideas. *Necessary Doubt* echoes *Ritual* in
a number of ways, particularly in granting to its point-of-view
character the privilege of withholding testimony by which he
would cooperate with official charges against an acquaintance,
who is other than perfectly innocent. The protagonist in
Necessary Doubt is Professor Karl Zweig, an existential
theologian of Austrian origin whom Wilson models in part on
Paul Tillich. Zweig's relation to the dubious and off-putting
Gustav Neumann is somewhat analogous to Gerard Sorme's
relation to Austin Nunne in *Ritual* although Neumann differs
from Nunne in his degree of social pathology (less acute than
Nunne's) and intelligence (higher than Nunne's). As for *The
Philosopher's Stone, Necessary Doubt* anticipates it in the notion
that access to intensified consciousness might be mediated by
psychotropic drugs or by neurosurgery. The metallic substance
that accomplishes this goal in *The Philosopher's Stone* is called the
Neumann Alloy, in a direct backwards link to the earlier work, as
Nicolas Tredell has noted (Tredell 1982, p. 88).

In addition to being a pivotal work in the development of

Wilson's novelistic *oeuvre*, *Necessary Doubt* also serves to remind readers that its author bears a resemblance (perhaps while owing a happy debt) to an earlier British novelist. Wilson had called attention to H. G. Wells as early as *The Outsider*, his first book. One would not wish to propose Wilson as Wells' successor in some narrow sense; yet elements of Wells' novelistic art have correspondences in Wilson's. One of those elements is the motif of a substance, natural or artificial, which alters consciousness and conduces towards the emergence of a new type of human being, something not unlike the Nietzschean *Übermensch*. Thus, for example, Wells' novel *In the Days of the Comet* (1906) has the earth's atmosphere infiltrated by a cosmic aerosol that allays the aggressive impulse and throws reality into objective relief for the affected individual. Another element common to Wells and Wilson is reliance on dialogue as the medium for intellectual narrative, the prototypes being Plato's *symposia*.

I. *Zweig as Unlikely Übermensch.*

Zweig, the sixty-five-year-old, Teutonic-professorial main character of *Necessary Doubt*, differs markedly from the focal character of *Ritual in the Dark* and its immediate sequel *The Man without a Shadow* (also known as *The Sex Diary of Gerard Sorme).* A widower, an author-philosopher, a man of modest but established reputation (he is even a minor television personality), Zweig feels weighed down by the torpor of age: "Compressed by fatigue," (Wilson 1964, p.57) as he thinks, a victim of "exhausted attention," "tired," and "not awake yet." (p.50, 57 & 63) The falling snow that blankets Christmastime London in the novel's opening sequence reinforces the hibernal melancholy that has – as readers may assume – been stealing on Zweig gradually without his being sufficiently conscious of it. In his thirstiness for schnapps and whiskey, Zweig perhaps responds subconsciously to this creeping spiritual crisis; but then

25

everyone in *Necessary Doubt* drinks too much. Stimulating where alcohol is anesthetizing, and positively provocative of intensified awareness, abrupt impingements on consciousness from the outside world – moments of elevated meaning – occasionally and providentially call Zweig back to himself. In the first of these incidents, Zweig experiences the sudden recognition of a long unseen but powerfully familiar face, caught in a swift glimpse as the percipient's taxicab passes another parked curbside while admitting two passengers who have just emerged from a hotel.

The longtime unseen face belongs to Neumann, son of an old colleague, a former student, and the man whose presence in England will provide the occasion of Zweig's spiritual renascence: In the flood of specific memories and evaluations triggered by the glimpse, Zweig will rescue himself from his slough of despond. Zweig knows immediately on catching sight of Neumann that he must make a "decision" – must act *with* the opportunity that existence has offered – whether to accost the man (p.3). He decides positively. Various contingencies prevent Zweig from making immediate contact, but the "sudden interest" nevertheless heralds the revitalization of his spirit (p.3). While spending Christmas Eve in the flat of his old friends Sir Charles Grey and Lady Grey, Zweig gives evidence of mental quickening, of redeeming in and for himself the "debt" of which, as he says, "Western civilization is dying." (p.2) Seated at table, Zweig responds to another – this time to a *visionary* – recollection, generic but powerful: "The dining room always made him think of a lake in autumn. This may have been due to the brown, polished expanse of the table, in which reflections of the candle flames lay like yellow leaves." (p.10)

This luminously metaphoric state of mind compels Zweig to the consideration that, "Our whole concept of happiness needs revising" because, as the professor thinks, "a man could be happy while suffering pain – provided the pain strengthened his vitality." (p.10) Zweig experiences another memory, of bombed-out Hamburg after the war, which, representing "brutality and decadence," provides the polar contrast to his idyll of hushed Alpine waters (p.10).

Later, during Zweig's first, testy direct confrontation with Neumann, in response to Neumann's unrelenting rudeness and provocation, the philosopher suppresses his rising anger by a studiously minimal expedient: "With an effort [Zweig] took a drink from his lager glass, stared at the surface of the beer as he drank, and allowed his mind simply to contemplate the pattern of foam on its surface." (p.139) Readers of Wilson will discern in both "the lake in autumn" and "the pattern of foam" in the pint of beer the phenomenological trope of *intentionality*. The term *intentionality*, in Edmund Husserl's particular usage, lies at the heart of Wilson's philosophical project of the *New Existentialism*, as he has called it. In the book of that name (1966), Wilson writes: "Husserl suggested... that as man loses all the false ideas about himself and the world through scientific analysis, and as he comes to recognise that he himself is responsible for so much that he assumed to be 'objective,' he will come to recognise his true self, presiding over perception and all other acts of living." (Wilson 1980, p.58)

Whether in imagining the calm surface of a lake or in concentrating his perception on an ordinary and otherwise banal object (the foam on the lager), Zweig flexes his intellect, so as to restore its tone. By deliberate mental self-restoration Zweig thus wrests back control of the situation from Neumann's attempted domination of it through the lifeless mechanics of insulting behaviour.

Zweig's personal history of spiritual progress resembles in outline a sustained combat with the forces of a reductively mechanical and inhumane order. Wilson's craftily placed, pseudo-bibliographic allusions to Zweig's authorship enable readers to grasp a philosophical maturation that puts the philosopher increasingly at odds with the modern anti-spiritual attitude. In Heidelberg in the 1920s, Zweig participated in the post-Nietzschean, post-"War-to-End-War" skepticism of the time, taking its tone from Oswald Spengler's *Decline of the West* and Martin Heidegger's *Sein und Zeit* (1927). Zweig lets on to Grey that he was writing his own Spenglerian-sounding *End of an Epoch* at the time that Heidegger's book appeared. Zweig's *Necessary Doubt* seems to have followed *End of an Epoch* in 1931. The title, with resonances of Søren Kierkegaard, indicates its author's movement towards Christianity; or, more generally, towards something other than a purely immanent view of existence. Zweig wrote an essay on "Vision" around the same time. Citing the case of how Ramakrishna's despair generated an epiphany, Zweig "argued that this vision is the aim of all philosophy, and that no amount of thinking can reveal it." (p.26) This emergent visionary thesis of Zweig's coincided with his dawning sense of debilitating clumsiness in "academic philosophy," as expounded in "long-winded books." (p.10 & 25)

Zweig's *Protestant Theology* belongs plausibly to his more recent work, locating it in the late 1940s or early 1950s. As the events of *Necessary Doubt* unfold, Zweig is at work on his commentary on *Sein und Zeit*. In that commentary we read that, "the state in which human beings have lived for thousands of years has been analogous to sickness."(front matter, before p.1) In an exchange with his admirer Natasha Gardner, Zweig answers her mention of his *Creative Nature of the Sexual Act* with the observation that it was "one of my earliest works." (p.105) The late discussion of Heidegger might thus be said to revisit an early insight about vitality and existence. In describing his essay on "Vision," Zweig nearly invokes Nietzsche's superman-perspective: "A philosopher has to be like an eagle – to plunge down on truth from a great height, from sudden moments of vision, and to try to seize it... Nietzsche had said the same kind of thing many times." (p.25)

Zweig became a convert to Christianity, either shortly before or shortly after leaving Germany. Zweig's conversion is possibly connected with the death of his wife in circumstances that *Necessary Doubt* never divulges, but it also communicates with his intuition about the restricted character of reason, as modernity tends to use that term. The topic of conversion emerges early in the novel, when Grey mentions that his wife is a Catholic convert and cautions Zweig to avoid theological discussion over dinner. One notes that conversion is a special – an especially powerful – instance of intentionality: It is an experience of meaning so *epochal* as to transform the percipient in his entire world-orientation. Conversion is, moreover, not logical, but epiphanic; it involves acknowledgment of something that argument from facts cannot demonstrate. Conversion is linked in Wilson's system of metaphors in *Necessary Doubt* with such notions as *redemption* and *original sin,* the latter of which Zweig uses in an idiosyncratic way.

II. *Neumann as Botched Übermensch.*

Having been jolted into a tumult of memories by his catching sight of Neumann, and having experienced an access of *élan vital* through the encounter, Zweig tells the Greys over dinner Neumann's story, explaining as he does so why Neumann's presence in London with an elderly male companion strikes him as worthy of investigation. A suspicion of criminality attends Neumann. Zweig and Neumann are the novel's two principle persons. Wilson articulates his narrative around the dialectic of their relation, both intellectual and moral; and their two extended conversations form the heart of *Necessary Doubt.* If Zweig, as I have just argued, were an "unlikely *Übermensch,*" then one might best describe Neumann as a botched *Übermensch,* the disparity between whose insight and practice makes him tragic in a qualified way. Zweig never thinks of

29

himself as a superman; while he is never falsely modest, neither is he boastful although he exhibits the forgivable susceptibility to being admired.

Neumann, on the other hand, displays egomaniacal and narcissistic traits, characteristics that make plausible the hints of nefarious activity accompanying his known itinerary. Zweig's own duality whether the evidence convicts Neumann is the novel's titular dubiety, which Zweig will eventually classify as occupying a higher order than Grey's forensic certainty. Zweig even dreams about his interrupted correspondence with the one-time student, seeing the two of them pitched tensely against each other in a gigantic chess match, surrounded by ominous fog.

Zweig first knew Neumann as the son of a colleague, Alois Neumann, at Heidelberg in the 1920s. The elder Neumann was a physiologist who specialized in brain-research. Gustav's mother had died when he was ten, leaving him a quasi-orphan, likely indulged by the grief-stricken parent-survivor; he is by natural endowment an intellectual prodigy, who appears initially more interested in Zweig's department, philosophy, than in his father's department, neurophysiology. After the first meeting with Neumann, Zweig says to Natasha Gardner, "You cannot understand the forces that turned Gustav into... a nihilist." (p.168) Among those forces was the utopian optimism of the ex-soldiers, now become professors: "It seemed to many of us that the world had entered a new era"; Zweig believed with his friend Ernst Cassirer "in the future age of reason and enlightenment." (p.168) When Hitler came, Zweig says, "it was as if all our faith had been the most childish kind of illusion"; the students – including Neumann – "felt... betrayed twice... and some of them became nihilists." (p.168)

At private school, the thirteen-year-old Neumann becomes a target of anti-Semitic hazing. He wreaks vengeance on the ringleader by devising nearly to scald him to death in a gymnasium shower. Confessing his deed to Zweig, he seems not even to understand the professor's statement that *someone other than the perpetrator* might have entered the shower stall. When Nazi thugs beat to death Neumann's friend Georgi Braunschweig, Neumann reverses character and attempts suicide, after which "he was sullen" and "hardly ever spoke." (p.21) He does, however, read voraciously, "the English philosophers, and Kant and Schopenhauer and Hegel," until one late evening he knocks on Zweig's door "in a state of tremendous excitement," apparently having "stopped hating the world." (p.21) They talk through the night. Yet on the subject of anti-Semitism, which implicates his friend's beating-death, Neumann tells Zweig that both the Nazis and the Jews are at fault, "the Nazis for being idiots, the Jews for being weaklings." (p.22) Neumann publishes his "brilliant paper on Husserl... in the phenomenological *Jahrbuch*," but abruptly loses interest in philosophy and takes up research into brain physiology. (p.22)

In 1931, Neumann's behavior veers towards the bizarre. He steals a car and drives it over a cliff; he all but strangles Zweig's pet kitten. He conceives the theory that, "the Gods had created the human race as a kind of joke." (p.27) On a train, he sees the two *bourgeois* men sharing his compartment as "fat bankers with faces like pigs," as "self-deceivers," and as "insects trying to help other insects." (p.28) Likening himself to "Paul on the road to Damascus," Neumann divulges to Zweig his ambition to become "a real criminal," someone beyond good and evil, "who is not just an underprivileged victim." (p.28) Breaking contact, Neumann goes to ground. Bits of information coming Zweig's way suggest that the former student and would-be master criminal has become a confidence man who specializes in persuading elderly men to designate him as heir, after which, in a disturbing pattern, they commit suicide.

Neumann strikes Zweig in confidence-man fashion as having pulled an elaborate swindle on himself, bypassing conscience for egoistic reasons; he has done so by buying into the same pseudo-Nietzschean doctrine that was exploited by the Nazis. At their first meeting, Neumann advances his old grudge against Zweig, accusing him of having sold out his commitment to Nietzschean realism for the false comfort of a fideistic creed: "I would like to know why you call yourself a Christian?" (p.143) Thus, as Neumann sees it, Zweig traded the prospect of the superman for the middle-class ease of slave-morality. Neumann wants to know how Zweig squares belief in the Gospel with triumphant brutality under Hitler. Zweig answers: "Imagine human history without Christ. There would be *nothing but* the Nazis." (p.144) Zweig's assertion brings readers to the crux of the matter.

In Braunschweig's death, his own father's suicide, and the rise of Nazism Neumann has had his *Blick in Chaos*, and he has concluded, like the protagonists of Sartre and Camus, that absurdity reigns over existence supremely. Neumann reasons that people avert their awareness of this frightening fact in the myths of consolation, which proves their weakness. Neumann proves his strength by facing up, as he sees it, to the nothingness. He is *certain of the nothingness*. Zweig, on the other hand, believes that "man's capacity to doubt is his greatest dignity, and that even a saint would never discard his ability to doubt." (p.23)

Doubt conditions faith. Doubt probes towards truth in the necessary acknowledgment that it has not yet seized truth or under the premise that truth provides the subject with the horizon of openness in respect to which he engages the creative project of the Self. He who goes forth in doubt in quest of truth demonstrates courage. He also demonstrates *love*, which is etymologically constitutive of the term *philosophy*. It was Christ finally, more than Socrates, who "had given a form and expression to the idea of love," Zweig tells Neumann (p.145). Seen this way, Neumann's posture of superiority appears as the imposture of an evasive and haphazard (a *loveless*) life dissimulating itself under the formulas of cynicism. Zweig behaves from the beginning of the novel's action to its end as a consistent character; Neumann by contrast shifts from deliberate rudeness to a simulacrum of candor in a way troublingly suggestive both of a guilty motive and a knack for manipulation. Near the end of Wilson's novel, Zweig speaks of Neumann to Natasha, saying: "Oh, he is cunning. And a consummate actor." (p.145 & 302) Yet Zweig not only refuses to condemn Neumann; he actually abets Neumann's escape from justice.

III. *The H. G. Wells Connection.*

Tredell mentions that Wilson acknowledges Friedrich Dürrenmatt as an influence on *Necessary Doubt* (Tredell, p.80). I would stress what I call the H. G. Wells connection. Writing in *The Strength to Dream* (1962) on the subject of Wells, Wilson, referring to a passage from Wells' *Experiment in Autobiography* (1934), observes the following: "Self-enjoyment is synonymous with purposeful evolutionary activity of the intellect and the sense; and the notion of a living creature capable of absolute enjoyment is the notion of a man-god, no longer plagued by tiresome necessities over which he has no control. When a man commits himself to this definition of meaning, the 'value of life' ceases to be a matter of material symbols... it becomes instead a function of the limitless realm of the intellect and imagination, of the creative will." (Wilson 1966, p.105) Also in *The Strength to Dream*, one finds rare appreciation of one of Wells' least-read scientific romances, *In the Days of the Comet*. Wilson summarizes Wells' fantasy this way: "He imagines that a comet made of gas strikes the earth, and the gas has the effect of completely reforming human nature." (Wilson 1966, p. 110)

The moment of reformation is worth examining. Wells' first-person narrator has just attempted jealous murder, firing his pistol wildly, as the comet strikes. He falls unconscious only to

33

awaken in a state of heightened mentality. The dreary sky, for example, has become "the sky of a magnificent sunrise" illuminating and intensifying a field of poppies into "an archipelago of gold-beached purple islands floating in a sea of golden green." (Wells 1963, p.364) The narrator says: "I held up my left hand before me, a grubby hand, a frayed cuff; but with a quality of painted unreality, transfigured as a beggar might have been by Botticelli." (Wells 1963, p.365)

That the comet's "green vapors" amount to a *Deus ex machina* is no reason not to notice the real interest in the passage: Wells' description, which goes on for pages, of the metamorphosis of consciousness that permits his narrator to see the world at last, as if the Blakean "Doors of Perception" had been flung wide. The narrator has ascended to a new order of existence – he is now a kind of superman. The state of heightened consciousness is a recurrent motif in Wells' *oeuvre;* so is the Nietzschean *Übermensch.* In *Kipps* (1905), the priggish Walsingham, who "had been reading Nietzsche," lectures the ingenuous title-character on "the non-moral Overman," which Walsingham fancies himself to be (Wells 2005, p.157-8). In *Tono-Bungay* (1909), the clownish Uncle Edward likewise sees himself reflected in the "Overman Idee." (Wells 2005, p.264) In a non-comic context, the protagonist of *The Research Magnificent* (1915) experiments with opium but finds that he best evokes the mood of intensity by mental concentration applied to realizing ideal goals; the same is true of the male protagonists of *Meanwhile* (1927) and *Babes in the Darkling Wood* (1942).

A synthetic counterpart of the "green vapor," the "gas of peace" from the film-scenario for *Things to Come* (1935), ushers in utopia by subduing neo-barbaric bellicosity; as the people of Everytown rise from their swoon, John Cabal's voice is heard announcing the brave new world.

Commenting again on *Experiment in Autobiography*, Wilson writes these words in *The Strength to Dream*: "Wells suggests that a new type of man is appearing, who wants a third dimension of imaginative consciousness for its own sake, not for his survival. This type of man, as Wells points out, demands imaginative consciousness – as distinguished from observational and reflective consciousness – as his *sine qua non.*" (Wilson 1966, p.179) Wilson presumably wrote these speculative remarks coevally with his work on *Necessary Doubt*. It will be readily seen, then, that what is an interesting notion in Wells becomes an explicit discussion in Wilson. Ordinary life, the regime of habit endowed on the *Homo sapiens* by the evolutionary process, entails frustrating mental circumscription. Impatience to transcend ordinary consciousness can press so severely on the attuned subject that bypassing the natural, neurological limitations by recourse to the pharmacy begins to seem justifiable.

Gustav Neumann – assessed by Zweig as being, or at least as having once been, a finer mind than himself – has glimpses into elevated awareness, but no reliable access to such exaltation on his own. He therefore applies himself to clandestine pharmaceutical research to produce an elixir that will generate visionary intensity, as it were, on request. His *neurococaine* and *neuromysin* are the result. Neumann's exploitation of elderly millionaires has provided him both with funds for developing the two drugs and, as Zweig remarks, with "guinea pigs" for evaluating them (p.299). Neumann incidentally resembles Wells' Walsingham in being a prig and Uncle Edward in being a charlatan. One should not forget Ponderevo's enterprise of selling useless tonic to gullible consumers.

Zweig, while cautious about pharmaceutical transcendence, grants to Neumann that *he* has pursued the avenue that Zweig eliminated by choosing philosophy: "Gustav has returned to the body." (p.301) Wilson nevertheless gives a good many hints in *Necessary Doubt* that chemical prosthesis is the least attractive portal to expanded awareness; or, as Zweig likes to say, to the overcoming of "original sin." (p.300)

During the action of the novel Zweig experiences a number of Maslovian peak experiences; he recollects his past experience of some others. Reflections of candlelight in a table precipitate a powerful dream-image of a lake in autumn when he goes to dine with the Greys on Christmas Eve. Music moves him. While driving Zweig, Grey, and Natasha to reconnoiter Neumann's cottage in the North Country, Gardner switches on the radio: "The full orchestra gave out the Thunderstorm motif [from Wagner's *Rheingold*]." (p.191) Zweig remarks how "we had a society in Göttingen – a Nietzsche society – in 1910" whose members "used to meet and talk about the superman"; he adds, "we had piano scores of all Wagner's operas... our favorite piece was that storm music." (p.192) The professor speaks these words "looking past" Natasha, as though in a state of abrupt detachment from the present (p.192). Here the act of recalling a moment of vision from the past becomes an actual moment of vision *in* the present. The word "detachment" occurs elsewhere in *Necessary Doubt* in connection with the quickening, the "freshness," that the chance sighting of Neumann triggers in Zweig (p.75).

Zweig fights fatigue continuously. Exhausted by his first meeting with Neumann and by Natasha's solicitousness, he relishes the asylum of his hotel room. Wilson writes: "He took out his heavily marked copy of *Sein und Zeit* and his own manuscript, held together by a bulldog clip... A calm intense joy took possession of him. His brain leaped forward like a horse that is released into a meadow after a long winter." (p.152) By contrast, Zweig's neuromysin experience asserts itself with noticeable artificiality. Instead of a vital metaphor (the "horse"), Wilson provides a mechanical metaphor: In Zweig's apperception, "his brain felt like an electric generator working a searchlight." (p.266) The sensation does not strike Zweig unpleasantly, but the figural difference remains significant. Overuse of neuromysin produces, moreover, a nasty side effect of severe fatigue that Zweig has observed up close in the case of Timothy Ferguson, Neumann's latest client. This is a limitation, not of consciousness, but of the philter.

IV. *Dialogue, Imagination, and the Übermensch.*

In a reprinted review, from *Books and Bookmen* (July 1973), of Norman and Jeanne Mackenzie's biography of Wells, Wilson writes: "I cannot accept the shallow, rather facile view... that Wells was a major writer until he wrote *Tono Bungay* – say, around 1910 – and then that he became a windbag, endlessly repeating himself." (Wilson 2009, p.249) Wilson takes the contrary view that Wells continued to create remarkable fiction, well into the 1930s at least. Wilson cites *The Undying Fire* (1919), for example, as "one of the most powerful statements of Carlyle's 'eternal Yes versus eternal No' in all literature" and mentions *The World of William Clissold* (1926) with approval (Wilson 2009, p.249-50 & 251). In Wilson's assessment: "Where Wells scores is in the power of his intuition and intelligence," which is "as intuitive as Lawrence's," so that "the perceptions are like a shower of sparks"; Wells "can face a problem as big as a mountain; and then, with a few leaps and somersaults like an acrobat, he is standing on top of it." (Wilson 2009, p.250). I happen to share Wilson's judgment. I would add that the interest in Wells' later prose has a good deal to do with the novelist's willingness to let the dialogue take over, as it does almost entirely in *Meanwhile* and *Babes in the Darkling Wood.* Now *Necessary Doubt* comes close to being a dialogue novel: The heart of the book consists in the two extended conversations between Zweig and Neumann (p.131-148 & 256-297). Conversation dominates the story.

Failed conversation, like Zweig's first parlay with Neumann, contributes to the abasement of mood, to pessimism, and to a sense of ineradicable *limitation*. Successful conversation, such as

Zweig's second parlay with Neumann, is itself tonic, lifting the participating spirit while opening vistas of meaning and possibility.

A moment from *The Mind Parasites* (1967), more or less contemporary with *Necessary Doubt*, bears appositely on this part of the discussion. Austin Gilbert and his colleagues – they have all undergone a type of ramped up phenomenological training – *join minds* to exert psychokinetic force on the moon. Gilbert remarks, "There was immense exhilaration as our minds combined"; and a bit later, "our wills locked like a great searchlight beam." (Wilson 1972, p.202) The metaphors that *Necessary Doubt* employs are less *outré* than those of *The Mind Parasites*, but they mean the same thing. The "Thunderstorm" motif from *Das Rheingold* galvanizes Zweig not only because of its striking intrinsic beauty but also because it once formed the focus of shared attention of the likeminded talkative members of the Nietzsche Society. When Zweig revisits the topic of the Nietzsche Society in private exchange with Natasha, he links it to the trope of *conversion*.

A man named Haller (shades of Hermann Hesse) once read a paper before the society in which he asserted that, "we need not accept all Nietzsche's ideas, because a lot of them are the screams of a sick man," but even so, "Nietzsche is expressing something that is happening to man's spirit in this century"; Haller, at the same time, "converted to Roman Catholicism." (p.228) In a kind of Hegelian synthesis, *conversion* means seeing another point of view objectively and assimilating it, productively or creatively. At their second parlay, Neumann, supposing that he is sincere, repents his earlier rebuff of Zweig. He tells Zweig, "I was impressed by the opening sentence of your Heidegger book [that] man's experience of the world is basically an experience of limitation." (p.265) Zweig replies that he remarked a similar idea in Neumann's article in a criminology journal. It is as if the two men were resuming a conversation that malign events interrupted decades before. The reader is therefore *in doubt* whether the exaltation that Zweig feels comes mainly from the neuromysin or mainly from his *joining minds* in dialogue at last with the prodigal student Neumann.

Two subordinate plot-developments – Zweig's relation with Joseph Gardner and his relation with the psychiatrist Stafford-Morton – support the "dialogue" answer to the just posed ambiguity. At Zweig's first meeting with Neumann, the former student rebuffs the former teacher. While Zweig feels friendly toward Gardner, and while he accepts Gardner's help in tracking down Neumann, he initially rejects the opportunity of dialogue. Gardner writes books devoted to Atlantis, Hans Hörbiger's World Ice Theory, extrasensory perception, and the like. Zweig tells Natasha, "Your husband has a completely untrained mind," but he admits that Gardner "is not an ungifted man"; Natasha has earlier characterized Gardner to Zweig as "enthusiastic" and prone to "get carried away by things." (p.161 & 151) By the end of the novel, partly because Gardner seems so sympathetic to the professor (more so than Grey), and partly because he has grown appreciative of the occultist's enthusiasm, Zweig subtly but positively changes his attitude to his new acquaintance.

When Zweig first encounters Stafford-Morton, he rebuffs him as rudely as Neumann first rebuffs Zweig. The psychiatrist strikes Zweig as *too certain* and *too narrow* in his view. On a second encounter, he finds that Stafford-Morton is actually insightful and he apologizes for his earlier bad behavior.

Zweig's assessment of Neumann also undergoes complex alteration. On the basis of their second parlay, Neumann strikes Zweig as a quasi-criminal and immoralist who nevertheless possesses a mind capable of sporadic insights. Neumann resembles in this way the actual eccentrics in whom Wilson had already begun taking a biographical interest in the mid-1960s: George Gurdjieff, Peter D. Ouspensky, H. P. Lovecraft, Wilhelm

Reich, and the mystics and "New Age" types who were to come under discussion in *The Occult*. Yet Zweig no longer regards Neumann's mind as finer than his own. He tells Natasha, "His brain is no better than mine – in many ways it is worse." (p.301) But, in Zweig's new wager, Neumann's selfishness, duplicity, and confidence-man tricks are *accidents* and, as such, *irrelevant* to the discoveries that he has made despite his impulsiveness and narcissism. For this reason Zweig schemes to shield Neumann from the law.

The discoveries are what motivate Zweig, especially where it concerns Neumann's declaration that man needs *"a vision of purpose."* (p.281) The trick of intensified consciousness is to imagine a worthwhile goal and *to hold it steady* so that it becomes a transcendent purpose. Zweig knows this abstractly but had ceased to feel it vitally until the coincidence of Neumann's emergence from *status incognito*. "The way we see the world," Zweig tells Natasha, "is a lie"; he adds, "I suppose this is what I came to mean by original sin." (p.300) The *rencontre* with Neumann after so many years has revived Zweig's flagging conviction that, as he says, "it is the work of the philosopher to undo original sin." (p.300)

Necessary Doubt is a novel of masterly composition and remarkable psychological subtlety that has perhaps not received the attention it deserves. It is the kernel of much of what would subsequently come from Wilson's audacious and always-vital mind.

References:

Tredell, Nicolas (1982) *The Novels of Colin Wilson*. Barnes & Noble.

Wells, H. G. (1963) *Three Science Fiction Novels by H. G. Wells*. Dover.

Wells, H. G. (2005) *Kipps*. Penguin.

Wilson, Colin (1964) *Necessary Doubt*. Trident Press.

Wilson, Colin (1966) *The Strength to Dream*. Abacus.

Wilson, Colin (1972) *The Mind Parasites*. Oneiric Press.

Wilson, Colin (1980) *The New Existentialism*. Salem House.

Wilson, Colin (2008) *The Death of God and other plays*. (ed. Colin Stanley). Paupers' Press

Wilson, Colin (2009) *Existential Criticism: selected book reviews* (ed. Colin Stanley). Paupers' Press

The Mind Parasites (1967)

The Mind Parasites: Wilson, Husserl, Plotinus

Stephen R. L. Clark

Plot and character:

The archaeologist Gilbert Austin learns that an old friend, Karel Weissman, has committed suicide, and left him the task of sorting through his papers. Unwilling to engage with this task, he leaves for a dig in Turkey, where he and another friend, Wolfgang Reich, slowly uncover the remains of a great city, buried two miles in the earth, which seems to be much like the cities described by H.P.Lovecraft (1890-1937). The suggestion is made that Lovecraft's "Great Old Ones" might be woken from their sleep by the archaeological disturbances, and Austin, at last beginning to read his dead friend's papers, catches sight (as it were) of alien presences, "mind parasites", in the depths of his own mind. With the help of phenomenological exercises derived from the writings of the philosopher Edmund Husserl (1859-1938), Austin and his colleague develop telekinetic and telepathic powers, enlist other scientists in their enterprise, and decide to alert the public to the dangers posed by "the Great Old Ones" (who may or may not be the mind parasites or their makers). The alien presences fight back, driving the conspirators to suicide or madness, and eventually inciting racial war between a United Africa and Europe. Austin defeats their attempt against him, enlists the American President as an ally, educates other scientists in the new techniques, discovers the malign influence of the Moon on the human mind, and finally halts the war between Europe and Africa by creating a shared hallucination of extraterrestrial invaders. They also dispose of the Moon. Rather than remain as masters of the human world,

Austin and his companions leave Earth behind to join a "universal police force". The novel in which all this is imagined is composed of documents created at one time or another by Austin, and gives all the signs of being related by an unreliable narrator who (amongst other things) deliberately fogs the relationship between the builders of the buried city and the mental parasites that control and feed on human emotion.

The Mind Parasites (1967) began as Colin Wilson's response to a challenge from August Derleth (1909-71), who was Lovecraft's literary executor. He also composed a shorter story, "The Return of the Lloigor" (1971), in which the monsters embody a deeply rooted, "rational" pessimism. The challenge itself was a response to Wilson's critical remarks, in *The Strength to Dream* (Wilson 1963, pp.1-9, 102-6), about Lovecraft's style and his failure to understand where his greatest strength really lay: not in horror fiction so much as in an evocation of the immense span of time and space in ignorance of which we conduct our usual lives. In the event, the merely Lovecraftian elements of Wilson's fable turn out to be irrelevant, "a gigantic red herring to keep man looking for his enemies *outside* himself" (1967, p.185): pre-historical and possibly non-human civilizations, invasions from "space", hidden cults, and the fancied return of powers inimical to living creatures whether of human or non-human kind. Some of those themes are treated at more length in Wilson's later "Lovecraftian" fables: *The Philosopher's Stone* (1969) or *The Space Vampires* (1976). The closer cousin of *The Mind Parasites* is rather Eric Frank Russell's *Sinister Barrier* (1939; expanded edition 1948). There may also be an allusion to a work by Bernard Newman (1897-1968), *The Flying Saucer* (1948), in which a group of scientists stage a mock invasion by extraterrestrials with the aim of uniting humanity against the alien threat – which is what Wilson's scientists are, rightly, accused of doing (though the accusation, we are to understand, is driven by the parasites' need to discredit their new enemies). Newman had offered a similar scenario before the war, in *Armoured Doves: a Peace Novel* (1931): there the scientists unite humanity by the threat of a death-ray. G.K.Chesterton commented acidly (1987, p.644) that:

> We have all read shockers and sensational stories, in which a white-haired and wild-eyed Professor, alleged to be idealistic and instantly recognized to be insane, is at work on producing a Death-Ray or some deadly explosive or destructive machine, so terrific as to lay the nations prostrate with panic, and thus achieve the happy result of imposing peace on the world. ... To remain at peace, out of sheer panic about a professor with a death-ray or a tyrant with an instrument of torture, would be to die daily and even then not be secure against death.

In Wilson's fable, the effort is not entirely successful: many people simply disbelieve the story that the "Tsathogguans" of Lovecraft's fantasy have been awakened; many others quarrel about the best way to respond to the imagined threat; some fall into despair; a few begin to devise new ways of making war upon the heavens, or each other. The main battle is halted by sending a huge experimental airship over the warring armies, and causing mass hallucinations (almost as many die in the panic as would have died in battle), but there is no real prospect of a genuine or permanent peace. Some measure of calm is restored only by a magical dislocation of the moon – imagined, in the fable, to be a constant irritant, a source of "lunatic" emotions in the human soul.

Wilson's narrator is a middle-aged, unmarried, overweight archaeologist, with a liking for fine food and wine. But just as the merely Lovecraftian elements of the plot are a red herring, so also are the archaeological interests of the narrator: the important truth about ourselves and our situation are not to be found by excavations, nor even by burrowing miles down into the earth to uncover ancient cities, but by burrowing down into the mind, through "layer upon geological layer of response to experience, habit patterns", to borrow a phrase from a later novel (1969, p.129). This is to be done, we are to suppose, by really attending to Husserl's insights rather than by then-fashionable experiments with drugs or sleep deprivation. In later Lovecraftian novels, the route is rather through neuropsychology and the accidental discovery of a metal that speeds up neural processing (*The Philosopher's Stone*) or through the conscious use of sexual desire (*The Space Vampires; The God of the Labyrinth*). In all the stories the effects of enhanced intelligence include telekinetic and telepathic powers – and especially the power to control all "lesser" minds, whether they are wasps or reporters. In *The Mind Parasites* the narrator and his companions, having engineered world peace (at least for a moment), depart to join an imagined galactic police force. It remains uncertain whether their departure is motivated more by boredom and disgust with the merely human condition, or by a genuine love of all the creatures with whom we share a cosmos, a wish to be of service and a delight in something new. In Eric Frank Russell's story we are to suppose that the Earth, once rid of its tyrants, will be free to join the larger community: in Wilson's, only a very few (and almost entirely male) will do so.

The parasites of Wilson's fable, sometimes referred to as Tsathogguans (after Lovecraft's monsters), first slither into sight when the narrator's friend kills himself after writing what at first seem paranoiac ramblings about the enemies that lurk within our minds. The narrator, protected at first by his own ignorance, inattention and automatic disbelief, gradually learns that there are indeed such enemies, and that they can be identified and even defeated. The first attempt to gather together scientists and scholars to face this danger is a fiasco: most kill themselves, or are killed; one is engulfed by the parasites. Much the same pattern fills Eric Frank Russell's

45

Sinister Barrier, which draws (like Wilson) on the stories collected by Charles Fort, and the Fortean hypothesis that we are property (see Fort 1941). Both also identify the sensation that 'someone is walking on my grave', a shiver down the spine, as a signal of the parasites' presence. The stories are also alike in invoking such staples of classic 50s science fiction as telescreens, stratospheric expresses, rocket-powered automobiles and rock-chewing mechanical moles – all the expected devices of advanced technology as it was imagined in those days. But this background is also mostly irrelevant. The focus in both stories is on the *mental* effects of the infestation. It is true that Russell's parasitical intelligences (called "Vitons") are visible – after appropriate medication – as ball lightning, and can be destroyed in the end by beams of polarized radio-waves. In Russell's fable the parasites engineer an assault upon the West by Asians persuaded that Vitons are their ancestors. In Wilson's the open war is between Africa and Europe, each animated by racialist delusions. But the real battle in both cases is fought in the human mind and heart. Wilson's exist *only* "in the mind" (which is not to say that they are merely imaginary), and must be defeated entirely by moral effort, aided by careful phenomenological analysis of our moods and internal promptings (though they have sufficient "physical" existence to be affected when the heroic band of scientists and scholars rotate the moon away from us). Russell's polarized radio-waves are replaced by a "polarized beam of attention" (1967, p.105). The moral effort is supported by a power deeper within the mind than even the parasites can travel: indeed, their chief sustenance is gained from tapping the flow of energy from that deep source into our individual existences. This idea is one also to be found in Lindsay's *Voyage to Arcturus* (1920) and – more recently – in Doris Lessing's *Shikasta* (1979). Russell's parasites, by contrast, exist externally, although they have as great a power over our emotions as Wilson's, Lindsay's or Lessing's. Moral and electrical energy are equated in Russell's world, but perhaps not in Wilson's – though 'the Philosopher's Stone' of the later novel subverts that distinction.

In both Wilson's and Russell's stories the parasites may possibly have arrived fairly recently. Wilson, indeed, seems to suggest that they have only been with us since the late eighteenth century, when the hopes and ideals of the Enlightenment began to be sapped by creeping nihilism.

A strange change comes over the human race. It happens towards the end of the eighteenth century. The tremendous, bubbling creativity of Mozart is counterbalanced by the nightmare cruelty of De Sade. Suddenly we are in an age of darkness, an age where men of genius no longer create like gods. Instead, they struggle as if in the grip of an invisible octopus. The century of suicide begins. In fact, modern history begins, the age of defeat and neurosis (1967, pp.57-8).

But this is a strangely skewed view of history, as is the later claim that "the men of previous centuries [before about two centuries ago] ... were more unified than modern man: they lived on a more instinctive level" (1967, p.188), and so suffered less from mental or corporeal cancers. It would be far more plausible to suppose that the parasites have been with us for millennia, experienced as spirits, demons or gods. In *The Philosopher's Stone* Wilson offered a more optimistic account of the supposed change from one century to the next: that it is only in the romantic movement that people experience a visionary "freedom from one's own personal little problems" (1969, p.58) – a freedom sabotaged, perhaps, by the parasites. But this too neglects the long past history of just such a notion of freedom, and what threatened it. In Russell's story, more plausibly, the parasites have been the originators of every form of madness, from paranoid schizophrenia to nationalism and religion. It is

47

they that have filled the human heart and mind with superstitions, hatreds and obsessive loves – though romantic love, scientific curiosity and ordinary human companionship are allowed a more natural origin. In Russell's world our safety lies in legwork (the title of one of his minor stories): the unimpassioned accumulation of information and its careful sifting by many working together rather than inspiration or unusual genius on the part of a creative few, "the creative minority" mentioned also in *The Philosopher's Stone* (1969, pp.46-7). In Wilson's world salvation comes only from those few, scientists and scholars inspired by phenomenology, and contemptuous of the ordinary mass of people.

Husserl, Phenomenology and Plotinus:

Russell's heroes are usually engineers or private investigators, "practical people" given to mocking authority figures. Their loyalty is to the freedom of humankind, without any reasoned account of why they should be loyal, or what is valuable in freedom. Even the telepathic hero of *Three to Conquer* (aka *Call Him Dead*), who is also confronted by alien intelligences (bacterial in bodily essence, and Venusian in proximate origin) who threaten to take us over, has little interest in any *theory* about the alien and human minds he listens to. Much the same is true of the many 50s SF stories featuring alien infiltration, mind control and the like, by Robert Heinlein, Jack Finney, Philip Dick and others. The dangers are usually, in the end, defeated by bodily courage and technological know-how. In Wilson's stories it is the theory that matters, and whatever defeat his heroes inflict upon the enemy is moral more than material. "Freedom is the most important experience that can happen to human beings" (1967, p.178) – but the freedom of which Wilson is speaking is only ever enjoyed by the few. The rest seem "alien and repulsive, little better than apes" (1967, p.199), though the narrator and his friends do occasionally feel a little patronizing pity for them. As Tredell (1982, p.103) observes, this seems like just the sort of "petty, personal emotion" that an evolved humanity should have discarded, and far too much like Lovecraft's talk of human beings as "crawling and miserable vermin" (Wilson 1963, p.9).

So what is being recommended? And why should *The Mind Parasites*, despite its obvious flaws as a novel, still be worth reading? Northrop Frye's comment is apt: "Silly book in many ways, which is a pity, because its central idea is a genuine Promethean archetype, the Gospel driving out of the devils symbolized as malignant small creatures like insects" (Frye 2002 p.215). But first we have to *notice* the devils.

"By luck, Reich and I had quickly picked up the techniques of phenomenology; because neither of us were philosophers, and had no preconceptions to get rid of, Husserl's seed fell on fertile ground." (1967, p.82). Whatever it is that Wilson's heroes pick up, of course, it cannot have been simply Husserl's technique: Husserl himself, after all, was not transformed into a telekinetic, telepathic, ruthless manipulator of lesser beings, and scornful saviour of humankind! The invented documents that make up Wilson's novel are, as I remarked before, deliberately unreliable: sometimes the Tsathogguans really are Lovecraftian monsters; sometimes they are more like Russell's Vitons; sometimes they are hardly more than cancerous elements of the human mind, or inappropriate habits. Whatever it is that Reich and Austin do remains, deliberately, obscure: Wilson himself may not have any clear idea, and certainly his heroes don't provide one. Not that this is surprising: being "initiated" will always demand more than book-learning, and whatever it is that is to be conveyed about our situation we can't simply be *told* it.

Husserl's particular contribution to philosophical methodology was a variant on Cartesian meditation: a reflexive examination of what we are doing in thinking, feeling, desiring and the like. The essence of *mental* activity is that it is *intentional*, directed at some object, with some particular feeling tone. To see this clearly we need to "bracket off" any question about "external" reality, and let ourselves notice the *internal* object of the activity. Material existents exist alongside and outside each other, at different times and locations: mental existence is ineradicably relational. In our ordinary, "natural" state we pay little or no attention to the activity by which we are reaching out to things, and entertain no questions about their reality or their lack of it.

> Husserl's great contribution was to point out that if you look at something without reaching out to grasp it (i.e. if you glance absent-mindedly at your watch while in conversation) you don't register it. In all perception there is this element of reaching out and grabbing – of intention. ... But, said Husserl, if something inside me has this power to 'attend' to experience, imposing more or less meaning and unity on it, surely this indicates some principle in me that wasn't written on the slate by my experience? (2009, p.202 (first published 1972))

In becoming aware of our own mental involvement in the construction of the internal objects of that activity, we may also experience a sudden enlightenment – that there is a world outside our ordinary consciousness, and that ordinary life is indeed constructed for us by something that is not quite our ordinary self, and is itself a part of that reality. This revelation shows how little we know about the source of our own thoughts and actions. "I speak of 'my mind' as I speak of 'my back garden'. But in what sense is my back garden really 'mine'? It is full of worms and insects who do not ask my permission to live there. It will continue to exist after I am dead...." (1967, p.40).

Noticing how few of "our own thoughts and feelings" are simple products of our own thinking, how few are under our own control, is the necessary beginning of any properly disciplined thinking. We are infested by "mental microbes", as D.G.Ritchie noted (1891, p.22) – though C.S.Lewis may have been right to suspect that they are rather "macrobes", demons under another name (1945, pp.315-6). Unsurprisingly, ascetics have long known about them, since it is only ascetics who make much effort to resist them!

> We can infer from the object appearing in the mind which demon is close at hand, suggesting that object to us. ... All thoughts producing anger or desire in a way that is contrary to reason are caused by demons (Evagrios Pontikos (345-99): Palmer 1979, p.39).

Noticing how much of what we think and do is simply a matter of habit, a lazy agreement with some demon, is the moment when we might learn or attempt some new thing – including the creation of a better habit. Habits are at once the enemies' tool (1967, p.81) and necessary for life (1967, p.130). "Most of your actions are carried out by a host of unconscious zombies who exist in peaceful harmony along with you (the "person" inside your body)!" (Blakeslee & Ramachandran 1998, p.228).

Like other animals, we inhabit a "life world", what Jacob von Uexkuell (1957) called an *Umwelt*, such that only a fraction of what is "really" going on is immediately present to us. Unlike other animals (or at any rate, unlike what we suppose to be true of other animals), we can occasionally notice that there is a larger world, and do so especially when we attend, reflexively, to our own imaginative and constructive mentality. As one of Wilson's heroes remarks in another novel, "Man is the first *objective* animal. All others live in a subjective world of instinct, from which they can never escape; only man looks at the stars or rocks and says 'How interesting...' instantly leaping over the wall of his mere identity" (1969, p.129). But the most interesting thing of all is the realization of that wider identity.

Such moments of "objective realization" are not necessarily comfortable. "The suicide rate was increasing because thousands of human beings were 'awakening', like me [that is, the original author of the discovery, Karel Weissman, who kills himself in the opening pages of the book], to the absurdity of human life, and simply refused to go on. The dream of history was coming to an end. Mankind was already starting to wake up; one day it would wake up properly, and there would be mass suicide." (1967, pp.21-2) The narrator himself experiences this sort of awakening a little later in the story:

> Suddenly, abysses of emptiness were open beneath my feet. It did not even produce fear; that would be too human a reaction. It was like contact with an icy reality that makes everything human seem a masquerade, *that makes life itself seem a masquerade* (1967, p.113).

This is after all more or less the real opinion of most self-styled moderns, though they are usually content to hide from it and its more disagreeable implications. There is no reason, it seems, to think *our* life-world is any closer to reality than that of a sea-slug, a spider or an albatross: we sense only a tiny segment of what we "know" is happening, and divide it up according to our personal and social values in a way that, we suppose, receives no universal warrant. We may see sermons in stones and books in the running brooks, but "really" they aren't there. Neither the world at large, nor the human frame, has any objective meaning. All that we do and think is no more than a mask over emptiness. The vision of futility is almost enough to drive Austin to suicide. The same vision is used in James Blish's *Black Easter* (Blish 1969, p.87) – and it is there, explicitly, a weapon in the hands of a black magician:

> Thou shalt straightaway go unto him, not making thyself
> known unto him, but revealing, as it were to come from his
> own intellectual soul, a vision and understanding of that
> great and ultimate Nothingness, which lurks behind those
> signs he calls matter and energy, as thou wilt see it in his
> private forebodings, and that thou remainest with him and
> deepen his despair without remittal, until such time as he
> shall despise his soul for its endeavors, and destroy the life of
> his body.

The "cosmic pessimists", the Lloigor, of Wilson's shorter fable
(1971), are too "rational" to be able to disregard this thought.
Fortunately, most human beings have other resources (as Dr
Johnson's friend remarked: "I have tried in my time to be a
philosopher; but cheerfulness was always breaking in" (Boswell
1953, p.957: 17 April 1778)) – but as long as they are unconscious
and irrational we cannot easily make use of them. The next turn
of the argument – and of enlightenment – is to recognize that
this story too is a fiction. "Since these creatures [the parasites]
had deliberately induced this feeling of total meaninglessness,
they must be in some way *beyond* it." (1967, p.114). If we really
knew nothing of the world "out there" we could not know that
it was meaningless. Conversely, if the world of our experience is
constructed for us, so also is this sudden revelation of a world
larger than our previous petty concerns. The vision of futility
itself demonstrates that we are more than the simple animals it
seeks to make us. "The basic concepts of existentialism are 'the
nausea' and its opposite, man's sense of his interior power, his
reality", so Wilson remarked in an essay on "existential
criticism" in 1959 (2009, p.31; 1st published 1959, 1965).
"Nausea" is the response imagined for his anti-hero Roquentin
by Sartre at the sudden realization of the "alien facticity" of a

tree-root. Austin's imagined response (that is probably also Wilson's response) is happier: he had been reading about Nineveh in his youth while staying at a farm, when it occurred to him to bring in some clothes drying on a line:

> Just inside the farmyard there was a large pool of grey water, rather muddy. As I was taking the clothes from the line, my mind still in Nineveh, I happened to notice this pool, and forgot for a moment where I was or what I was doing there. As I looked at it, the puddle lost all familiarity and became as alien as a sea on Mars. I stood staring at it, and the first drops of rain fell from the sky, and wrinkled its surface. At that moment I experienced a sensation of happiness and insight such as I had never known before. Nineveh and all history suddenly became as real and as alien as that pool. History became such a *reality* that I felt a kind of contempt for my own existence, standing there with my arms full of clothes. (1967, p.18)

It may be doubted whether Roquentin's or Austin's response is the "truer". There is little doubt which is the healthier and happier! What is strange in Wilson's commentary is his belief that moments such as these come late in human history. Far otherwise: on the one hand, "accidie", the noon-day demon of boredom and disillusion, has been the curse of intellectuals for as long as there have been intellectuals (see Norris 1985; Klibansky et al 1964); on the other, the shock of delight that Plotinus calls love is a response to beauty. Beauties "exist and appear to us and he who sees them cannot possibly say anything else except that they are what really exists. What does "really exist" mean? That they exist as beauties" (Plotinus 1966, p. 247: *Ennead* I.6 [1].5, 18f). "Or rather, beautifulness is reality" (Plotinus 1966, p.251: *Ennead* I.6 [1].6, 21). The shock of the real reminds us that we are alive. It is reality that may jolt us out of accidie.

Finding that reality, outside and underneath our usual preoccupations, may also gradually create or reveal in us a "real self" behind or beyond the self we thought we were. So Austin, after his phenomenological discoveries, can say, "I was quite detached from the human being I would have called 'Gilbert Austin' two months earlier, as detached as a puppet master from his puppet" (1967, p.79). Plotinus proposes a similar story: "every man is double, one of him is the sort of compound being and one of him is himself" (Plotinus 1966, vol.2, p.75 : *Ennead* II.3.9 [52], 31-2). It seems that Plotinus himself wished not to be identified, even for the convenience or interest of his disciples, with his bodily form and personal history: "he could never bear to talk about his race or his parents or his native country", and flatly refused to have his portrait taken (Plotinus 1966, vol.1, p.3: *On the Life of Plotinus* 1). Similarly Wilson (commenting on one of J. L. Borges's stories, "Funes the Memorious": Borges 1970, pp.87-95): "to be possessed by a strong sense of purpose is to ignore ninety-nine per cent of your experience, and to forget all the unimportant things that have happened to you" (2009, p.56). This too was Plotinus's goal: to become, or retrieve, the form of consciousness enjoyed, he imagined, by the star-gods. Heracles' shadow, maybe, might recall his earthly life, but Heracles himself no longer minds such things (Plotinus 1984, vol. 4, p.135: *Ennead* IV.3 [27].32). The souls of the stars need not remember where they've been (Plotinus 1984, vol. 4, p.135: *Ennead* IV.4 [28].8, 41ff). This was not, we can be fairly sure, because Plotinus "despised" the natural world: on the contrary, he reserved his most critical commentary for those who did exactly that. "Despising the universe and the gods in it and the other noble things is certainly not becoming good. ...For anyone who feels affection for anything at all shows kindness to all that is akin to the object of his affection, and to the children of the father that he loves. But every soul is a child of That Father"

(Plotinus 1966, vol.2, p.285: *Ennead* II.9 [33].16). Austin would have done well to remember it.

Interestingly, whereas no-one has suggested that *Husserl* had any occult powers, it was widely supposed that Plotinus did: he could identify thieves by immediate intuition, recognize depression in his disciples, and repel magical attacks. When he was persuaded by a disciple to attend a séance intended to reveal his higher self or guardian *daimon*, this turned out to be a god! What exactly any of these stories meant at the time, and especially to Plotinus, is uncertain. Nor are his preferred techniques for stripping away presuppositions, clarifying the motive powers within our souls, or allowing ourselves to be drunk with love of beauty, at all easy to expound or explain. But some of his conclusions seem close to those that Wilson (through his various imagined narrators) also wishes. *Feeling* is a form of perception (1967, p.82). It is through the focusing of our attention that we can progress (1967, p.104). "In the mental sense, all the space in the universe is somehow compressed to a point" (1967, p.124): distance is an illusion. The world we perceive has been built, is being built, by Soul. It is unfortunate that Wilson internalized too soon the popular notion of "Greek" (or more precisely Platonic) thought: as a Neo-Platonist rather than an eccentric phenomenologist he might have developed Plotinus's account in an interesting direction.

Austin and his colleagues, as I have already remarked, often despise ordinarily foolish people (though with a little effort they remember that they were themselves once just as foolish). Similarly, Shakespeare (who is identified, for reasons that escape me, as a front man for Francis Bacon) is unbearable to the hero of *The Philosopher's Stone:* "I felt from the beginning that these people [the characters in *Macbeth* or *Antony and Cleopatra*] are fools, and that consequently nothing that happens to them can possibly matter" (1969, p.152). It would be easy to conclude that both characters are rather too like the "right men gone wrong"

(Tredell 1982) in some of Wilson's other stories. It would be easy, indeed, to suspect that Austin in particular is not just an unreliable narrator, but wholly self-deceived. We have only *his* word that he and his colleagues have defeated the Tsathogguans: another reading of the story would be that the parasites, knowing far more of the human mind than he, have subtly reinforced their self-conceit and petty irritation with the human world. Like others of Wilson's ambiguous heroes Austin and the others kill without pity, though (unlike others) also without much pleasure. Even their apparent victory is tainted: thanks to them, the rest of humanity, united in a hierarchical World State, is fixed in xenophobic terror of the wider world. We are led to suppose that Austin and his colleagues leave to join the universal police, but there is no hint that the police are any more benevolent than Austin, or than the long-ago priest-king of *The Philosopher's Stone*, who instigated mass murder simply to keep the populace from being too happy!

But though this critical re-reading is worth considering, we might also try to understand the overt moral more sympathetically. Whereas most contemporary ethicists are concerned with the simple "welfare" of human beings (or possibly of the wider class of sentient beings), Wilson's heroes share an older philosophical suspicion that nothing of that sort matters.

> The man who belongs to this world may be handsome and tall and rich and the ruler of all mankind (since he is essentially of this region), and we ought not to envy him for things like these, by which he is beguiled. The wise man will perhaps not have them at all, and if he has them will himself reduce them, if he cares for his true self. He will reduce and gradually extinguish his bodily advantages by neglect, and will put away authority and office. He will take care of his bodily health, but will not wish to be altogether without experience of illness, nor indeed also of pain. (Plotinus 1966,

vol. 1, p.205: *Ennead* I.4 [46].14, 14ff).

He will not mind these things for himself, and rather little for others – though Plotinus was trusted to look after the material interests of the orphans trusted to his charge ("in case they should turn out *not* to be philosophers": Plotinus 1966, vol.1, p.31: *Life* 9). Wars and tumults are no more than children's games or theatrical displays, not to be taken seriously: "We should be spectators of murders, and all deaths, and takings and sacking of cities, as if they were on the stages of theatres" (Plotinus 1966, vol.3, p.93: *Ennead* III.2 [47].15, 44f). Plotinus supposed that his soul was larger and older than his current bodily self – a notion at which Wilson's Austin only briefly hints, in a reference to his memory of "previous lives" (1967, p.121). But even without that addition, the philosophical tradition on which Plotinus draws prefers the exercise of our vital powers to the amassing of material or social goods. In this, incidentally, Aristotle was entirely in agreement with Plato: the best form of life is not "the political" but the "theoretical", the life of God. In some later allegories, to achieve this goal the soul must ascend past the moon, and at last past all the planetary spheres, shedding its unhelpful passions as it goes (as of course Wilson's heroes also – perhaps – do). According to the Hermetic text, *Poimandres* (2nd or 3rd century), in its ascent "the soul gives back the power of increase and decrease in the first sphere (i.e. the moon), evil plotting in the second (Mercury), lust in the third (Venus), the proud desire to rule in the fourth (the sun), impiety and audacity in the fifth (Mars), greed for wealth in the sixth (Jupiter) and malevolent falsehood in the seventh (Saturn), and escapes the rule of Fate" (*Poimandres* 1.25: cited by Scott 1991, p.89).

It is easy to misunderstand the Aristotelian (and Platonic) claim, as though they preferred to *think* about living rather than actually *live*. One mode of enlightenment is the discovery of something so far more impressive than our usual petty concerns that we cease to be troubled by them, and by the self industriously constructed so as to deal with them. This is close to the cult of academic objectivity: merely personal beliefs and prejudices should be set aside, and whatever is worth saying must be said "impersonally". But this latter is really a failure of nerve. "The disease of our time is the diffidence, the sense of personal insignificance, that feels the need to disguise itself as academic objectivity when it attempts to philosophise" (2009, p.2). A failure of nerve – or rather an example of bad faith. The attempt to *hide* our own commitments, from ourselves and others, merely leaves them unexamined, and inordinately powerful: the very prejudices that we *should* put aside simply persist as unconscious axioms, even when they are really at odds with each other, or with our professed beliefs. By insisting, for example, that merely *moral* claims are not properly "scientific" or "rational", the investigator is free to act out the moral prejudices he has internalized from childhood. No moral claims are rationally grounded – but it is irrational to doubt that "human beings", just as such, have rights that the non-human don't, and irrational to doubt that "advancing science" justifies just about anything the scientist feels like doing. Education should be entirely "rational" and "progressive" – and it is just obvious that human welfare consists solely in respectable employment and the enjoyment of material goods. The only forms of altruism that creatures like us can be expected to display are nepotistic or manipulative – but we are outraged if officers of the state do what we expect everyone to do.

The moral confusion involved in this refusal to bring our assumptions into the light, and actually examine them, rests on an unexamined conviction that moral heroism is impossible for us. The same conviction lies behind much mainstream fiction (including soap opera) – that "heroes" are unrealistic, and that "ordinary lives" are lived only for the moment, in obedience to transient impulse. Anything else is "fanatical" (and fanatics must all be hypocrites in any case). There are alternative visions, mostly in genre fiction (as Wilson 1963, p.113) – but genre writing only becomes respectable if the supposed heroes are themselves needy, corrupt or incompetent. Aristotle offered a simple division between "tragedy" and "comedy", as these were once understood: tragedies offer characters better or larger than life; comedies concern characters worse, smaller, pettier than life. By this criterion almost all mainstream fiction is comedic – without having really happy endings. As Wilson remarked in the course of complaining about the "unheroic premise" of too much modern art and literature, "the hero is the man who overcomes the obstacles peculiar to his own age" (2009, p.34: 1st published 1959). Why do we so readily relegate "the hero" to the outskirts, to genre literature or popular films? Why not understand that it requires heroism to deal, exactly, with the "great and ultimate Nothingness" that seems to lurk behind the everyday?

Wilson's writings generally, like the best science fiction, follow the pattern of Chesterton's "romantic fiction": "a mixture of the familiar and the unfamiliar, ... picturesque and full of a poetical curiosity" (Chesterton 1908, p.10), respecting common humanity, courage, loyalty, and imagination. Heroes are born from unexpected characters: whether the plump, food-loving archaeologist of *The Mind Parasites*, the death-fearing nerd of *The Philosopher's Stone*, or the space-ship captain of *The Space Vampires*. Wilson commented, in 1963, that he had "come to feel that [Tolkien's *The Lord of the Rings*] may be one of the greatest books of this century" (2009, p.107), perhaps for exactly this reason, that it celebrated an appropriate heroism, without ever losing sight of the perils – including the moral perils – besetting heroes. Notoriously, the literati continue to be appalled that popular judgement agrees with Wilson in this! Austin is an unreliable narrator, and un-satisfactory as a true hero-figure (being too forgetful of the affection owed *all* children of the

Father), but he is nonetheless at least an image of the heroism that we need, unafraid to face the implications of what he knows, and ready to appeal beyond his ordinary self to something altogether other, on the far side of the parasites.

Bibliography:

Blakeslee, Sandra & Ramachandran, V.S. 1998 *Phantoms in the Brain*. London: Fourth Estate

Blish, James 1969 *Black Easter, or Faust Aleph-Null*. London: Faber

Borges, J.L. 1970 *Labyrinths*, edds., Donald A.Yates & James E.Irby. Harmondsworth: Penguin

Boswell, James 1953 *Life of Samuel Johnson*. London: Oxford University Press.

Chesterton, G.K. 1987 'Torture and the Wrong Tool': *Collected Works* vol.5. San Francisco: Ignatius Press; from *The End of the Armistice*, ed. F.Steed (1940).

Fort, Charles 1941 *The Books of Charles Fort* (comprising *The Book of the Damned, New Lands, Lo!, Wild Talents*), intr.Tiffany Thayer. New York: Henry Holt & Co.

Frye, Northrop 2002 *The"third book" notebooks of Northrop Frye 1964-1972*, ed. Michael Dolzani Toronto: University of Toronto Press

Klibansky, R., Panofsky, E., & Saxl, F. 1964 *Saturn and Melancholy* Edinburgh: Nelson

Lessing, Doris 1979 *Shikasta: Archives re Colonized Planet 5*. London: Jonathan Cape.

Lewis, C.S. 1945 *That Hideous Strength*. London: John Lane

Lindsay, David 1920 *A Voyage to Arcturus* London: Methuen

Newman, Bernard 1948 *The Flying Saucer* London: Gollancz

Norris, Kathleen 2008 *Acedia and Me: a marriage, monks and a writer's life*. New York: Riverhead Books

Palmer, G.E.H., Sherrard, P. and Ware, K. 1979 edds., *The*

Philokalia, vol.1. London: Faber

Plotinus 1966-88 *Enneads,* tr. A.H.Armstrong. London: Heinemann, Loeb Classical Library

Ritchie, D.G. 1891 *Darwinism and Politics.* London: Swan Sonnenschein & Co.

Russell, Eric Frank 1986 *Sinister Barrier.* London: Methuen; 1st published 1939, 1948.

Russell, Eric Frank 1957 *Three to Conquer.* London: Denis Dobson

Scott, Alan 1991 *Origen and the Life of the Stars.* Oxford: Clarendon Press

Tredell, Nicholas 1982 *The Novels of Colin Wilson* Barnes & Noble; a second edition, *Existence and Evolution: the novels of Colin Wilson* (Maurice Bassett: Richmond, CA 2007), is available through Amazon Kindle.

Von Uexkuell, Jacob 1957 "A stroll through the worlds of animals and men" in C.H.Schiller, ed., *Instinctive Behavior,* New York: International University Press, pp.5-80.

Wilson, Colin 1963 *The Strength to Dream: literature and the imagination.* London: Gollancz

Wilson, Colin 1967 *The Mind Parasites* London: Barker

Wilson, Colin 1969 *The Philosopher's Stone* London: Barker 1969

Wilson, Colin 1971 "The Return of the Lloigor" (1969), in A.W.Derleth *Tales of the Cthulhu Mythos.* New York: Ballantine Books

Wilson, Colin 1976 *The Space Vampires* London : Hart-Davis MacGibbon.

Wilson, Colin 2009 *Existential Criticism: selected book reviews,* ed., Colin Stanley. Nottingham: Paupers' Press

The Philosopher's Stone (1969)

The Philosopher's Stone: a cosmic adventure story for
the 21st century.

Simon Brighton

I first read *The Philosopher's Stone* in 1982, it was, I think, my
third Colin Wilson book after *The Occult* and *Mysteries*. At the
time I was working near the British Museum and so at lunch
time, or on the way home, I could immerse myself in a 'Colin
Wilson World' of the museum, second hand bookshops and the
numerous pubs in the area. These had been frequented by
Wilson himself and then by the heroes in his books including
the protagonists of *The Philosopher's Stone*.

Re-reading the book after nearly thirty years I am struck by
just how many ideas, facts and philosophies are contained
within its 268 pages. I had forgotten how much I learnt from the
book, for instance I am pretty sure this was the first time I came
across the 'Voynich Manuscript'.

I notice I paid two pounds for my copy, the cover of the now
battered paperback states the book is 'a novel of occult terror in
the chilling H. P. Lovecraft tradition', it also strangely describes
the hero as 'Howard Newman', but in the text he is called
'Howard Lester'. I am not sure how this discrepancy occurred[*].
The cover art of my copy is fairly crude and has a sort of psychedelic impression of some aspects of the story with a bit of artistic
license thrown in. It features a cairn of rocks, atop of which is a
giant purple head spitting fire, its forehead inset with green
jewels. Behind the cairn are a dinosaur and a UFO; a strange eye

---

[*] In fact this originates from the blurb on the dust-jacket of the original British
edition (London: Arthur Barker, 1969) where 'Howard Newman' is named as the
hero whilst on the inside flap he is called 'Harry Lester'! [Ed.]

peeps out from the cairn and the whole scene is set on a dusty desert plain.

The other Wilson novel in the H. P. Lovecraft tradition is the earlier *The Mind Parasites* (1967). Wilson describes in the preface to *The Philosopher's Stone* that he wrote the two books after corresponding with August Derleth, Lovecraft's friend and publisher. Derleth had objected to Wilson's estimation in *The Strength to Dream* (1962) that Lovecraft had some qualities but being a good writer wasn't one of them so he took Wilson to task and suggested if *he* was so good *he* should attempt a 'Lovecraftian' novel himself.

In truth, although they have some points of comparison Wilson's two books are very different to Lovecraft's work. Lovecraft was a writer of fantastic tales, published in magazines. He was writing to grab the reader's attention, while Wilson uses the format to develop his own thoughts and provide a rich panorama of ideas, from the romantics to criminality, poltergeists to genetics.

Lovecraft described his stories as 'cosmic horror', and today he is cited as a hugely influential writer. Authors such as Clive Barker and Stephen King acknowledge him as the creator of a particular style of horror. One significant aspect across his stories is the invented history and Lovecraft's historical 'facts', such as *The Necronomicon*, have achieved such a presence that some argue that they are actually real and that Lovecraft was privy to hidden knowledge.

In one way Lovecraft's stories are directly opposite to Wilson's, as Lovecraft suggests that knowledge of the universe is a dangerous pursuit and his heroes usually come a cropper and lose their minds as a result of foolish ambition. This pessimism — and Lovecraft really was a 'grumpy old man' — is at odds with Wilson's view that man's journey will take him to greater knowledge, understanding and ultimately wisdom. Lovecraft saw the modern age as decadent and aimless, Wilson would perhaps say that the modern age has given man time to think, and it is up to him what he thinks about.

The principle Lovecraftian element of *The Philosopher's Stone* are the 'Ancient Old Ones' the race of disembodied beings that had existed in the universe before life invaded matter. Once they had ruled the earth but now they were forgotten and lost to normal humans existing in a state of suspended animation with the potential to awake at any time.

The pacey style of *The Philosopher's Stone* owes much to classic adventure stories such as the Sherlock Holmes novels, but here it is Holmes doing the narration. Tales of exploration such as Conan Doyle's *The Lost World* are also an influence.

The Philosopher's Stone could be seen as having two parts, part one being the lead up to the Silbury Hill encounter, and part two what occurs subsequently. On reflection I found that I had remembered the book mostly from what happens in part one, and a lot of part two I had forgotten. This is perhaps because the first section is a kind of psychological thriller which engages the reader; while part two of the book develops into a science fiction adventure. Part one creates a great anticipation which part two only partially resolves.

Part one is also a study in the nature of consciousness and the possibilities of transcending normality, portraying the mind as a point in space which, given the tools to 'really' see the universe, would experience a wonderful reality. Part one could be read as a guide to the ideas of Colin Wilson.

The book was written in the late 1960s and the action occurs mostly in the 1970s. It is set in the England of big manors, remote cottages, second hand bookshops and of course the British Museum; there is the occasional excursion over to a university campus in the USA and a scattering of European destinations. The protagonists also eat and drink well: lobster, artichoke hearts with parmesan, huge breakfasts and a great fruit cake are just some examples of the food described, most washed down with a bottle or two of fine wine.

The book begins in the future with the hero Howard Lester writing an account of his life from the perspective of having achieved a state of enlightenment, and the knowledge of how to achieve a longevity previously unknown to humans.

He reflects on his early life which has many similarities to Wilson's own, growing up in a stifling post war Midlands atmosphere which was bereft of ambition, where people 'knew their place' and should not dare to dream (see: Wilson 1968, chapter 2).

Lester feels out of place, as did Wilson, living with the feeling that he is destined for more than being recycled as another member of the working class with little more to look forward to than getting a wage and maybe retiring before death.

At the start of the story it is music which provides stimulus to the young Lester. Pausing outside a church he hears a choir rehearsing, they repeat a choral phrase again and again; it is this repetition that creates in Lester the feeling of detachment and emotional release: 'The effect was almost incantatory, and in the cold night air the voices sounded distant and mysterious, as if mourning for man's loneliness' (Wilson 1974, p.10). He breaks down in tears and has an experience which will take a—very long—lifetime to understand.

The immediate effect of this experience is depression, the young man has seen a glimpse of joy which makes ordinary life seem empty, and he reflects that existence seems futile. This again is straight out of Wilson's own account of his youth where he recalls his brief thoughts of suicide (see: Wilson 2004, p.1-4).

But at 13 Lester meets an older man, Alastair Lyell, who is to be his mentor and provide the direction in life that perhaps Wilson would have wished for at the time. Lyell is a great polymath with his own museum and access to all disciplines of learning. Through him, Lester develops his own knowledge and gains the thirst for learning that would sustain him and take him away from his monochrome Midlands existence.

Lester visits Lyell and his museum whenever possible and begins to ruminate on existence and the nature of time. Occasionally he finds he is able to grasp the 'reality of history', and transcend normal divisions between what is 'now' and what was 'then'. This is a recurring theme in Wilson's books which he sometimes calls 'Faculty X', the ability to perceive and understand other times and dimensions (see: Wilson 1973, p.75-77).

Lester continues his relationship with Lyell through to his young adulthood and during that time he accompanies him on trips around the world to visit the great historical sites.

There were some disagreements though, Lyell failing to agree with Lester's suggestion that mental powers might be heightened in a 'scientific' manner; Lester uses the observations of T. E. Lawrence to support his assertion. Lyell sees this as *un*scientific: "'My dear Howard, you really can't reason like that. It's not scientific. How do you know Lawrence was right...can you devise an experiment to test your theory?'" (Wilson 1974, p.21). Lester is disappointed that Lyell wouldn't at least entertain the notion that 'scientific' methods might be employed in this area.

Lyell dies suddenly and this affects Lester greatly, he sinks into a depressed state and although he is left a sizable inheritance including a seaside cottage, he initially does nothing with it, using the house as a retreat and lapsing into a self-obsessed state of *ennui*.

The light at the end of the tunnel appears when he visits London to attend to matters related to Lyell's will. While at dinner with the lawyer overseeing the estate he accidentally gets drunk and realises that his inebriation has the effect of freeing him from his morose mood; in fact this section of the book has a succession of boozy incidents as Lester consolidates his ideas with a drink in hand. He describes the 'bird's eye view' of consciousness, a sense of clarity and freedom and begins to ponder on the question of whether there might be a methodical way of achieving this enlightenment, and whether these 'breathing spaces' might be summoned at will and without alcohol.

One of Lyell's relations gets in contact, Aubrey Lyell, who invites Lester to Alexandria. Aubrey is fairly hedonistic in his lifestyle and Lester avoids most of the offered excesses preferring to spend his time in the huge library Lyell has inherited from one of his predecessors.

During this month long stay in Egypt he discovers that mathematicians live statistically longer than others and, with a little further research, Lester realises that, on average, all 'thinkers' tend to outlive their fellows.

Lester returns to his cottage and listening to the radio one day, by chance hears a lecture by the scientist, Henry Littleway. Littleway suggests that man's potential has hardly been realised. Lester contacts Littleway who sends him some books by Aaron Marks, a psychologist based on Abraham Maslow (1908-1970) with whom Wilson corresponded and eventually wrote a book about (Wilson 1972). Marks has theories around the 'Value Experience', a phenomenon based on Maslow's 'Peak Experiences'. These are the occasional random moments of affirmation when we seem to transcend our normal mood, feelings of 'absurd good news' as Wilson likes to say.

Lester consolidates his ideas around what he describes as 'otherness'. This 'otherness' is the opposite of the depression he suffered previously at his cottage, a focused perception rather than a world-weary, 'channel-flipping', mentality. Lester sees that Mark's 'Value Experiences' are comparable to his 'otherness'.

Marks also posits that there is a 'dominant minority' of people, corresponding to 5%, who feel there is more to life, those who are unsettled in their regular existence and feel the need to 'progress'. This psychological dissonance often causes frustration, which can be released through crime or creativity.

Lester and Littleway arrange to meet and Littleway states that he feels that progress will only be made in studying the gene code (a prescient observation considering modern preoccupations with decoding the genome and all the claims that have been made for the potential of such an accomplishment).

Lester is invigorated and he feels he is making progress so he throws himself into a frenzy of work and creativity.

He visits Littleway in the Leicestershire countryside, where he meets Roger, Littleway's brother; Roger is a man who sees his own pleasure as the main aim in life whatever the consequences for others.

Littleway and Lester visit a farm-worker, Dick, who has had a brain injury as the result of getting a spike through his head. Dick is loosely based on the case of Phineas Gage who on September 13, 1848 managed to fire a steel pole through his temporal lobe while he was dampening dynamite for blasting a rail track route. Gage managed to survive but with a dramatically changed personality for he no longer seemed to 'care'. This incident was used as the 'evidence base' for later lobotomies attempting to treat depression.

As a result of his accident Dick proves to have developed a 'second sight' together with *idiot savant* traits. The *idiot savant* is a phenomenon that Wilson refers to in a number of books. To him the skills of the *savant* prove that 'everyday consciousness' comes about through a process of filtering-out much of what is available, but 'everyday consciousness' is only one version of consciousness among potentially many more.

The *idiot savant* has lost his ability to filter what is available and is thus handicapped by the amount of information on offer, this results in a need to channel attention into specific areas, often related to numbers or art, and they can often calculate, draw or play music at a supernaturally high level.

Dick had attained his enhanced mental state unintentionally

and therefore has not developed any discipline, being childlike and easily distracted.

Lester and Littleway carry out various tests on Dick, proving that mental vitality has an effect on physical health, but when Dick becomes ill, and dies of a brain tumour, Lester feels he is back to square one since the tumour seems to counteract his theory that a heightened consciousness would protect against illness.

Lester once again retreats to his cottage in a state of pessimism and ruminates on the consequences of his research. During this time he absently fills the days until he experiences a moment of insight into the nature of 'value experiences'. He realises that he had been under the misconception that VEs are an end in themselves, he had presumed that the cultivation of VEs should bring about physical and mental super-health, but he now realises that this is not the case, the VE is just an associated symptom of the 'spider's web consciousness'; the perception that Wordsworth experienced on Westminster bridge, when his mind radiated through time and space; a moment of great transcendence, when past present and future seemed to come together in one. Lester realises that this capacity for transcendence is what needs to be developed. What Wilson is describing here is the mechanism of mysticism, the nature and process of the religious experience.

Wilson often uses the example of Swann in Proust's *Du côté de chez Swann* (*Swann's Way*, 1913) to describe the VE. Swann dips a small cake, a madeleine, in his tea, the taste and smell immediately transport him back in time to his childhood when he enjoyed the same cake. The experience is as overwhelming as it is elusive.

Wilson maintains that artists as a rule do not turn to crime, because the artist has developed his own mechanism for VEs and is able to understand the futility of crime. Because they live mostly in the imagination, artists often have little regard for material possessions whereas the criminal can see no further than his immediate surroundings, and lacks the capacity for the positive feedback that the VE would provide, seeing robbery or rape as a way of meeting his need for self-esteem.

Lester comes to the realisation that there 'is no such thing as normal death, only suicide' and humans could live forever if they could grasp the implications of VEs and develop their consciousness accordingly.

He comes to the conclusion that the prefrontal cortex of the brain is where man's 'hidden powers' can be found. Working with Littleway they come across the 'Neumann alloy', a (fictional) substance developed in early 20th century brain surgery. They insert a minute piece of the alloy into the brain and use a weak electric current to activate it. Employing this method they are able to instil transcendent experiences in their subjects, an alcoholic and a depressed young woman.

Lester decides to have the operation himself, a small piece of the Neumann alloy inserted into his cortex. After this has been done he experiences a heightened superconsciousness, which he realises is in fact 'normal' consciousness, the everyday version a poor relation to what he is now experiencing.

With a little practice Lester trains himself to enter this state without the electric current and is soon experiencing a continuous state of alertness, with this change also come insights such as the knowledge that he has now overcome the restrictions of the usual life expectancy and 'knows' he will be able to live as long as he likes.

Lester's colleague Henry Littleway then decides to have the experiment. Littleway, for much of the book, provides the Dr Watson element, a foil making observations which allow Lester to expound on his own ideas. Littleway is 'converted' by the operation, and starts to appreciate the world in the same way as Lester; previously he had been a little suspicious.

The pair take to driving around the Midlands collecting

obscure books from second-hand bookshops. During one of these trips they take the opportunity to drop in on two elderly ladies, friends of Littleway's family. While relaxing in the garden of their rambling cottage, Lester realises he has the ability to 'see' into the past, a skill, he finds that has developed with his expanding consciousness. He is able to detect the presence of a ghost, and has his psychically gained intuitions confirmed when he checks out the history of the house. Over the next few weeks Lester uses his psychic abilities to look further into the past of the cottage and ultimately manages to decode the Elizabethan intrigue of who really wrote Shakespeare's plays!

During this period he attends a house suffering from a haunting by a poltergeist and finds that he can 'tune in' to the vibrations and either amplify them or cause them to cease; he leaves the house poltergeist free.

While on one of their excursions the pair visit Stonehenge and, employing their ability to divine the past, they are alarmed when they briefly have a vision of giants and an associated feeling of dread. They experiment with psychometry, (the ability to psychically gain knowledge of an object's past by handling it) and they find they are able to establish the true origins of some artefacts, noting that they are far older than thought.

The last section of the book begins with a brilliant description of a climb up Silbury Hill. Lester attempts to mentally dowse the mound but finds that it is unresponsive, all he perceives are pleasant summer sensations, the smell of grass and the noise of a tractor in the next field. He feels a desire to relax in a local pub with a beer and the whole experience provides a warm security, a reassurance that everything is alright with the world. But Lester is suspicious, the impressions from the hill are too benign, he makes an effort and realises that he is being resisted, there is something out there!

While the two are driving back to the Midlands they are involved in a series of near-accidents that make them understand that they are in fact under attack and, as further events demonstrate, the power of these forces is far reaching. Lester and Littleway have to take defensive measures to make sure they are not vulnerable to accident or attacks from people suffering from temporary insanity.

The final section of the book is the account of the battle with the 'Ancient Old Ones'. Lester goes in pursuit of *The Necronomicon*, the legendary text mentioned in Lovecraft's book, and comes to the conclusion that the mysterious (real) text, the 'Voynich Manuscript', is *The Necronomicon*, but like Silbury Hill it is psychically defended.

While studying the illustrated manuscript, Lester and Littleway make a concerted mental effort and, for the first time, glimpse through the defences and encounter one of the terrifying Ancient Old Ones, and finally understand the power of the beings they are up against. They realise, however, that this Ancient Old One is not aware of them, as it exists in a permanent slumber, as do all the Ancient Ones. But while they sleep they have activated 'robot forces' which are designed to repel any inquisitive beings that get too close. It is these robots that maintain the processes which hide the past, and mask sites which have links to the Old Ones such as Silbury Hill and Stonehenge.

Both men are now overcome with a fearful pessimism, for the first time since their operations they are unable to summon the will to persist and for the moment it all seems pointless. Lester realises that the cause of their malaise is the Ancient Old Ones and knows that, as they get close, this oppression will increase. Once he understands this he starts to feel more motivated.

On returning to England Lester and Littleway accidently discover that the robot forces which obscure the past are not aware of photographs and they realise that they can divine from photos without any resistance. So by using photos of ancient objects they are able to mentally travel back seven million years to the continent of Mu. Mu is home to the first humans who were created by the Ancient Old Ones.

They gain knowledge of Mu's birth and violent decline. The great leader of Mu was K'tholo, (an obvious version of Lovecraft's 'Cthulhu'), and after another visit to the British Museum they are able to find a ceremonial basin, which they know originally belonged to the great K'tholo.

While dowsing this basin they discover that K'tholo was the intermediary between the Ancient Old Ones and humans; he was unique and effectively ruled Mu for centuries. Lester learns of the great underground cities the Ancient Old Ones created as they sought to evolve, but this evolution was to bring about their downfall. As they pursued knowledge and attempted to comprehend the universe through science they developed an awareness, a conscious ego, but below this was a powerful subconscious, it was this that revolted. Essentially left to its own devices the collective subconscious of the Ancient Old Ones wrecked their cities and almost destroyed everything, but just in time they comprehended their plight and brought about a mass sleep, inducing unconsciousness across their population, which was the only way to quieten the forces accidently unleashed.

K'tholo watched all this, and, after the Ancient Old Ones slept, he and a small group of survivors from Mu established a foothold on the earth that was the beginnings of human society.

The book finishes with Lester reflecting on his knowledge of the Ancient Old Ones and their situation. He realises that they will not sleep forever and when they awake will, once again, want to rule the world. Man has a choice to either be slaves or masters. So Littleway and Lester take the decision to induct others into their 'super-consciousness'. They aim to form a society of masters who will meet the Ancient Old Ones on equal terms. But will they have enough time before the Ancient Old Ones awake and arrive to claim their world back?

In an essay entitled 'Science Fiction and Existentialism: a

personal view' (1978), Wilson wrote:

> In...*The Philosopher's Stone*, I was less concerned to try to symbolise the forces that oppose our freedom than to express the nature of that freedom....The interesting thing...is that when I set out to express it as *directly* as I could, the medium had to be 'science fiction'. In ordinary fiction, with its reflection of a familiar reality, the characters and events tend to overshadow the ideas—assuming there are any. In science fiction—or speculative fiction—the idea can be reflected clearly, as in a mirror. (Wilson 1989, p.30 & 31)

The critics of the time were undecided as to whether Wilson had utilised the genre effectively. Peter Buckman in the *Times* (June 28, 1969, p.23), praised his "narrative style that can make the pursuit of any idea, however abstruse, seem exciting detective work" and noted that Wilson "...pleases the reader with his skill [and] like the best craftsmen [also] succeeds in making him think about his limitations, his laziness and apathy, his lack of an enquiring interest in ideas and knowledge". In the *Spectator* (222, June 28, 1969, p.857), Barry Cole declared that "In its own idiosyncratic genre, *The Philosopher's Stone* can have few competitors" and considered it to be Wilson's "...best novel to date..." David A. Harsent, in the *Times Literary Supplement* (July 10, 1969, p.745), during the course of a short but dismissive review, made the fatal error of using Howard Newman (the incorrect name of the hero as printed on the dust-jacket), resulting in a rejoinder from Wilson (*TLS*, July 24, 1969, p.820) accusing him of not having read the book! Nicolas Tredell, in his essay for the *Literary Encyclopedia* concludes:

> the novel remains interesting in the twenty-first century for its challenge to a powerful cultural and literary tradition in which the attempt to avoid death or prolong life indefinitely

is seen as inevitably doomed. (Tredell 2008).

References:

Tredell, Nicolas. "The Philosophers Stone". *The Literary Encyclopedia*. 16 July 2008.
http://www.litencyc.com/php/sworks.php?rec=true&UD=23931 (subscription necessary to view full article)

Wilson, Colin (1968) *Voyage to a Beginning*. London: Cecil & Amelia Woolf.

Wilson, Colin (1972) *New Pathways in Psychology*. London: Victor Gollancz.

Wilson, Colin (1973) *The Occult*. St Albans: Mayflower Books

Wilson, Colin (1974) *The Philosopher's Stone*. St Alban's: Panther Books

Wilson, Colin (1989) *Existentially Speaking*. San Bernardino: Borgo Press

Wilson, Colin (2004) *Dreaming to Some Purpose*. London: Century.

The Non-Fiction

The Outsider (1956)

The Outsider: From Existentialism to Enlightenment

Steve Taylor

My discovery of *The Outsider* was a life-changing event – so much so that I can remember it completely clearly. I can even remember the act of pulling the book down from the shelf, in the University of Warwick library, in May 1987, just a few days after my 20th birthday. I was a second-year undergraduate, studying English and American literature – at least I was officially a student, but I had long since stopped going to lectures and only went to the occasional seminar. (I only went to three lectures in the second and third years of my course.) Rather than attending my course, I spent most of my time reading in libraries, or on my own at home, listening to or playing music, writing songs, poems and stories, and feeling depressed and alienated. I often couldn't bring myself to get up in the mornings, and stayed in bed till the afternoons. I frequently fantasised about committing suicide, although I only came close to doing it once.

My alienation was partly due to social differences. Coming from a lower class northern English background, I found it difficult to relate to the more privileged and confident middle class southern students I was surrounded with at the university. But more than that, my alienation had a psychological source. I felt a constant sense of frustration, as if I wasn't the person I was supposed to be, even though I had no idea who that was. I found it difficult to communicate with anybody – every sentence I spoke sounded inappropriate and inauthentic. I had a sense of being trapped inside my own head, alone inside my own mental space with thoughts and feelings that no one else would ever be able to experience. I felt this isolation painfully, and the thought that it would endure for the rest of my life seemed terrible.

Everybody else around me seemed to have one goal in life: to have a 'good time,' to go drinking and socialising, or to smoke cannabis and entertain each other with anecdotes and jokes. I thought I was supposed to be like that too – that was how I'd been brought up – but because of my frustration and depression, I couldn't operate at that level. As a result, I thought that there was something wrong with me, that I was a social failure.

On top of that, I had grown to loathe my course. I hated the cold intellectual way my professors read literary texts, the way they analysed and dissected them as if they were dead animals. It seemed absurd that they had made a career out of writing books about other people's books, presuming to interpret them as if they had written them themselves. I agreed with Flaubert, who complained that literary criticism was the lowest form of literature, even lower than a limerick – since at least that required a degree of creativity.

As a consequence, *The Outsider* came as a revelation to me, at exactly the right time. It hooked me from the first few lines. I took it home and carried on reading until the early hours of the morning. I was captivated by the fluency of Wilson's style – I'd never read a non-fiction book written with such clarity, pace and verve. But what impressed me most – and still impresses me now – is the power and simplicity with which Wilson expresses his ideas. So many philosophers are poor writers, and cloak the core meaning of their words with layers of subterfuge, as if they're afraid that their ideas will appear too simplistic in their naked form. But Wilson had the ability – and the courage – to communicate profound existential and spiritual ideas with great clarity and enthusiasm. I had already been groping towards some of these ideas myself, and to see them expressed so clearly was exhilarating – and also a relief, to discover that I wasn't mad; or at least that if I was, dozens of other distinguished Outsiders were too.

As I read the book, I felt somehow that I was coming home,

that a path was slowly forming in front of me. The next day, when I finished it, I felt like a different person. My image of myself had changed, and I knew that my life was going to change too, that that bleak period I'd been living through was drawing to a close.

Of course, I'm not alone in being so affected by *The Outsider* – apart from its impact on thousands of alienated young people such as myself, in its time it had a massive cultural impact too. Appearing in the mid-50s, it was at the spearhead of what Marilyn Ferguson (1980) called the 'Aquarian Conspiracy,' the wave of self-development and spirituality which became most visible during the 1960s, and has been a major part of Western culture ever since. It was part of the same cultural shift as the Beat poets, psychedelic drugs, Timothy Leary and Carlos Castaneda, Zen and TM, and the hippie movement. In fact, to some degree *The Outsider* actually helped to create this movement, with its advocacy of mysticism and spiritual development, and the attention it gave to previously obscure figures like Hesse and Gurdjieff.

The Outsider as Literature

One of the reasons why *The Outsider* had such a powerful impact is that – as I became aware 24 years ago – it has an outstanding *literary* quality. Even now the book has an amazing freshness. The books of many of Wilson's contemporaries seem sadly dated – Angus Wilson's novels, for instance, or *Lucky Jim*, even *Room at the Top*. You only need to read a few lines to realise that these books belong to a different era. But *The Outsider* is somehow timeless; it could have been published 5 years ago, rather than 55. There are only a few authors whose prose has this fresh quality – for example, Schopenhauer, Henry Miller or F. Scott Fitzgerald. Authors like D.H. Lawrence, Aldous Huxley and George Orwell belong to the 'time-bound' camp. And Wilson is indisputably a member of the former group.

The book's structure also has a literary quality. Wilson originally thought of himself as a novelist, and one reason why *The Outsider* works so well is because of its novelistic structure, its strong narrative arc, and compulsive forward flow. The whole book proceeds in logical, linear fashion. First Wilson deals with the most neurotic and least developed Outsiders (such as the narrator of Barbusse's *L'Enfer* and Sartre's Roquentin); then he moves on to the romantic Outsiders (such as Steppenwolf and Nietzsche), whose isolation was relieved by occasional spiritual experiences; then the artistic Outsiders (such as Van Gogh and Nijinsky), whose art was a means of self-transcendence; and finally, the 'visionary Outsiders' who have truly solved the 'Outsider problem' and reached a permanent state of integration and transcendence.

This narrative arc is the developmental journey of the Outsider, from self-division and alienation, through temporary transcendence to permanent spiritual awakening, or enlightenment. Or in philosophical terms, this is the journey from existentialism, through to romanticism towards mysticism. Unfortunately though, as Wilson shows, many Outsiders don't make the whole journey, but become stuck at the earlier stages, due to a lack of self-understanding or self-belief.

At the centre of the book is Wilson's astonishing, magisterial command of a vast array of literature from a dizzying range of sources. One can scarcely imagine how obscure and esoteric some of the figures must have seemed in 1956, such as Berdyaev, Heidegger, Gurdjieff and Ramakrishna, together with esoteric philosophies such as the Kabbala and Vedanta. As many reviewers remarked at the time, it seems incredible that a young man of 24 (particularly one from a poor working class background) could have been so erudite, and possessed such a powerful, organising intelligence.

The Philosophy of The Outsider

But of course, the main impact of *The Outsider* lies in its ideas, and the evolutionary impetus behind them.

The Outsider prefigures all of Wilson's philosophical work. It's clear from the outset that he's an existentialist – like Sartre and Camus, only with more clarity, he analyses the apparent meaninglessness of human life in an indifferent, empty universe. He describes the existential Outsider's self-division, his 'sense of strangeness, or unreality' (Wilson 1978, p. 25). As he puts it eloquently, 'The outsider's sense of unreality cuts off his freedom at the root. It is as impossible to exercise freedom in an unreal world as it is to jump while you are falling' (ibid., p. 49).

At this stage, the Outsider's defining characteristic is that he can't accept the surface-level realities of the world, the seemingly rational and ordered world of the 'bourgeois.' He 'sees too deep and too much' (ibid., p. 25). The everyday world seems meaningless to him; all its values seem baseless, and its conventions absurd. He needs something more, but his drive is blind; he doesn't have enough insight or self-knowledge to understand it.

If this were the end of it, *The Outsider* would still be a cogent existential analysis of the 'world without values.' But of course, Wilson moves beyond existentialism, and beyond Sartre and Camus. As far as 'solutions' to the 'Outsider problem' go, Sartre advocates authenticity and commitment, while Camus suggests a simple acceptance of absurdity of life, both of which are hardly satisfactory. The difference between them and Wilson is that their philosophies are based on the assumption that the vision of reality which normal human consciousness reveals to us is objective, that it tells us the truth about reality. However, Wilson senses that consciousness is a continuum rather than a static point (although he expresses this idea more clearly in the later books of the Outsider cycle). For him – as for William

James – there are varieties of conscious states, some of which are more intense and expansive than others. Wilson doesn't trust the existential vision of meaninglessness and indifference, because he is aware of the existence of higher states of consciousness in which this vision is transformed, where the 'world without values' becomes a radiant, meaningful and benevolent place. This is where the solution to the 'Outsider problem' lies: in gaining access to the world of meaning beyond the limited reality of normal consciousness.

For me, this is the most important insight of the book – and indeed, of all Wilson's work: his core intuition that there is something wrong with normal human consciousness. What we think of as our 'optimum' state of being is in fact a near patho-logical state of discord, disconnection and alienation from reality. Our normal consciousness is so narrow and limited that we're cut off from the essential wonder and meaning of the world, and from the well-springs of optimism and vitality within our own being. As a result, we're trapped in a dangerous subjec-tivity, suffering from a sense of unreality and inner frustration. (In one of his later major works, *A Criminal History of Mankind*, Wilson describes how this pathological psyche gives rise to crime and violence, and is responsible for the constant conflict and discord which has filled the last few thousand years of human history.)

The imperative, then, is for us to 'unpick' this normal psyche, and transcend it, allowing a new, higher state of consciousness to manifest itself. The Outsider isn't a self-help book, so Wilson doesn't tell us how to do this in any great detail, but he does offer some useful guidelines. The Outsider overcomes his self-division and alienation through self-knowledge and self-disci-pline – most significantly, by learning to discipline his vital energies. The artistic Outsider disciplines his vital energies through his art, but often doesn't manage to heal his divided psyche, because of his lack of self-understanding. Wilson offers

Van Gogh and Nijinsky as examples of this – although they had regular peak experiences, they never overcame their self-division and alienation.

What is really needed is some form of *spiritual* discipline which provides what Wilson describes as 'a deliberate policing of the vital energies' (ibid, p. 113). The Outsider-mystic uses techniques like meditation and prayer to still his 'energy-stealing emotions', in order to 'steadily increase his supply of surplus vital power' (ibid.).[1] This is what 'successful' Outsiders such as George Fox, Blake and Ramakrishna did. At this point the Outsider becomes a visionary, a mystic, with a permanent sense of purpose and meaning. After struggling through confusion, self-loathing and isolation, he realises the spiritual potential latent within every Outsider, and ends 'that long effort as an Outsider' (ibid., p. 295) as a saint.

As Wilson himself became aware later on, what he has created here is a *positive* existentialism – or what might be more accurately described nowadays as a kind of 'transpersonal existentialism.' Whereas philosophers such as Sartre and Heidegger busy themselves with diagnosing the problem, he offers a cure.

This philosophical content seems remarkably prescient, and is another reason why *The Outsider* seems strangely modern for a book written more than half a century ago. In fact, its message seems even more relevant, now that the wave of self-development and consciousness expansion has intensified so much, despite the currents of post-modernist superficiality and scepticism which oppose it.

In recent years, the American philosopher Ken Wilber has been praised for his attempts to bring Western and Eastern psychology together, by integrating the developmental schemes of psychologists such as Piaget and Erickson with Eastern development paths such as Vedanta and Buddhism (see, for example, Wilber's magnum opus *Sex, Ecology and Spirituality*, 1995). And it strikes me that, three decades before Wilber, Wilson was trying to do something similar: to integrate Western existentialist philosophy with the spirituality of Christian mysticism and Eastern philosophy, and in doing so, take existentialism out of its impasse, and find a solution to the *Lebensfrage*.

The Outsider and Evolution

Despite their highly positive tone, some initial reviewers complained that Wilson's use of term 'Outsider' was so broad that it became virtually meaningless. As J.B. Priestley noted, for example, '[The Outsiders'] personalities are so widely various, they present so many different psychological types, that any discussion of them based on their common likeness does not takes us very far' (1988, p.94). This is even truer of Wilson's 'sequel', *Religion and the Rebel*, where figures such as F. Scott Fitzgerald and George Bernard Shaw sit uneasily next to Rimbaud and Wittgenstein. (In his introduction to the 1984 reprint of *Religion and the Rebel*, Wilson himself notes that 'many people I discuss as Outsiders...could just as easily be labelled Insiders' [Wilson, 1984, pp. viii-ix]).

Nevertheless, I believe that the term 'Outsider' is valid, and does identify a real phenomenon. In fact, this is one of the reasons why the book is so significant – because it was the first detailed examination of a new human type, or at least a new kind of consciousness.

Of course, Wilson wasn't the first author to identify this new human type. Nietszche meant something very similar with his distinction between the 'Ultimate Man' and the Superman. The Ultimate Man is completely satisfied with himself as he is, and strives only to make his life as comfortable and enjoyable as possible. But in reality, says Nietzsche, the human being is not fixed and complete, like the Ultimate man, but a process, a bridge and not a goal: 'a rope fastened between animal and

Superman.' (Nietzsche, 1985, p. 43) The potential Superman, like the Outsider, is the person who is not self-satisfied, who has the urge to 'overcome himself.' For him, life is an attempt at 'going across' the gulf between animal and superman.

In his novel *Demian*, Hermann Hesse makes a similar distinction, dividing human beings into a majority for whom life is just a question of keeping themselves comfortable and secure and maintaining the status quo, and a small minority who have an urge for self-transcendence. (Strangely enough, although he discusses *Demian* at some length, Wilson doesn't mention Hesse's use of this distinction.) As the novel's narrator Emil Sinclair says:

> We were 'awake' or 'wakening' and our striving was directed at an ever-increasing wakefulness, whereas their striving and quest for happiness was aimed at identifying their thoughts, ideals, duties, their lives and fortunes more and more closely with that of the herd…Whereas we, on our conception, represented the will of nature to renew itself, to individualise and march forward, the others lived in the desire for the perpetuation of things as they are. For them humanity…was something complete that must be maintained and protected. For us humanity was a distant goal towards which we were marching (Hesse, 1969, p. 137)

The main distinction here is that the potential Superman (or Outsider) feels somehow incomplete and unfinished. He has a dynamic urge to develop, whereas 'ordinary' people are 'static' in the sense that they don't feel this need for growth.

Abraham Maslow's concept of 'self-actualisers' is obviously closely linked to this too. Maslow was puzzled by the fact that only a small minority of people seemed to progress to the highest level of his 'hierarchy of needs', the level of 'self-actualisation.' Most people, he observed, stop striving once their material and emotional needs are satisfied. But self-actualisers keep growing. According to Maslow, whereas 'the motivational need of ordinary people is a striving for the basic need gratifications that they lack', for self-actualisers 'motivation is character growth, character expression, maturation and development' (Maslow, 1970, p. 165).

Self-actualisation is a process which leads to the goal of being 'self-actualised.' This is equivalent to the stage of the 'successful' Outsider – the point where the individual becomes completely integrated, and free of any psychological discord. According to Maslow, the 'self-actualised' person has a constant freshness of perception, is free of negative thoughts or feelings, and lives spontaneously and freely, without any prejudice towards others. He or she has a greater need for peace and solitude than other people, and a sense of duty or mission which transcends their personal ambitions or desires.[2]

But are these distinctions really accurate? Are there really two types of human beings – the poor, unfortunate, ordinary civil servants and factory hands who take the world for granted and are content to repeat the same experiences again and again, and the dynamic few who feel a powerful urge for self-development?

I don't think anyone would seriously suggest that we're dealing with two clear-cut human types. This is another issue which Wilson takes his younger self to task for, admitting the miscalculation that 'I talk about "the Outsider" as if he is a precisely definable type of human being, like an Eskimo or a cannibal. The truth is, of course, that most people contain an element of 'Outsiderism'…For me now, this constant use of the term Outsider gives the book [*Religion and the Rebel*] an element of oversimplification.' (Wilson, 1984, viii-ix).

Rather than a distinct human type, we're dealing a new kind of psyche – or a new kind of consciousness – which is beginning to develop in more human beings, and which manifests itself in different people to a greater or lesser to degree. This new kind of consciousness is more intense and expansive than ordinary consciousness in that it includes a heightened perception of the is-ness and beauty of the world, a heightened sense of connection to other people, nature and the cosmos as a whole, and a sense of the meaning, harmony and ultimate spiritual essence of the universe. The 'Outsiders' (or 'self-actualisers') are simply people in whom this new kind of psyche is strongly developed. The dynamic urge for self-development these people feel is the impulse to allow this new consciousness to manifest itself. In many people, it is latent rather than fully formed, in the same way that the state of a butterfly is latent in a caterpillar. The Outsider's struggle is to bring this latent consciousness to full fruition, and emerge as a higher 'butterfly' self.

As Wilson pointed out later, this struggle is essentially an *evolutionary* urge. From the inner point of view – as opposed to the outer, physical level – evolution is a process of living beings becoming progressively more *conscious:* more aware of their surroundings, of their own selves and their predicament as living beings in the world, with more autonomy and freedom to control their own actions and their environment. And so by intensifying and expanding his own consciousness, the Outsider is contributing to this process. He is effectively an *agent* of evolution, attempting to carry the evolutionary process further forward. His urge for self-transcendence is an individual manifestation of the evolutionary impulse to move forward to more complex and conscious life forms. As Wilson wrote in 1967, 'Evolution has been trying [through the Outsider] to create a human being capable of travelling faster than sound. Capable, that is, of a seriousness, a mental intensity that is completely foreign to the average human animal' (Wilson, 1978, p. 303).

The evolutionary movement which the Outsider is a part of has, I believe, been clearly visible for around 250 years. In my book *The Fall*, I suggest that since roughly the mid-eighteenth century, major cultural changes have occurred which can be seen as the result of a general inner psychological shift. At this time, a new wave of empathy seemed to emerge, a new ability to sense the suffering of other human beings – and animals too – and a new emphasis on the *rights* of other individuals. This led to the women's movement, the animal rights movement, the anti-slavery movement, more humane treatment of disabled people and homeless children, and the abolition of brutal forms of punishment. This empathy spread to nature too, resulting in the Romantic movement, based on the feelings of ecstasy and transcendence which nature induced. More recently, this new sense of connection to nature has given rise to the environmental and ecological movements, a return to the empathic and respectful stance towards nature of many of the world's indigenous peoples. The old duality between the ego and the body – and the sexual repression this gave rise to – has begun to fade away too, resulting in a more open attitude to sex and the human body. And of course, over the last few decades we have also had the 'Aquarian Conspiracy' – a massive upsurge in interest in eastern spiritual traditions, and self-development.

These changes show a movement beyond the separate ego – the separateness which has led to environmental abuse and sexual repression, and the narrowness of consciousness which has led to brutality, oppression and exploitation. In my opinion, they are too significant to be merely the result of social or cultural factors. I believe that they are the visible effects of an evolutionary change – a collective intensification of consciousness, and a progression towards a more integrated, less pathological state.

This is the evolutionary movement which has been – and still is, of course – creating Outsiders, and which they are contributing to.

The Reputation of The Outsider

Even in the 1950s, *The Outsider's* impact was limited by the media backlash against Wilson. (Partly this was his own doing – he has never done himself any favours in his relations with the media, often appearing self-absorbed and arrogant). At the time, nothing did him as much harm as his protestations of his own genius. However, on the evidence of *The Outsider*, it's hard to dispute that something approximating to genius was at work. At any rate, the book shows massive intellectual precociousness, almost to the extent of a child prodigy or an autistic savant.

Wilson is probably one of the few authors whose first book – and in fact, first few books, if we take the Outsider sequence as a whole – was (were) his most fully realised and important. His later works have never quite reached the same level of power and insight, although some have come close (in my opinion, *New Pathways in Psychology* and *A Criminal History of Mankind*). In fact, I should admit that I'm not a great fan of Wilson's books on crime and the supernatural, most of which lack the intellectual rigour of his early work, and sometimes show a lack of critical judgement, too much openness towards the irrational and unproven. The plethora of such books has also tended to weaken the long-term impact of *The Outsider*, and the other books of the 'Outsider Cycle.'(Happily, however, his most recent book, *Super Consciousness*, rekindles some of his insight and power.)

My guess is that, while some of Wilson's more popular work – the many books he has written for financial reasons – will be forgotten, future generations will view him as an important philosopher of human development; someone who saw very clearly – perhaps more clearly than anyone else before him apart from Nietszche – that human beings are incomplete and even subnormal as we presently are, and who helped to facilitate the shift to a healthier and higher state.

For me though, *The Outsider*'s real importance will always lie in its effect on my *own* evolution. In his 1978 introduction to a new edition, Wilson writes that the early success of the book gave him 'a feeling like leaving harbour', (1978, p. 19). And the book had a similar effect on me. It was like being given a code which allowed me to decipher my mental confusion and understand myself. It was a matter of self-esteem too – *The Outsider* told me that there wasn't something wrong with me after all; on the contrary, it was a positive thing to be different. Together with the other books of the Outsider cycle which I devoured soon afterwards – particularly *Beyond the Outsider* and *Introduction to the New Existentialism* – it gave me a sense of identity and clarity, a notion of the path that I was meant to follow through life. I'm still following that path – and I will always be grateful for Wilson's guidance.

References:

Ferguson, M. (1980). *The Aquarian Conspiracy*. New York: Tarcher.

Hesse, H. (1960/1989). *Demian*. (Trans, W. J. Strachan). London: Paladin.

Maslow, A. (1970). *Motivation and Personality* (2nd Edition). New York: Harper & Row.

Nietszche, F. (1985). *Thus Spoke Zarathustra*. (Trans. R. J. Hollingdale). London: Penguin.

Priestley, J.B. (1988). In *Colin Wilson: A Celebration* (Ed. Colin Stanley). London: Cecil Woolf.

Rogers, C. (1980). *A Way of Being*. Boston: Houghton Mifflin.

Taylor, S. (2005). *The Fall: The Insanity of the Ego in Human History* O-Books.

Taylor, S. (2010). *Waking from Sleep: Why Awakening Experiences Occur and How to make them Permanent*. London: Hay House.

Wilber, K. (1995). *Sex, Ecology and Spirituality*. Boston: Shambhala

Wilson. C, (1956/1978). *The Outsider*. London: Picador.

Wilson, C. (1984). *Religion and the Rebel*. (Reprint edition). Bath: Ashgrove Press.

Wilson, C. (1984). *A Criminal History of Mankind*. London: Grafton.

Wilson, C. (2009). *Super Consciousness*. London: Watkins.

Notes:

1   In re-reading *The Outsider* for this essay, I've realised that I may be indebted to Wilson for one of the basic ideas of my own recent book, *Waking From Sleep*. The central concept of the book is that higher states of consciousness – or awakening experiences, as I call them – have two basic causes. Firstly, they can occur when the normal homeostasis of our physiology is disrupted e.g. through fasting, sleep deprivation, self-inflicted pain or psychedelic drugs. Secondly, they can occur as a result of what I call an 'intensification and stilling of life-energy.' This happens when certain activities or situations have the effect of halting or reducing our normal 'outflow' of energy, so that our vitality becomes concentrated inside us. This can happen through meditation, contact with nature, listening to music, sex, general relaxation and so on. As far as I was aware, I developed this idea from Evelyn Underhill's study *Mysticism*, and partly from my observations of how my own awakening experiences occur. But it's possible that the germ of the idea was planted in my mind many years ago, by this passage:

The concentration of the energies is undoubtedly one of the most important conditions of the state the saints call Innigkeit, *inwardness. The saint achieves inwardness by a deliberate policing of the vital energies. He comes to recognise the energy-stealing emotions, all the emotions that do not make for inwardness, and he sets out to exterminate them in himself. As he moves towards his objective, he increases steadily his supply of surplus vital power, and so increases his powers of foresight and hindsight, the sense of other times and other places; there is a breaking free of the body's sense of imprisonment in time and a rising of warm life-energy that is spoken of in the Gospel as 'to have life more abundantly' (Wilson, 1978, p.113).*

If I had been aware of it at the time, I would certainly have quoted this passage and credited Wilson. Hopefully I will be able to for a later edition.

2   Carl Rogers – Maslow's fellow humanistic psychologist, and the founder of person-centred counselling – had a similar concept too, of 'the person of tomorrow.' Like Maslow, Rogers believed that this person was a member of a small but growing minority. He described them as striving for 'a wholeness of life, with thought, feeling, physical energy, psychic energy, healing energy, all being integrated in experience... These persons have a trust in their own experience and a profound distrust of external authority. They make their own moral judgements, even openly disobeying laws that they consider unjust.' (Rogers, 1980, pp. 350-51)

Introduction to the New Existentialism (1966)

Intentionality is the key.

Colin Stanley

Introduction to the New Existentialism is the seventh, and final, volume in Colin Wilson's *Outsider Cycle*. It was published by Hutchinson & Co. in April 1966 and by Houghton Mifflin Co., a year later, in the U.S. In his Preface to the 1980 Wildwood House reprint (re-titled *The New Existentialism*) he explains:

> "I decided that it was a bit too much to expect my readers to read the [previous] six volumes of my 'Outsider Sequence', and that I would try and summarise its essence in one short volume. The result was...perhaps the best and clearest summary of my central ideas...." (8*)

And in the Preface to the original edition, he adds:

> "The purpose of this book is described in the title. The philosophy that is at present known as existentialism...is fundamentally pessimistic—even nihilistic—and a limit seems to have been reached in its development ....Existentialism has halted in a *cul de sac*....In the six volumes of my 'Outsider Sequence' I have attempted to outline a 'new existentialism' that will possess...the possibility of future development." (9)

The book is divided into two parts: 'The Crisis in Modern Thought' and 'The New Existentialism'. In a short introduction to Part One, Wilson outlines his own approach to the problem. He first of all defines existentialism and explains how it came into being. He regrets that: "It seems to be generally accepted that existentialism is necessarily a philosophy of pessimism or at least, of a very limited, stoical kind of optimism"(14) and feels that there is a "...certain atmosphere of gloom..." (14) which pervades books on the subject:

"All the existentialist texts that I know—whether by [Jean Paul] Sartre [1905-1980] or [Gabriel] Marcel [1889-1973], [Karl] Jaspers [1883-1969] or [Albert] Camus[1913-1960]—seem to share this atmosphere. It is an atmosphere we encounter a great deal in modern literature, even in writers who could not be described as existentialists—Aldous Huxley [1894-1963] and Graham Greene [1904-1991], Samuel Beckett [1906-1989] and Eugène Ionesco [1909-1994], Ernest Hemingway [1899-1961] and T.S. Eliot [1888-1965]. It is completely unlike the atmosphere we encounter in [H.G.] Wells [1866-1946] or [George Bernard] Shaw [1856-1950] or [G.K.] Chesterton [1874-1936], whose suppositions are optimistic." (14-15)

[Wilson deals with this tendency in modern literature at greater length in *The Age of Defeat* (1959), the third volume in the *Outsider Cycle*.]

He feels that Sartre's theory of man's contingency ("...[the] sense that he is somehow not 'necessary', that he is an accident" (16)) is denied by the 'peak experience'—that sudden rush of pure happiness that we all experience in moments of delight—as described by the students of the American psychologist Abraham Maslow (1908-1970):

"Modern literature and psychology play a considerable part in forming the picture that we have of ourselves; but according to Maslow they have been guilty of an underestimation of man's character and potentialities." (17)

In Chapter One: 'The Old Existentialism', Wilson assesses the contributions of Søren Kierkegaard (1813-1855), Jaspers, Martin Heidegger (1889-1976), Sartre and Camus and explains why he thinks that existentialism is a failure:

"Existentialism, like romanticism, is a philosophy of freedom. It has reached a standstill because no existential thinker can agree that there are any values outside man— that is, outside man's ordinary, everyday consciousness. Man is free, says Sartre...but the world is empty and meaningless—this is the problem. While this sentence remains a summary of existentialism, there is nothing further to be done." (33)

In Chapter Two 'What is Phenomenology?', Wilson attempts to show that a way out of this *cul de sac* can be achieved by using the philosophical method of phenomenology, founded by Edmund Husserl (1859-1938), to study the structure of consciousness:

"Consciousness must not be taken for granted as something too obvious to need further questioning. Consciousness itself must be studied.... While philosophy confines itself to the external universe, it is only half a science." (39)

Intentionality, the central concept of phenomenology, is seen as "...the key not only to phenomenology, but to a new existentialism" (40)

"Consciousness itself...is intentional. It is not a plane mirror, merely reflecting the world. It makes its own distortions, quite apart from our natural human tendency to distort the world through our emotions and prejudices" (41)

The result is that:

> "We 'read' the world around us; it is actually a confused
> mass of sights and sounds. Our senses filter out about
> ninety per cent...so that we do not even have to notice
> them...[and] learn to find their way among the confusion
> of the remaining ten per cent by inventing convenient
> short-cuts. It sorts the world out into convenient symbols,
> and attaches more or less importance to various symbols
> according to its inclination." (48)

So life is "largely a matter of habits...and habit means taking for
granted" (49):

> "An existential philosopher cannot even begin to be
> objective until he knows something about his habits of
> thought—what he takes for granted because it happens to
> be the most convenient way of grasping the world" (49)

Wilson believes that Husserl's phenomenology has made it
possible for "A philosopher [to] be self-critical enough to keep
his actual prejudices out of his philosophy"(50) thereby creating
the possibility of existentialism becoming a "true philosophy"
(50).

In Chapter Three, 'The Meaning of Husserl's Revolution',
Wilson explains the aim of phenomenology and how it has been
variously applied (in particular by a group of American psychologists known as Transactionists). He concludes with a short
section on Alfred North Whitehead (1861-1947) whose
suggestion that we possess *two* modes of perception—
'immediacy' and 'meaning'—is seen as a significant development.

In Chapter Four 'The New Picture of the Universe', Wilson
suggests that:

"...the fundamental drive of human life is not some Freudian libido or death-wish, nor the fear of the unknown and the need for security, but an *evolutionary appetite* of which the other appetites are minimum-manifestations..." (78)

And that:

"The chief characteristic of the human being is that his interests extend far beyond mere survival and comfort. The need for survival is a mere sub-department of the appetite for fruitful activity and a high quality of life" (80)

This was obviously not always the case. Wilson believes that roughly the turn of the nineteenth century is the time when "Large numbers of these creatures with a new 'minimum requirement' begin to appear in the western world..." (80). Equating this progress to that of amphibians struggling to breathe in a new way, he nevertheless sees that man has a long way to go before he becomes a fully fledged land animal: "The truly human will indicate an entirely new degree of freedom. The problem that is of importance at the moment is how this can be *made* to happen" (81).

For the remainder of the chapter, Wilson turns his attention to existential psychology: "The existential psychologist is inclined to accept that creative frustration may be as important a cause of neurosis as the usual negative fears and anxieties" (83). He explains how Maslow cured alcoholics with the aid of the drug LSD. Apparently all those cured had peak experiences under the drug, induced by music or visual stimuli:

"Alcoholism is based on a misconception...it is a failure to recognise that the passive attitude towards pleasure is indissolubly connected with the law of diminishing returns. The peak experience destroys this misconception in those intelligent enough to grasp its significance" (89)

Wilson does not advocate the general use of LSD for this purpose but he sees that occasional application can provide a "stimulus to phenomenological self-analysis" (90)

> "Peak experiences are necessary; they recharge the creative batteries. A psychologically healthy person has, to some extent, mastered the art of inducing peak experiences without the aid of drugs. Phenomenological analysis is an attempt to discover the conscious structure of *any* experiences...If drugs like LSD can help to provide peak experiences, and phenomenological analysis can help to uncover their structure, the significance of the method may go far beyond its possibilities as a cure for alcoholism." (90-91)

Part Two, 'The New Existentialism' commences with a chapter entitled 'The Man in the Fog':

> "The first half of this book has been little more than a clearing of the ground. In this second part, I shall try to show that existentialism, far from being a dead philosophy, is in fact the only modern philosophy with a long and clear road of development ahead of it" (95)

He acknowledges that "...the basic impulse behind existentialism is optimistic..." (96) but feels that in the work of Heidegger and Sartre "...the great trumpet call of optimism no longer sounds. There is no clear road ahead" (97). They are like men sitting in a boat surrounded by fog: "...the 'old existentialism' is a failure only because it cannot penetrate *far enough* into the fog...It is 'negative' only through certain errors of judgement" (97).

Wilson sees the central problem of existentialism as man's contingency: "Contingency is passivity, the opposite of will...Man takes it for granted that his consciousness is a *passive* observer of the world..." (99). But "...phenomenology points out that consciousness is intentional" (99) and the first step towards the 'new existentialism' is the recognition of this. "The most basic mistake of both Sartre and Heidegger was to misinterpret this intentionality, and consequently to fail to see its implications" (99-100).

In the final section of this chapter, Wilson suggests that: "The first *practical* necessity for the existential philosopher is to learn to become constantly aware of the intentionality of all his conscious acts" (100). We need to accept the fact that we are constantly observing the world "...through the coloured spectacles of some mood or other" (100).

"We cannot talk about contingency until we are in full possession of the facts about the intentionality of consciousness. For what is subject to contingency is the 'false self,' the idea of ourselves built upon the fallacy of passive perception...Every man is a Jekyll and Hyde; a Jekyll of 'passive consciousness,' a Hyde of intentionality. The aim of phenomenological discipline is to destroy the duality..." (102)

He assures us that "to become aware of the continual intentionality of consciousness is to produce a change in consciousness..." (101-2) for "Jekyll is a dwarf; Hyde a giant" (102).

Chapter Two, 'The Extension of Consciousness,' examines those mystical, aesthetic or poetical experiences which produce the effect "of the fog lifting, and the sudden vision of 'increasing ranges of distant facts' standing up like mountains" (104) and cause us to ask: "Why are we forced to live in this depressing slum of consciousness when our perceptions are perfectly capable of grasping the wider horizons?" (105). Because "the delusions of passive consciousness make man particularly susceptible to pessimism...to 'intentionalising' his perceptions so that they take on a negative flavour" (107), Wilson answers that it would not be safe for human beings to live in a broader state of consciousness until they learn to "achieve a phenomenological discipline that enables them to recognise how far pessimism is intentional" (108).

In the final section of this chapter, Wilson addresses the problem of boredom. In an effort to create a centre of security, human beings deliberately limit their consciousness. But:

"The psychological 'blinkers' that are designed to protect our energy and vitality may have the opposite effect. Too much security becomes boredom, and boredom leads to a decline in vitality. Man has surrounded himself by walls, and has built his narrow 'human world' as a centre of security; but the security has begun to stifle him" (111)

Here Wilson introduces one of his favourite characters from literature: Faust [created by Johann Wolfgang von Goethe (1749-1832)]—the intellectual who contemplates suicide before the Easter bells suddenly evoke the essence of his childhood:

"The episode of the Easter bells is of symbolic importance. Faust...has examined his life and decided it is not worth living. He has certainly examined it to the best of his ability *with his intellect*. What the bells teach him is that, in this matter, the intellect is a false guide. It is the fallacy of all intellectuals to believe that intellect can grasp life. It cannot, because it works in terms of symbols and language. There is another factor involved: consciousness.

If the flame of consciousness is low, a symbol has no power to evoke reality, and intellect is hopeless...The Easter bells are a symbol of the 'beyond,' the assertion of the *real existence* of a world of beauty and intensity beyond our narrow human consciousness" (112)

This, Wilson asserts, is what is missing from the world of the 'old existentialism': "The 'philosophical equation', as propounded by Sartre and Camus, insists on sticking to 'this world,' as revealed to us through our limited consciousness" (113). Inevitably, he feels, this can only end in a *cul de sac*. To avoid this we must make "phenomenological analysis a second nature, and to make it a fundamental premise of our lives that the world of beauty and intensity has a real existence." (113).

In Chapter Three, 'Inside the Dark Room', Wilson furthers his investigation of the problem of limited consciousness by looking at the results of sensory deprivation experiments conducted at Princeton University in the early 1960s. Subjects were asked to stay in a completely dark, soundproofed room (containing a bed, a supply of food and a chemical toilet) for as long as possible. Some pressed the 'panic button' after just a few hours but others, who stayed in for up to three days, reported that colds cleared up quicker than usual and chain-smokers lost the desire to smoke.

"The subject in the dark room feels boredom and a vague sense of discomfort. Having nothing to distract his attention from it, the full battery of his powers of 'intentionality' are turned on it, magnifying it tenfold, with a result that can turn to panic.

On the other hand, if we have a cold or some other physical ailment, the sheer distractions of everyday life prevent us from turning the full battery of intentionality on it—in this case, to cure it. The dark room releases these

inner powers, which 'melt' the ailment like the sun on ice"
(117)

It is clear to Wilson that "man possesses enormous powers which
he prefers not to use" (118). His 'new existentialism' is founded
upon the belief that 'ordinary' consciousness is voluntarily
restricted:

> "Man has evolved to his present position by his capacity to
> narrow his attention, to 'exclude' whatever has nothing to
> do with the business in hand. This excluding has become
> a habit, so that when he ceases to strive, he becomes
> bored." (123)

Sometimes, after long periods of concentration, our excluding
faculty can get jammed and we continue to look at things with
indifference to the extent that not even pleasure can stimulate us.
Yet, paradoxically, the prospect of pain or inconvenience can
administer a jar to the 'excluding faculty' and unjam it. "I have
called this state in which we can be stimulated by pain (or inconvenience) but not by pleasure 'the indifference threshold'" (122).
He has also labelled this phenomenon 'the St Neot Margin'.

Wilson believes that the time has come "for man to evolve to
a new level, in which contemplation comes naturally, in which
he explores the world of his own being" (123). However:

> "The world itself is a gigantic 'dark room' that proves that
> we are too dependent on physical stimuli. The countries of
> the mind may be vast, but man cannot get a visa to stay
> there. He can only get a day ticket that forces him to return
> every night" (125)

This was the conundrum that confronted and destroyed many of
the nineteenth-century poets and romantics:

"The major mistake of the nineteenth-century romantics—
and it is repeated by existentialism—was to look for a
'practical' solution: religious conversion, political
engagement.... The idea that philosophy might provide
the answer struck them as somehow too cold and
uninviting. And yet it becomes increasingly apparent that
this is where the answer lies" (131)

So, "what now remains is the problem of method, of the tools for
attacking it...the main problem for the 'new existentialism' is to
create a tool of philosophical analysis..." (132-3).

[At this point it is interesting to note that Wilson, as was often
the case in the 1960s, was concurrently expressing his philosophical ideas in the form of a novel. Thus a first draft of the
'spy' novel *The Black Room* (London: Weidenfeld & Nicolson,
1971) appeared as 'Margin of Darkness' in *The Minnesota Review*
(vol. 6, no. 4, p. 268-295) in 1966].

In Chapter Four, 'Language and Values,' Wilson sees the need to
"invent new words to describe effects for which the old
language is inadequate" (135)—a language to describe those
"glimpses of horizons of distant fact" (143)—and asserts that "a
'new existentialism' must begin with the rather pedestrian task
of pushing its scaffolding of language into these new realms"
(142). Returning to the analogy of the man in the boat
surrounded by fog, he feels that the philosopher must be able to
extend his scaffolding into this fog and concludes that "...the
'new language' of existentialism will be created out of a patient
attempt at phenomenological description of man's inner
states..." (148).

Chapter Five, 'Everyday Consciousness is a Liar,' was
considered important enough to be included by Wilson in his
self-edited collection *The Essential Colin Wilson* (London:

Harrap, 1985). "Let us be quite clear about the implications of all this," he writes, "for they constitute a revolution in philosophy" (151). Peak experiences make us aware of the weakness and the inadequacy of our everyday consciousness: "Everyday consciousness is a liar, and most people have insights to this effect at least once a week" (152). In these moments we become aware of a "...deep sense of purpose.... Such a sense of purpose cannot exist unless we first make the assumption that our sense of contingency is a liar, and that there is a standard of values external to everyday consciousness" (153). This highlights the difference between the 'old' and 'new' existentialism:

> "The old existentialism emphasises man's contingency. It says that since there is no God, there are no 'transcendental values' either. Man is alone in an empty universe [his] actions are of no importance to anyone but himself" (152)

Like a blinkered horse, mankind has narrowed its consciousness, concentrating on the present and its problems:

> "For several centuries now, the direction of our culture has been a concentration upon the minute, the particular. In the field of science, this has produced our present high level of technological achievement. In the field of culture, we have less reason for self-congratulation, for the concentration on the particular—to the exclusion of wider meanings—has led us into a *cul de sac*" (154)

Wilson feels that an objective study of human values would be of use here but there is a problem:

> "A value is a response, an immediate flow of vitality and optimism. But since our consciousness is so limited, it is

precisely our 'ultimate' values that are *not* responses. A saint like Ramakrishna may be able to establish immediate vital contact with his deepest values; but most of us have to work in the dark." (156)

Nevertheless:

"The new existentialism consists of a phenomenological examination of consciousness, with the emphasis upon the problem of what constitutes human values. And since moods of optimism and insight are less accessible than moods of depression and life-devaluation, the phenomenology of life-devaluation constitutes the most valuable field of study" (157-8)

But "The analysis of consciousness is only half the task. The other half consists in the analysis of language" (158). This "...implies the creation of a language and a set of concepts in terms of which we can discuss it" (152):

"Not the least important feature of the 'new existentialism' is that it is able to unite the two major traditions of twentieth century philosophy: linguistic empiricism and phenomenological existentialism" (159)

In the final chapter, 'The Power of the Spectre,' Wilson explains:

"One of the reasons that the 'old existentialism' found itself immobilised was that it tried so hard to compromise with academic philosophy. To a large extent, the difficulties encountered in a text of Jaspers, Heidegger or Sartre are the difficulties that the author feels to be necessary to an academically respectable philosophy.

The truth is that existentialism has more in common

with science fiction than with academic philosophy." (160-
61)

To illustrate his point, Wilson introduces the concept of the 'mind
parasites':

"To express this problem in science fiction terms: it would
seem that there is some mysterious agency that wishes to
hold men back, to prevent them from gaining full use of
their powers. It is as if man contained an invisible parasite,
whose job is to keep man unaware of his freedom.
[William] Blake [1757-1827] called this parasite 'the
spectre.' In certain moments of vitality and inspiration, the
spectre releases his hold, and man is suddenly dazzlingly
aware of what he *could* do with his life, his freedom" (161)

Wilson feels that, in our age of increased leisure, the spectre
seems to be making even greater efforts to defeat us: "...we have
never been so bored and depressed, and the increased rate of
suicide and neurosis is becoming one of our major social
problems" (162). But "...if man can become fully conscious of [it]
and turn the full battery of his attention on it" (162) the enemy
can be defeated and the problem solved: "...and a new phase of
evolution will have begun, the phase of the truly human—or
superhuman, as Nietzsche called it" (162).

[This concept became the central theme of Wilson's 1967 novel
The Mind Parasites (London: Arthur Barker) written in the science
fiction genre. In an extended essay entitled *Science Fiction as
Existentialism*, he describes *The Mind Parasites* as: "...an attempt
to state symbolically what I felt to be wrong with human beings:
that through art and mysticism, we obtain glimpses of a
tremendous freedom which seems, in effect, to be beyond our
reach" (Wilson (2); 13). This remains, without doubt, the novel

that most clearly conveys Wilson's ideas about the human condition. R.H.W. Dillard suggests that it is "...a most effective and comprehensive metaphor" (Dillard; 147) and I have elsewhere described *The Mind Parasites* as "the ultimate allegory" (Stanley; 25)]

For Wilson "It is extremely important to grasp the notion that *man does not yet exist*. This is not intended as a paradox or a play on words; it is literally true" (163). Most animals are like machines with consciousness, they live in a perpetual present. So, says Wilson, does man but his imagination and intellect give him the means to live life "...at a level of intensity and purpose that is impossible for the mere animal" (164). The question is "...how can man learn to use this imagination to conquer the 'fallacy of passive consciousness,' to reach out to the 'ranges of distant fact'?" (164).

We can only achieve this, he believes, by totally changing our viewpoint and he spends the rest of the chapter trying to convince the reader to adopt a positive, and therefore purposive, attitude:

"Man is instinctively aware that he is a 'purposive' animal, that he was not intended to live passively in the present. He therefore feels an instinctive protest against the present and its values. If he is not far-sighted enough to see new horizons of purpose, he may still feel a deep dissatisfaction with his present values" (165-66)

Consider the poetic experience: "The mind hovers above objects, and sees them freshly, as on the first day of a holiday" (176). Contrast this with the phenomenon of boredom. To illustrate this Wilson provides the example of starting a routine office job. At first the surroundings are fresh and the job new but soon boredom sets in:

"My 'automatic pilot' has taken over my perceptions. The usual role of this 'automatic pilot' is to free my mind for more important tasks; but since I am condemned to the trivial, his only effect is to hand me over to my defeat. If this canker of boredom is allowed to eat deeply enough into me, it will rob me of all my energy, all my creative delight, so that even a beautiful scene will fail to arouse any response" (178)

Sartre is criticised for "...his assertion that to see the world as meaningless and indifferent is to see it 'truthfully'...." (178):

"Like misery and pain, boredom is a projection on to my surroundings. It is true that my surroundings are neutral. But if I experience beauty, I am not *projecting* beauty on to my surroundings. I am simply experiencing my *real inner freedom*, which the complex nature of my response to existence usually conceals from me." (178)

[This important concept of the 'automatic pilot' was later re-labelled by Wilson 'The Robot': "[The] Robot is a labour-saving device....When an activity has been performed often enough, he takes it over and...does it a great deal more efficiently than I could do it consciously...." However, "Whenever I acquire some new skill, it gives me pleasure, but the moment the Robot takes over, the pleasure vanishes.... The consequence is that when life is peaceful, we find it difficult to feel really alive...." (Wilson (3); 38-40)]

So:

"The 'new existentialism' accepts man's experience of his inner freedom as basic and irreducible....[It] concentrates the full battery of phenomenological analysis upon the everyday sense of contingency, upon the problem of 'life-devaluation.' This analysis helps to reveal how the spirit of freedom is trapped and destroyed; it uncovers the complexities and safety devices in which freedom dissipates itself. It suggests mental disciplines through which this waste of freedom can be averted." (180)

Wilson's conclusion is inevitably optimistic:

"Sartre and Heidegger are mistaken; it is not true that there is 'no exit' from the human dilemma.' There is a very clearly marked exit. Any man who can see this, and is capable of making the choice that the insight demands, has already taken the first step in a new phase of human evolution." (181)

Although *Introduction to the New Existentialism* is currently out-of-print, an excellent précis is available as *An Essay on the New Existentialism* (Nottingham: Paupers' Press, 1986).

Contemporary reviews of *Introduction to the New Existentialism* were mixed—a very similar response to the previous four volumes in the *Outsider Cycle*. In the *Times Literary Supplement*, the anonymous reviewer, whilst begrudgingly admitting that "Mr Wilson has some things which are worth saying...," went on to argue "...but his positive thesis will appeal only to those who, like himself, have rejected traditional religious and ethical systems but still demand an "answer" to life..." ('Only Exist', *Times Literary Supplement*, Jan 26, 1967, p.72). In a largely unfavourable review for *The Spectator*, Christopher Ricks starts off encouragingly:

"A protesting admirer of Colin Wilson might speak for him like this: 'Whatever his faults, he is a cosmopolitan. His mental background, insofar as it is not English,

is predominantly French and German. His cast of mind reflects the mutual interplay of two Continental European traditions: German Hegelianism and French Existentialism. His writings are proof that he is familiar with the work of Daumal, Frankl, Husserl and Kimmel...'"
('The Latest Wilsons' *New Statesman*, May 13, 1966, p.695)

But adds: "Of course, he might be all of that and not very good." The reviewer in *British Book News* (July 1966, p.484-5) concludes that the book has "...the belligerent and engaging air of a do-it-yourself philosophy." William Tonks, in *The Aylesford Review* (Summer 1966, p. 67-8), writes "This seems to me the best book Mr Wilson has written," and considers it to be "...lively, provocative and readable...." In America, Walter Kaufmann in the *New York Times Book Review* ('Existentialism, New and Old' July 30, 1967, p. 6) dismissed the new existentialism as "...a gimmick rather than a philosophy" and asserts that Wilson's "...brisk chatter and constant name-dropping cannot allay the impression that his optimism is as shallow as his unreflective contrast of 'optimism' and 'pessimism.'" No contemporary reviewer, however, was more enthusiastic than Grattan Freyer in *The Irish Times* ('Outsiderism' June 4, 1966, p.8):

"...I shared the critical enthusiasm for *The Outsider* when it first appeared. But I only read reviews of the later volumes, and formed the impression that Wilson was "written out"...I now realise how wrong I was—which shows how foolish it can be to judge a writer by the reviews he gets!...Anyone seriously concerned with twentieth-century values must make themselves familiar with Colin Wilson."

John A. Weigel adds:

"The work is a readable and informative guide.... Although most of his arguments are familiar to those who know the earlier essays and novels, this volume is unusually lucid....Wilson is intent on opening the door that Sartre marked 'no exit.'" (Weigel; 131-2)

But what of Wilson's philosophy as expressed in the *Outsider Cycle* as a whole? In a recent article, Matthew Coniam wrote:

"...the *Outsider Cycle* (along with some of the later books, notably the simply magnificent *A Criminal History of Mankind* [London: Granada, 1984]) does offer solid grounds for taking seriously Wilson's assertion that his ideas constitute a mini-revolution in philosophy, for he has managed to winch the worldview of humanist existentialism free of the impasse of despair in which it had been reluctantly abandoned by Sartre and Camus" (Coniam).

The philosopher John Shand adds:

"What strikes me as distinctive about Colin Wilson's philosophy is that it does give one some clue as to how to answer the much vexed question, "How should I live?"... Wilson's philosophy in fact tries to answer questions which are eminently practical, and which could well affect one's everyday actions" (Shand; 4)

Whilst Howard F. Dossor believes that:

"...the seven volumes of the Outsider cycle is a single work and it is one of the most seminal works of our century. Even then, it must be acknowledged that it does not stand alone. It is the cornerstone of a profound literary production...that is stunning in its consistency and its vitality." (Dossor; 56)

However, the final word should go to Wilson himself who wrote in his Preface to the 1980 reprint of *Introduction to the New Existentialism*: "If I have contributed anything to existentialism — or, for that matter, to twentieth century thought in general, here it is. I am willing to stand or fall by it." (8)

* All quotes are from the 1980 edition of *Introduction to the New Existentialism* (re-titled *The New Existentialism* London: Wildwood House Ltd).

References:

Coniam, Matthew 'The Forgotten Existentialist' in *Philosophy Now*, June/July 2001, p.20.

Dillard, R.H.W. 'Toward an Existential Realism: the novels of Colin Wilson' in Stanley, Colin (ed) *Colin Wilson, a celebration: essays and recollections*. London: Cecil Woolf, 1988, p.137-149.

Dossor, Howard F. *Colin Wilson: the man and his mind*. Shaftesbury: Element Books, 1990.

Shand, John 'Colin Wilson as Philosopher' in Shand, John & Lachman, Gary *Colin Wilson as Philosopher & Faculty X, Consciousness and the Transcendence of Time* (Colin Wilson Studies #9) Nottingham: Paupers' Press, 1996.

Stanley, Colin 'The Ultimate Allegory: Colin Wilson's *The Mind Parasites*' in Stanley, Colin *'The Nature of Freedom' and other essays* (Colin Wilson Studies #2). Nottingham: Paupers' Press, 1990.

Weigel, John A. *Colin Wilson* (Twayne's English Authors Series). Boston: Twayne Publishers, 1975.

Wilson, Colin (2) *Science Fiction as Existentialism*. Hayes, Middx: Bran's Head Books Ltd., 1978.

Wilson, Colin (3) *Poetry & Mysticism.* London: Hutchinson & Co., 1970.

Poetry and Mysticism (1969/1970)

Poetry and Mysticism

Gary Lachman

In March 1968, Colin Wilson and the Beat poet and publisher Lawrence Ferlinghetti sat in a bar in San Francisco, talking about a girl who died after taking an overdose of a psychedelic drug. In recounting their meeting, which he does in his book *Poetry and Mysticism*, Wilson remarks that the drug was 'new', and I'm inclined to wonder if it was 2,5-dimethoxy-4-methylamphetamine, or DOM, otherwise known as STP, which, according to one social historian, was 'distributed free in incautiously large doses throughout the Haight-Ashbury district of San Francisco in the summer of 1967'.[1] I'm also inclined to wonder what bar Wilson and Ferlinghetti sat at, as I know San Francisco fairly well. The North Beach district, where Ferlinghetti's City Lights Bookshop is located, is an old beatnik stomping ground, the Californian equivalent of Wilson's own Notting Hill and Soho from his 'angry young man' days in the late 1950s. While Wilson, Stuart Holroyd, Bill Hopkins, and Alex Trocchi were causing trouble at Chepstow Villas W11, Allen Ginsberg, Jack Kerouac, Gary Snyder, and Ferlinghetti himself were howling into literary history on the streets of San Francisco. The parallels were striking enough that in 1958, Gene Feldman and Max Gartenberg produced an anthology of work from both groups, entitled simply *The Beat Generation & The Angry Young Men*. In looking at the list of contributors, which includes William Burroughs, Kingsley Amis, and John Braine – not to mention Kerouac and Ginsberg – it's sobering to note that Wilson is one of the few who are still alive. He's even been able to tell the tale himself, as a look at his entertaining *The Angry Years* will show[2].

Wilson is always very good in writing about his encounters

with other writers, but there is something about this drink with the author of *A Coney Island of the Mind* – one of the 'must reads' of my teens – that I find significant.[3] It was, of course, the prompt for Wilson to write *Poetry and Mysticism* – which I will get to shortly – but it also affirms Wilson's roots in that rebellious literary world of the late 50s. Everyone knows that Wilson began his career in 1956 with *The Outsider*, but many of Wilson's contemporary readers know of him only through his 'ancient civilizations' books, or his books about crime and murder, or his many explorations into the occult. Indeed, Wilson has written a great deal *about* a great deal, so much in fact, that many of his readers today are sadly unfamiliar with his earlier work. What I like about imagining this drink with Ferlinghetti, is that it places Wilson in the literary world he started out in. It somehow – for me at least – affirms that he is first and foremost a *writer*. His topic might be philosophy, serial killers, mystical experience, Neanderthal Man, or sex, but he approaches these subjects – and many others – in what I can only call a 'writerly' way, trusting that the reader will grasp some idea of what I mean by this rather vague term.

Having said this, it seems a peculiarly apt remark for the book I promise to get to. *Poetry and Mysticism* is about writing; at least it's about one kind of writing, poetry. Wilson himself has said that he has never written poetry, but one doesn't have to be a poet to feel and understand the magic of a poem, just as one doesn't have to be a composer to appreciate great music, or a chef to enjoy a delicious meal. Wilson, of course, is a novelist, and he has also written plays; but in many ways I think that his best literary work is as a critic. He has a peculiar talent for opening up a writer's work – getting under its bonnet, as it were – and seeing what makes it tick, if I can be excused a mixed metaphor. Wilson has displayed this knack in many essays on individual writers – some of the best are collected in Borgo Press' *Existentially Speaking: Essays on the Philosophy of Literature* and Colin Stanley's fine collection, *Existential Criticism: Selected Book Reviews* – as well as in more general reflections on literature and literary form, such as *The Strength to Dream* and the 'nuts and bolts' *Craft of the Novel*. What these and Wilson's other critical writings show, is that he has an obvious and insatiable curiosity about and – I can think of no better word – love of literature. Or, if that seems too stuffy for an angry young man, writing.

The prompt for this particular book about writing came from that conversation with Ferlinghetti about the girl who blew her mind out in the aftermath of the 'summer of love'. Wilson notes that Ferlinghetti voiced some misgivings about the use of psychedelics. By this time they had become hugely popular throughout the youth culture through their advocacy by the Beatles and hippie demagogues like Timothy Leary, and Wilson himself remarked about his own unsuccessful psychedelic experience. In July 1963 – nearly five years earlier – Wilson ingested half a gram of mescaline sulphate – the psychoactive principle in peyote – in his home in Cornwall, having in mind Aldous Huxley's account of his own mescaline experiment in *The Doors of Perception*. His account of his 'trip' – in an appendix to *Beyond the Outsider* – is predominantly critical, and Wilson can, I think, if one wants to play Devil's Advocate, be accused of prejudicing the outcome, as he refers more than once to his belief that 'I don't need to take the stuff', which suggests a predisposition against it. At any rate, in the event, the drug made Wilson sick and the experiment was not a success, Wilson's remark that 'Oh God, I'll never touch this filthy stuff again', summing up his appreciation of it. In his early novel *Adrift in Soho* Wilson has similar words about cannabis, and it is curious that in most, if not all books devoted to writing and drugs – works such as Marcus Boon's *The Road of Excess* and Sadie Plants' *Writers on Drugs* – Wilson's mescaline account is never mentioned. Perhaps it's left out because it's a critical account, although Wilson did write a delightful book about his own favourite mind-altering substance, wine, appropriately called *A Book of Booze*.

Wilson himself has said that he pretty much sat out the 1960s. His popular 'come back', following the critical battering triggered by his second book, *Religion and the Rebel*, didn't happen until *The Occult* appeared in 1971. By the end of the 50s the angry young bubble had burst, and, fortified by the success of *The Outsider*, Wilson hunkered down in Cornwall, ignoring his critics, completing the books of the Outsider Cycle, and supplementing his income by teaching and lecturing in American universities. Although he is usually mentioned along with the Beats as a precursor to the 60s generation – Wilson was one of the first to write about Hermann Hesse in English, paving the way for the great Hesse craze of the late 60s and early 70s, of which I was a willing victim – his 'new' or 'evolutionary existentialism' was a tad too logical for the 'let it all hang out' sensibility of the time. In many ways, Wilson's take on the psychedelic movement was like that of an older writer with whom he has much in common, Arthur Koestler, although famously, Koestler had unkind words for *The Outsider*.[4] (That Wilson could later write so insightfully and positively about Koestler's work shows an admirable maturity.[5]) A few years before Wilson imbibed mescaline sulphate, Koestler tried some of Dr. Leary's magic (psilocybin) mushrooms, and like Wilson's mescaline, they did not agree with him. They were, he said, a way of 'buying one's visions on the cheap' and he likened the experience to a kind of extended, director's cut version of Walt Disney's *Fantasia*. Koestler's essay about his psychedelic experience, 'Return Trip to Nirvana'[6], is, like Wilson's 'The Mescaline Experience', also generally left out of most 'drugs and writers' accounts.

Wilson shared another criticism with Koestler: the overvaluing of 'Eastern mysticism' at the expense of 'Western thought'. Wilson is never as acid as Koestler – a chapter in

Koestler's *The Lotus and the Robot* is entitled 'A Stink of Zen' – but the impetus for *Poetry and Mysticism* is much the same; in fact, the first version of the book was called *Poetry and Zen*. And the comparison with Koestler is more apt still. The Lotus of Koestler's book about the early days of the 60s craze for 'the wisdom of the East' is the Hindu guru, soon to hit the big time with the Beatles' interlude with the Maharishi Mahesh Yogi. The Robot is the Zen master, unthinkingly perfect in every action. In *Poetry and Mysticism* Wilson equates much of the calm and equanimity of 'Zen consciousness' to the operations of a part of the human psyche that he dubs – guess what? – 'the robot.' I'm not suggesting Wilson got the idea from Koestler. What's important about the similarity is that it points to the common terrain both thinkers are mapping out.

By the time Wilson had his drink with Ferlinghetti, a whole generation had taken the 'journey to the East' – the title, of course, of one of Hermann Hesse's books – and the notion that the West could only be saved by imbibing the wisdom of the orient had become clichéd. It had already been a cliché much earlier, but now a younger generation was rediscovering what had been common knowledge since Madam Blavatsky and the Mahatmas. Swamis, gurus, and yogis had been part of the 'countercultural' scene since the late nineteenth century, and we could push the theme back even further. In the early nineteenth century the philosopher Schopenhauer was influenced by the *Upanishads*, and more than a century before that, another philosopher, Leibniz, wrote about the *I Ching* (Hesse's novel itself was written in the '30s). But now they were getting a new lease on life. To point out that the theme was clichéd is not to say the 'East' had nothing to teach us, merely that what it taught at the start of the 'Mystic Sixties' was not as new as many believed. In Ferlinghetti's neck of the woods, the hot import was Zen.

D.T. Suzuki's books on Zen Buddhism – which began in the sixth century AD in China – had been making the Western intellectual rounds for decades, but most people heard of *satori* through the work of Alan Watts. In 1935, at the age of nineteen, Watts made his name with the eminently readable *The Spirit of Zen*. More books followed, like *The Way of Zen* (1957) *Beat Zen, Square Zen, and Zen* (1959), and other well written popular essays on various forms of Eastern philosophy. Watts' presence among the North Beach Beats was so great – born in Chislehurst, he had moved to San Francisco in the 50s – that Kerouac used him as the model for the character Arthur Whane in his Zen novel *The Dharma Bums*. Another character, Japhy Ryder, was based on the poet Gary Snyder, who had spent time with a *roshi*, or Zen teacher, in a Kyoto monastery.

By 1968 and that drink with Ferlinghetti, Zen and other Eastern teachings were still the intellectual flavours of the month, but Wilson, ever the outsider, did not partake. Although Wilson recognized its importance, he nevertheless felt that there was 'no profound spiritual message to be drawn'[7] from the sort of effortless economy of movement that we associate with Zen. Zen, for Wilson, had 'nothing to tell us that we cannot say just as precisely in western terminology', and he remarked critically on the current 'revival of the fashion to exalt eastern modes of thought and disparage the western'.[8] Given that he was critical of psychedelic drugs and wasn't impressed with the 'wisdom of the East', it's no surprise Wilson 'sat out the sixties'. What Wilson did find important was Zen's 'shock tactics', the way in which a *koan* – most famously 'the sound of one hand clapping' – can jolt the literal, rational mind into a brief flash of 'freshness' or 'newness', a kind of 'clean' perception, unbiased by habitual ways of seeing. It was the difference between seeing, say, a tree and *seeing* it – what Huxley, borrowing from Meister Eckhart, had called seeing the 'is-ness' of things and what the German writer Gottfried Benn called 'primal perception'. The West, however, didn't need to import this method from the East, as it had already devised its own form of it: poetry. Wilson's inference is that it was only a kind of faddish snobbery, that sought all *lux ex oriente*, which prevented us from seeing this. Or *seeing* it.

But Wilson's mild criticisms of the Zen craze are not the essence of the book, and they are really only a means of launching his own analysis of the kind of inner 'shift' that proponents of Zen and other Eastern teachings were after. As the book was published by City Lights – at Ferlinghetti's request – we can assume it was sold in the shop, and must have reached at least a few readers familiar with Zen, the Beats, and psychedelic drugs. How Wilson's phenomenological account of poetic, aesthetic, and mystical experience went down among the North Beach hipsters is – barring some determined researcher – lost to posterity. Thankfully, his meticulous 'deconstructing' of poetry's ability to alter our state of consciousness is not. While not denying that both meditation and psychedelics were to a limited extent helpful, Wilson argued that there was 'no short-cut to mystical experience' and that what was needed was 'the scientific pursuit of the psychological mechanisms of the "intensity experience,"' so that 'at some point...man will achieve complete control over the floodgates of inner-energy that create the mystical experience'. With this in mind, Wilson aimed to produce 'detailed objective knowledge of what goes on in states of "intensity consciousness"'. I'm of the opinion that readers of *Poetry and Mysticism* will concur that that's exactly what he did.

Wilson thought that collecting his thoughts on the psychedelic craze, as Ferlinghetti suggested, might serve as a way of producing an 'interim report' on his ideas since completing the Outsider Cycle and its companion volume, *Introduction to the New Existentialism*, which he did in 1965. For the last decade Wilson had been trying to find a way out of the *cul-de-sac* in which Western philosophy had found itself, led there by the work of Heidegger, Sartre, Camus and other 'existential' thinkers. In the aftermath of WWII, existentialism had been a fresh, vital impulse in western thought. And although its roots can, as Wilson argues, be traced back as far as Plato, in the work of Sartre and Camus especially, it had acquired a peculiarly modern, urban character, and its influence was felt in practically all areas of modern culture, from literature to popular film. Film noir, in particular, seemed to share existentialism's sense of living 'without appeal', and the Montparnasse café crowd can be seen as the reigning hipsters prior to the Beats. By the 60s, however, existentialism had run out of steam, and as England's own 'home grown' existentialist, Wilson may have felt he had been saddled with an uphill battle. Although his 'new' existentialism offered a more optimistic, positive view of the 'human condition', it was like selling *do-wop* in the age of Jimi Hendrix, a situation made apparent when the modern 'occult revival' began in France in 1960, with the publication of Pauwels' and Bergier's *The Morning of the Magicians*, which I've described elsewhere as having the effect of 'a flying saucer landing at Café Deux Magots'[9]. It was also French, at least in the mind of the average reader, and while the English are notoriously immune to ideas – something Wilson never minds repeating – they are particularly resistant to French ones. Wilson's 'interim report', then, may have been a way to put a full stop to the purely existential stage of his work, to take stock of where he and the collective consciousness was at the end of the decade, and to reflect on fruitful new directions.

It isn't surprising, then, that much of what is found in *Poetry and Mysticism* also appears in other Wilson books of the same time, especially the Lovecraftian novels *The Mind Parasites* (1967) and *The Philosopher's Stone* (1969), two other works, incidentally, suggested by another writer, in this case Lovecraft's champion August Derleth. It also isn't surprising that in many ways it seems a kind of dry run for Wilson's first foray into the 'magical revival' triggered by Pauwels and Bergier, his mammoth *The Occult*. This was the first book of Wilson's I read, and it planted a 35 year long fascination with the untapped potentials of human consciousness, which has led to my making my own contribution to the modern 'occult revival'. By the time I read *The Occult*, in 1975, I was already familiar with existentialism and had made my way through the Beats – one of them, William Burroughs, could be found slinking into a New York rock club I played in at the time – and it was Wilson's enviable knack of linking existential thought to ideas about mysticism, occult powers, and esoteric philosophy that made the book, for me at least, a life-changer. As I've pointed out elsewhere, at the time I found other occult or mystical books leftover from the previous decade on friends' bookshelves, works by Leary, Castaneda, Crowley, and others; but it was *The Occult* that turned what might otherwise have been a passing interest into a serious pursuit.[10]

As is true of all of Wilson's books, *Poetry and Mysticism*, though a slim volume – the revised 1970 edition includes chapters on individual poets, but the insights they flesh out are found in the original version – is chockfull of ideas, and in the remaining pages I'd like to offer some thoughts on a few of them. I'm taking a risk here. Wilson is such a clear writer that, more times than not, in interpreting him one is usually saying the same thing, only more clumsily. Perhaps this is why he has never produced a 'school', which is usually the privilege of more 'difficult' writers; think of the reams written making sense (or trying to) of Heidegger, Foucault, or Walter Benjamin. Which isn't to say Wilson isn't influential; but his influence is to get his readers to think for themselves, and to apply his insights in new areas. And if, like myself, you are a reader who became a writer, it is to present your insights as clearly as possible.

One idea I've already mentioned, and it is perhaps best to start with it: the robot. The robot is our automatic pilot. The philosopher Whitehead said that 'Civilization advances by extending the number of important operations which we can perform without thinking about them,' and it is easy to see what he means. At some point in its evolution, life learned how to breathe. We can imagine that at first it had to put all its energy and attention into mastering this, which left little energy and attention for anything else. The same is true of walking, digesting, and other essential processes. Ages ago, through frustrating trial and error, I taught myself how to type. At first I had to focus on each key and stumble through error after error – it is, in fact, a sign of my determination that I became a writer at all. But over time the task of typing passed from my conscious mind to my automatic pilot, my robot, which left 'conscious me' free to consider other things, such as what I was writing about. As Wilson is eager to make clear, the robot is an absolutely essential tool, an indispensable helpmate, and we really can't do without it. But there's a catch. The robot is often *too* efficient. It not only types for me or ties my shoe laces – a welcome aid, remembering the agonies of mastering this – it also answers my children's questions, gulps down a meal, or, as Wilson often remarks, makes love to one's wife. Drugs like mescaline, cannabis, and alcohol produce their effect by shutting the robot down; this is why their initial effect can be delightful (except in Wilson's case), but prolonged use can lead to mere dullness. We need the robot – consider what life would be like if you had to focus all your will on taking each breath – but when we let ourselves become too dependent on it, life loses its savour. The robot lives, not us. Drugs are one way of getting some of it back.

Another is 'living dangerously', putting yourself into a crisis that demands your full participation. Both methods are very popular, yet both have major drawbacks. Drug dependency is one, and killing or at least badly damaging yourself through 'dangerous living' is another. Hemingway is one of Wilson's favourite examples of this. When throwing himself into danger – through big game hunting, bull fighting and other means – no longer did the trick, Hemingway put the full weight of the task of 'feeling alive' on drink, with the result that he eventually blew his brains out. What we need is not to sink *below* the robot, or galvanise ourselves into some sense of vivid life by flirting with death, but a method of rising *above* the robot. This would entail understanding the robot, and recognizing how it works.

Now, in a nutshell, the poetic, aesthetic, or mystical experience – I agree with Wilson that these are all markers on a gradient and that there is no *essential* difference between mystical and aesthetic experience – are moments when 'we' live, not the robot. Or, put more precisely, they are moments when we take control of living back from the robot, after lazily letting him do all the work. We have to remember, though, that the robot isn't a villain; he does not 'wrest' control of life from us. We *allow* him to take the wheel, through ignorance of our own psychology, and a certain natural indolence. This is why methods of 'escaping' from the robot – asceticism, even some forms of masochism – are unsatisfactory, as they merely take the wheel out of his hands for a brief time. The point, again, is to *understand* the mechanisms at work and to apply this knowledge, not beat our helpful servant off with a stick. And what does 'non-robotic consciousness' feel like? It is much like the sudden flash of 'is-ness' perceived in Zen, or the sparkling clarity of vision produced by good poetry. Both moments achieve the 'affirmation consciousness' that Wilson has doggedly investigated for more than half a century, and both deliver the 'absurd good news' the Zen master G.K. Chesterton spoke of many years ago.

How does poetry achieve this? If the robot reduces our perceptions to a functional sameness – it is severely economical and will only allow as much 'reality' into our awareness as is necessary to get on with things[11] – then 'non-robotic' perception is characterized by an awareness of the effervescent *difference* of things. This is not the 'difference' associated with Jacques Derrida and the school of deconstructionism, but the 'difference'

that P.D. Ouspensky speaks of in his classic work of philosophical mysticism – or mystical philosophy – *Tertium Organum*,
when he remarks on the *'incredibly vivid* sensation of the
difference between factory chimneys and prison walls, a
sensation that was like a blow or an electric shock'[12], which
sounds rather like a moment of Zen. To the robot – and, I must
add, a mainstream materialist scientist – bricks are bricks,
whether they form a factory or a chimney. Not to the poet or the
reader of poetry.[13] If the robot produces a kind of generalised
awareness in which 'all cats are grey in the dark', then 'non-
robotic' consciousness is a 100 watt bulb revealing a bevy of
Tabbys, Siamese, Manx, and a dozen other breeds.

This is the same as seeing the tree and *seeing* it, and it is a sign
of our lack of awareness in these matters that I have to use the
same word but italicized in order to convey my meaning. Our
language lacks the tools to express these distinctions. Poetry,
however, is precisely this, a way of using language to highlight
'difference'. It operates, as Wilson makes clear, by drawing
awareness to contrasts, something he calls 'the rainbow effect',
'the delight that comes after a storm, when the air is still full of
raindrops, and the sun emerges, creating a rainbow. The delight
here is a matter of the contrast with the storm, a feeling of
convalescence, of rebirth'.[14] Another example Wilson often cites
is the experience of the Indian mystic Sri Ramakrishna, who fell
into an ecstatic trance as a young boy when he saw a flock of
white cranes fly past a storm cloud: the sudden contrast
between the white birds and the dark cloud sent Ramakrishna
into 'affirmation consciousness', a bubbling feeling of 'Yes!', the
opposite of the diffidence normally felt in 'robotic
consciousness'. Another, less exotic example is how we feel on a
chilly morning when we are still wrapped in our warm blankets,
or the 'cosiness' produced by sitting by a warm fire when we
know it is raining outside. Wilson brings these insights to bear
on a fine analysis of Wordsworth's sonnet about crossing

Westminster Bridge in early morning en route to France. I cannot follow it in detail here, and suggest the reader taste a moment of 'non-robotic consciousness' by reading it for himself.

The perception of contrast produces what Wilson calls 'duo-consciousness', the *vivid awareness of two different realities*. In Wordsworth's case it is the reality of a London not yet wakened to daily life – 'Dear God, the very houses seem asleep' – and the bustling monster it will shortly be. Although Wilson does not use the term, 'duo-consciousness' is clearly an early formulation of the theme at the heart of *The Occult*, what Wilson calls 'Faculty X', the ability to perceive the 'reality of other times and places'. Robotic consciousness is fixed on the here and now, and tells us that 'reality' is what is at the end of our nose. 'Duo-consciousness', 'Faculty X', tells us that 'reality' – or perhaps I should say *reality* – is much more complex than that, and that its complexities branch out, like the dendrites of the brain. This 'branching out' Wilson calls 'relationality', and he adds to the philosopher Husserl's essential insight that 'perception is intentional' – the foundation of Wilson's 'new' existentialism' – the additional knowledge that it is also 'relational', an insight he embodied in fictional form in *The Philosopher's Stone* (which, with *The Mind Parasites*, can be called a work of 'phenomeno-logical fiction'). Although 'duo-consciousness' is the most immediate form of the mystical, poetic, or affirmation experience – we feel snippets of it more often that we realize – there is no reason why 'relationality' should stop at only two items. In certain mystical experiences – what R.M. Bucke called 'cosmic consciousness' in a book of that name – a seeming infinity of relations is perceived. Indeed, I recently finished a book about Hermeticism in which I relate Bucke's experience of cosmic consciousness – as well as that of Ouspensky and William James – to the 'gnosis' undergone by the Alexandrian Hermeticists of the first centuries following Christ.[15] The Hermeticists were urged to 'Conceive yourself to be in all places at the same time: in earth, in the sea, in heaven; that you are not yet born, that you are within the womb, that you are young, old, dead; that you are beyond death. Conceive all things at once: times, places, actions, qualities and quantities; then you can understand God'[16], which seems to me to be a way of expressing the insights of 'relationality' and 'Faculty X'.

Now, as 'Faculty X' is the perception of the reality of other *times* and places, it's clear that it is not only spatial, but also temporal, as the quote above from the *Corpus Hermeticum* indicates. This leads to another idea Wilson pursues in *Poetry and Mysticism*, and it is the one I will conclude with. Wilson talks of the difference between my 'short term self' and my 'long term self'[17]. My 'short term self' is the one that has let the robot do my living for me, and it is the one I am when I am 'angry, miserable, anxious, bored', the one, in other words, most of us are sadly familiar with most of the time. In moments of intensity, of 'affirmation consciousness', and poetry and mysticism, I become aware of – or actually I *become* – a 'long term self', a self not hemmed in by immediacies and entanglements, a self-aware of purpose, of otherwise dormant values, of 'strength and durability'. It is the self Proust knows when he tastes his madeleine dipped in herbal tea, or Hesse's Steppenwolf knows when he drinks a glass of wine and decides not to slit his throat. It's the self that rises above the vicissitudes of life and realizes the 'absurd good news' that 'all is well'. Recently I had a mini-experience of this. While re-reading *Poetry and Mysticism* to write this essay, a flat in a housing association, whose waiting list I had been on for some years, came through, and I soon found myself packing in order to move. While putting my library in boxes, I flipped through some of my copies of Wilson's books, and came upon some he had signed when I first met him at the Village Bookshop on Regent Street in 1981; it was a great shop and sadly, it is no longer there. I visited him in Cornwall a few years after that, and have kept up a friendship ever since. Throughout the 80s, 90s, and 2000s, I received other signed copies of Wilson's books, and during that time I went from being an ex-rock and roll musician turned academic living in Los Angeles, to being a full time writer living in London. I'm not saying it's his fault, but my penchant for Wilson's work had something to do with this. It was strange to look at a copy of one of his books autographed in 1981, and to grasp where I was, here, thirty years later, having written a few books myself, and contributing to this *Festschrift*. The persistence and durability of my 'long term self' seemed well in evidence, not to mention a not inconsiderable sense of 'absurd good news'.

Notes:

1   Stuart Walton *Out of It: A Cultural History of Intoxication* (New York: Harmony Books, 2002) p. 232.

2   For my review of *The Angry Years* see http://www.independent.co.uk/arts-entertainment /books/features/colin-wilson-its-time-to-look-back-in-anger- 446738.html

3   When I met Ferlinghetti sometime in the early 2000s, intro- duced by the poet Michael Horovitz, I mentioned how important his book was in my youth. He somewhat wearily replied that everyone told him that.

4   In his *Observer* 'Books of the Year' piece for 1956, Koestler called *The Outsider* the 'bubble of the year', and its author an 'earnest young man' who had discovered that 'genius is prone to *Weltschmerz*'. Collected in Arthur Koestler *Drinkers of Infinity: Essays 1955-1967* (London: Hutchinson, 1968).

5   See 'Arthur Koestler' in *Existentially Speaking* (San Bernardino: Borgo Press, 1989) pp. 60-70.

6   Koestler pp. 201-12.

7   Colin Wilson *Poetry and Mysticism* (San Francisco: City Lights, 1970) p. 44.

8   Ibid.

9   Gary Lachman *The Dedalus Book of the 1960s: Turn Off Your Mind* (revised 2nd edition, Sawtry: Dedalus, 2010) p. 15

10 In any case, I'd like to think it's serious. See my preface "Return of the Mind Parasites", to Colin Wilson *The Mind Parasites* (Rhinebeck: Monk Fish Publishing Company, 2005) pp.ix-xiv.

11 This is why 'psychedelic consciousness' can be so overwhelming, as, with the robot asleep, 'reality' floods in.

12 P.D. Ouspensky *Tertium Organum* (New York: Alfred A. Knopf, 1981) p. 128.

13 For a different but related take on the poet as mystic, see my essay "The Spiritual Detective: How Baudelaire invented Symbolism, by way of Swedenborg, E.T.A. Hoffmann, and Edgar Allan Poe" in *Between Method and Madness – Essays on Swedenborg and Literature* (London: Swedenborg House, 2005) pp. 31-44.

14 Wilson, p. 31.

15 *As Above, So Below: The Teachings of Hermes Trismegistus* (Edinburgh: Floris Books, 2011)

16 Book XI of the *Corpus Hermeticum* collected and translated by Clement Salaman in *The Way of Hermes* (London: Duckworth, 2001) p. 70.

17 Wilson p. 37.

New Pathways in Psychology: Maslow and the Post-Freudian Revolution (1972)

Colin Wilson's *New Pathways in Psychology.*

Colin Stanley

This book marks Wilson's brief return to his original publisher Victor Gollancz after an absence of nine years. It was published in the U.K. in May 1972 and in the U.S. by Taplinger Publishing Company the same year. In an article written to promote a new book *Super-Consciousness* (London: Watkins Publishing) in 2009, Colin Wilson wrote:

> "One day in the spring of 1963 I received one of the most important letters of my life. It was from a professor of psychology named Abraham Maslow [1908-1970], and he wanted to tell me about some researches he had been carrying out for the past ten years or so".

This, written nearly forty years after Maslow's death in 1970, reveals how important Wilson considers his association with the American psychologist has been and how much it has helped to reinforce his own ideas about the nature of human consciousness. It was, as the extract suggests, Maslow who made the initial contact:

> "Four years after the publication of my book *The Age of Defeat*—under the title *The Stature of Man*—I had received a letter from Maslow....He explained that he had been impressed by the optimism of *The Stature of Man*, and about the way I had pinpointed the sense of defeat that permeates our culture.
>
> Maslow had begun to have certain doubts about

Freudian psychology, feeling it had 'sold human nature short'. This was something I had felt strongly for years: Freud's view that all our deepest urges are sexual seemed to me to leave out some of the most important members of the human race, from Leonardo to Bernard Shaw...."
(Wilson (1), 208)

The book is divided into three parts with a lengthy introductory chapter outlining the ideas that Wilson and Maslow have in common. Part One provides a history of the major trends in psychology from its beginnings, through Sigmund Freud (1856-1939), to Maslow. Part Two deals exclusively with Maslow and Part Three discusses existential psychology in general.

In the Introduction, Wilson explains why he considers Maslow's concept of 'peak experiences' (PEs) — that sudden rush of pure happiness that we all experience in moments of delight — to be so important and asks whether they can be induced. Maslow felt that this was not possible but Wilson believes that PEs have "...a structure that can be duplicated. It is the culmination of a series of mental acts, each of which can be clearly defined" (21*). The basis of the PE is a state of "...vigilance, alertness, *preparedness*..." (22) and "...the first pre-condition is 'energy', because the PE is essentially an overflowing of energy" (21). In one of his typical analogies, Wilson sees healthy people as having surplus energy stored in their subconscious minds: "...like money that has been invested in stocks and shares" (22). Near the surface of the subconscious mind some of this energy is stored ready for use "...like money in a personal account" (22). When a delightful event is antici-pated large quantities of surplus energy is made available for use:

"...as I might draw a large sum out of the bank before I go on holiday...Peakers are people with large quantities of energy in the ready energy tanks. Bored or miserable people are people who keep only small amounts of energy for immediate use" (22).

However, both types of people have the same amounts of energy available to them, "...it is merely a matter of transferring it to your 'current account'" (22).

Both Maslow and Wilson see the need for us to live meaningful creative lives: "Meaning stimulates the will, fills one with a desire to reach out to new horizons" (26). The PE is a sudden surge of meaning and "the question that arises now is: how can I *choose* meaning?" (26). Wilson thinks that the secret lies in concentration and introduces an exercise which he later called 'the pen trick':

"...I discovered that a mild peak experience could easily be induced merely by concentrating hard on a pencil, then relaxing the attention, then concentrating again...After doing this a dozen or so times, the attention becomes fatigued—if you are doing it with the right degree of concentration—and a few more efforts—deliberately ignoring the fatigue—trigger the peak experience. After all, concentration has the effect of summoning energy from your depths. It is the 'pumping' motion—of expanding and contracting the attention—that causes the peak experience." (29-30).

[In his book *Access to Inner Worlds*, Wilson describes how he taught this trick to a class of students, combining it with a breathing exercise devised by Wilhelm Reich (1897-1957): "After a few moments, I noticed the curious sense of exaltation, followed by a sensation as if floating out of my body...Time became unimportant...we had been lying there for more than half an hour, and...no one showed the slightest inclination to get up" (Wilson (2), 38)]

Wilson highlights the importance of human imagination which, in most cases, only provides a poor copy of the original experience. The exception, however, is sex where the imagination can carry men and women to the point of sexual climax, achieving "a physical response *as if* to reality" (30). He feels that it should be possible for imagination to achieve this result, not just with sex, but in all fields.

In this chapter Wilson also introduces "...a concept that has become the core of my own existential psychology: the 'Self-Image'" (34) i.e. the way we view ourselves. This is a notion "of immediate relevance to Maslovian psychology" (37) because boosting one's self image can lead to the "promotion of the personality to a higher level" (35). It achieves this by providing a sense of external meaning. But, if this meaning is always there, why do I not experience it all the time?

"...because I allow the will to become passive, and the senses close up. If I want more meaning, then I must force my senses wide open by an increased effort of will. We might think of the senses as spring-loaded shutters that must be forced open, and which close again when you let them go...If I am not careful, the shutters close and I lose my objective standards. At this point I may wildly exaggerate the importance of my emotions, my private ups and downs, and there is no feeling of objective reality to contradict me." (37)

[As usual, Wilson also attempted to convey his ideas in the form of a novel. The Self-Image concept is central to his 1985 novel *The Personality Surgeon* (Sevenoaks, Kent: New English Library) in which the hero invents a revolutionary form of psychotherapy, involving the use of a video camera and digital paintbox, with the intention of improving the patient's self-image. Wilson speaks of the Self-image concept on the CD *The Essential Colin Wilson* (Wilson (3)). In the sleeve notes he writes: "I always intended to write a book called *The Self Image*, but never got round to it. Before a human being can live a creative and fruitful existence, he must have *a clear idea who he is*. It is as if we were all in need of a *mirror* in which we could see our own faces. Nietzsche meant the same thing when he said: 'The great man is the play actor of his own ideals.'"]

"'Reality' is the key word in existential psychology," (40) writes Wilson. We can always re-establish contact with reality by "an effort of reaching out to meaning" (41):

> "And the most important point for psychotherapy is that [we] can do this *by an act of will*. Mental illness is a kind of amnesia, in which the patient has forgotten his own powers. The task of the therapist is to somehow renew the patient's contact with reality." (41)

In Part One, Chapter One 'The Age of Machinery: from Descartes to Mill', Wilson writes: "It is one of the absurd paradoxes of psychology that it has taken three centuries to reach the conclusion that man actually possesses a mind and a will" (47). Starting with René Descartes (1596-1650) and progressing through Thomas Hobbes (1588-1679), John Locke (1632-1704) and David Hume (1711-1776), he traces how this came about. He considers Hume to be "one of the most significant figures in the history of psychology. For Hume's model of the human mind, has influenced every psychologist—directly or otherwise—since the publication of *A Treatise of Human Nature* (1739)" (49). Wilson attacks his theory that thinking and willing are illusions as "...ultimately unacceptable. One stage further, and he will be assuring me that I am not alive at all, and that there is no such thing as consciousness" (50).

This mechanistic view of man's mind was perpetuated by James Mill (1773-1836) and in spite of the work of Hermann Lotze (1817-1881) "and various other psychologists who accepted the reality of the will, psychology remained mechanistic" (60):

"...by...the late 19th and early 20th centuries...the great Freudian revolution was under way.... There seemed to be a general feeling that since psychology had attained the rank of a science, it had better stick to analysis and definition. The will...was allowed a small place among feelings, cognitions, memories, and so on, but it had to take its place at the back of the queue." (60)

Part One, Chapter Two: 'Towards a Psychology of the Will: from Brentano to James', concentrates on the work of Franz Brentano (1838-1917) and his pupil Edmund Husserl (1859-1938) whose concept of the intentionality of perception is central to Wilson's own ideas. In contrast to Hume they insisted that thoughts and feelings were always about things; in effect they *reach out* to things. "It is intentional. I look *at* something: that is, I do half the work." (63). This begs the question: "If thoughts are not blown around like leaves on a windy day, but directed by a sense of purpose, then who does the directing?" (62). The answer is the transcendental ego. "But...the intentional element in perception—the part *I* put into it—often distorts what my senses convey" (63). So, according to Wilson, Husserl's basic assertion could be summarized as follows:

"Philosophy has no chance of making a true statement about anything until it can distinguish between what the senses really *tell* us—the undistorted perception—and how we interpret it....The philosophical method that

Husserl called 'pure phenomenology' is an attempt to teach the mind to be objective" (64).

The rest of the chapter is devoted to the American philosopher and psychologist William James (1842-1910) who "...discovered the concept of intentionality at about the same time as Husserl, but made less practical use of it in his philosophy" (65). However, Wilson considers that he "...has provided more insights into the actual working of the human mind than any other psychologist or philosopher" (71) and feels that his *Varieties of Religious Experience* (1902) "...may well be the most important single volume in the history of psychology, since it is a direct attack on the problem of man's spiritual evolution" (81).

> "But although James asserted that there can be no psycho-logical proof of free will, he nevertheless goes straight to the heart of the matter when he points out that we become aware of free will when we are *making an effort*" (68)

This is an important point, one that Wilson emphasizes again and again throughout his work:

> "In order to grasp meanings, I must 'focus' —concentrate, 'contract' my attention muscles. Perception is intentional, and the more energy (or effort) I put into the act of 'concentrating', the more meaning I grasp." (68)

Most human beings, says Wilson, spend much of their lives with their attention "...vague, broad, diffused, unfocused, like a bored schoolboy staring blankly out of a window..." (68). It is only when faced with some crisis or emergency that they snap out of their dream:

> "Without emergency to keep them 'on their toes', their

general level of intensity diminishes; they take their comfort for granted; their responses become dulled. And, in a vague, distressed way they wonder what went wrong, why life is suddenly so unexciting....Why has life failed?

This is one of the most urgent problems for civilised man." (68)

With these statements we arrive at the heart of Wilson's message: "There is something wrong with 'normal' human consciousness. For some odd reason, we seldom get the best out of it" (87). The answer, he thinks, lies in higher levels of consciousness: "The higher one ascends on this scale, the more *self-sustaining* consciousness becomes" (69). In this sense Maslow's preoccupation with creativity is seen as a logical step beyond James and Husserl. However, "It is ironical," writes Wilson, "that after [James'] death in 1910, psychology should have been dominated by a new kind of determinism, that had no place for 'will' or 'values' (87).

The first chapter of Part Two delivers a biographical sketch of Maslow based on several tapes prepared by Maslow himself and sent to Wilson, after his death in 1970, by his widow Bertha:

"The paradox about Maslow is not simply that he was a reluctant rebel, but that he was unwilling to regard himself as any kind of rebel at all....He saw himself as a psychoanalyst and a behaviourist, not as the father of a revolution against them. He was a creative synthesiser, not in the least interested in dissension; this was his own way of making the best of his creative energies" (130).

The second chapter of Part Two is an account of the development of Maslow's ideas, commencing with his studies of monkey behaviour in the 1930s from which "He had evolved a new theory of evolution..., with dominance playing the central role, rather than sexual selection..." (157). He then went on to try and discover whether there was a close correlation between sexuality and dominance in human beings. It was in a paper *A Theory of Human Motivation*, published in the *Psychological Review* in July 1943 that he first proposed his important theory of the 'hierarchy of needs': "What Maslow stated in this paper is the essence of his life work" (162), writes Wilson:

> "Maslow's theory, then, is that there are five levels of needs: physiological, safety, love, esteem and self-actuali-sation, and as one becomes satisfied, another takes over....The really revolutionary point here...was that these 'higher needs' are as instinctoid as the lower, as much part of man's subconscious drives." (163-164)

[In a fascinating article on criminology 'A Doomed Society?' (published in the *Journal of Human Relations*, vol. 21, 1973, pp 395-410), Wilson describes how these levels correspond roughly to periods of crime: "Until the first part of the 19th century, most crimes were committed out of a need for food and security. Then came the age of sex crime...." Finally, "the self-esteem motive might explain more recent 'gratuitous' murders"]

Maslow's paper on self-actualising people, published in 1950 and later included in the book *Motivation and Personality* (1954; revised 1970), is described by Wilson as:

> "...probably Maslow's most important single work....It is revolutionary because this is the first time a psychologist has ignored the assumption that underlies all Freudian psychology: that psychology, like medicine, is basically a study of the sick..."(171)

Maslow discovered that a great many of these healthy self-actualisers:

"...have peak experiences, mystical experiences, 'the oceanic feeling', the sense of limitless horizons opening up to the vision. In the first edition of *Motivation and Personality* in 1954, Maslow speaks only of mystical experiences and the oceanic feeling; in the 1970 edition— issued after his death—he uses the term 'peak experience...' (171)

He was puzzled, however, by the fact that affluence does not project *everyone* toward self-actualisation. Wilson suggests that this is because it requires:

"...a different *kind* of development....Ordinary development can take place on a horizontal level; self-actualisation requires a kind of vertical movement.... The gap between ordinary human passivity and the active freedom involved in creation is absolute, as different as real activity is from dreaming." (201)

So despite the other needs—physiological, safety, love, esteem— being satisfied, human passivity is a bar to further development:

"What was really needed, to complete Maslow's theory, was the realisation developed by [Victor] Frankl [1905-1997] a decade later—that when human beings are passive, *neurosis tends to feed upon itself*....Neurosis, says Maslow, is a failure of personal growth. Frankl adds that healthy activity demands a goal, a sense of something worth doing, and that mental illness begins when men are deprived of the sense of 'something to look forward to'. Boredom, passivity, stagnation: these are the beginning of mental illness, which propagates itself like scum on a stagnant pond." (172, 174)

Summarising Maslow's achievement, Wilson states:

"Like all original thinkers, he has opened up a new way of *seeing* the universe. His ideas developed slowly and organically...; there are no breaks, or sudden changes of direction. His instinct is remarkably sound; none of his work has been disproved; none has had to be re-done...; in fact, I can see no single example in which he was definitely mistaken. He advanced with the faultless precision of a sleepwalker." (198)

In Part Three, Wilson asks the question 'Where Now?' and further examines the work of Frankl, along with that of Ludwig Binswanger (1881-1966), Medard Boss (1903-1990), Erwin Straus (1891-1975), Roberto Assagioli (1888-1974), Rollo May (1909-1994), R. D. Laing (1927-1989), and G. I. Gurdjieff (1866?-1949) whose "...importance in the history of psychology is not recognised; but as the 'existential' revolution proceeds, he is bound to become known as one of the greatest originators of the twentieth century" (209). He also considers the 'reality therapy' of William Glasser (1925-) and the 'attitude therapy' of Dan MacDougald (dates unknown).

"There is one obvious difference between the new movement in psychology—the trends and theories that can be loosely grouped together as 'existential'—and the older schools of Freud, Jung, Adler and Rank. The existential school adopts a more down-to-earth, empirical approach to mental illness. There is a notable absence of dogmatic underpinning, theories about the subconscious and its hypothetical contents. The psychiatrist tends to approach the patient with an attitude of self-identification: 'How could I myself get into that condition?' And, obviously, the answer will be in terms of conscious pressures." (213)

Wilson observes that man is not naturally static: "His mental being must be understood as something essentially dynamic, forward-flowing, like a river..." (220). This flow is:

"...not the Freudian libido or the Adlerian will to power, but a *sense of values* which operates rather like radar, by a kind of 'reaching out'....*Man is future-orientated*, not sex-orientated or power-orientated....What man craves is not power, but objective reality, values beyond himself" (220)

"The central need at the moment," writes Wilson, "is to develop a psychology of man's higher consciousness, a complete breakaway from Freudian pathology" (252). He introduces his own 'control psychology':

"The basic human problem is to maintain continually the state in which peak experiences are possible. This means, in practical terms, a certain forward-drive, and a deep seated refusal to accept depression, discouragement, all the various shades of defeat. We have got to realise that the 'pressure' we live at is too low to allow the development of our evolutionary potentialities." (247)

So we need to 'tighten-up' the controls. When we do this "...the world seems *more real*. New meanings appear. And it is the act of concentration *itself* that causes this intensification of consciousness." (245). For Wilson, this is an important point: meaning does not just come from 'out there', it has to be met with the full force of our attention.

In the last section of this long chapter, Wilson attempts to take the first steps towards creating a phenomenology for the new psychology. His starting point is the intentionality of consciousness. However:

"...consciousness is also *relational* by nature.... [J]ust as perception depends upon a subjective 'reaching out' towards the object, so the object-as-perceived is not a simple thing, but a complex structure depending on the relation between the object and the rest of the contents of consciousness." (256)

"...it is important to recognise that *all* perception involves a sense of relations, just as all perception involves intentionality....Nothing can be perceived in true isolation; all perception is relational.

Relationality is the meaning experience; intentionality is the will experience. They are intimately related, in that relationality can be increased by an act of intentionality, and meaning, in turn, stimulates and guides intention" (257)

This, according to Wilson, proves Maslow is right about his 'oceanic feeling' being proof of 'higher ceilings for human nature'. "When we recognise that perception must be both intentional and relational, then the 'oceanic feeling' is seen to be a wider state of relationality" (257).

But if perception is seen as an arrow fired towards its target, the bowstring needs to be taut. With effort, says Wilson, we can learn to do this but first we must restrain what he calls our 'Robot' from doing our perceiving for us. ["[The] Robot is a labour-saving device....When an activity has been performed often enough, he takes over and...does it a great deal more efficiently than I could do it consciously....Whenever I acquire some new skill, it gives me pleasure, but the moment the Robot takes over, the pleasure vanishes....The consequence is that when life is peaceful, we find it difficult to feel really alive..." (Wilson (4); 38-40)]. Also, a strong self-image, is seen to be important: "We might consider psychotherapy as a process of encouraging the patient to seek for a suitable self-image—one that is consistent with the highest level of self-esteem and creativity." (267)

> "The importance of this—for post-Maslow psychology— is immense. It means that *anybody* can become a 'peaker'. Provided they are willing to put a certain amount of effort into it. Non-peakers are either the habitually lazy or the habitually *discouraged*—those who do not realise how easy it is to become a peaker." (266)

Contemporary reviews were, as usual, extreme. Alan Hull-Walton in *Books and Bookmen* (July 1972, p. 50) wrote:

> "Here is no fuddy-duddy 'head shrunk' psychologist abiding by the rules and regulations of the enclosed academic establishment, but a man who has read and studied deeply, and is not afraid to say what he believes to be the truth....His superlative technique of breaking new ground in a controlled, concise, and easy prose, is absolutely incredible..."

Whereas the anonymous reviewer in *British Book News* (July 1972, p. 551) asks: "Colin Wilson's edifice upon Maslow's foundation is a provocative and interesting construction, but is it architecture or confectionery?" The psychologist Charles Rycroft (1914-1998) obviously thought the latter: "If there were, as there should be, an annual prize for the most pretentious and unscholarly book of the year, Colin Wilson's latest effusion would certainly be the winner for 1972." ('Still outside', *The*

Spectator, May 27, 1972, p. 818-819) although he later reluctantly admits that, despite all this, Wilson may be "...on to something." In a rather 'light-weight' review, considering the subject matter, Herbert Lomas ('Coffee Table Philosophy', *London Magazine*, Aug./Sept. 1972, p.148-149) declared: "It's not that one disagrees in general with his phenomenological premises; it's his vulgarization of them." In America, a rather more considered appraisal was provided by James S. Gordon (*New York Times Book Review*, Jan 28, 1973, p. 2-3) who nevertheless accused Wilson of smuggling into the book "...a naïve essentialism in the guise of existential theory...".

John A. Weigel comments:

"Wilson's goal as prophetic philosopher is more clearly defined than ever in his book-length exploration of the importance of certain psychological insights....*New Pathways in Psychology*, is an open-ended summary of what Colin Wilson is all about. Students, critics, and others interested in Wilson are well advised to make use of its select bibliography, index, heuristic summaries, case studies, and suggestions for research along these new pathways" (Weigel; 133)

Clifford P. Bendau sees the book as:

"...much more than a text on Maslow. *Pathways* represents an extensive survey of the history of psychology [and is] an accumulation of Colin Wilson's ideas on the topic of psychology and the future of man....It is important...because Wilson uses this opportunity to update his early ideas..." (Bendau; 54-55).

Finally, in his chapter on Wilson's psychology, Howard F. Dossor concludes:

"The existential psychology that Wilson embraces is one of the most exciting theories ever to have been created by the human mind....It makes all other psychologies appear inadequate because it is a profound synthesis of the best that each of them has to offer..." (Dossor; 113).

*All quotes taken from the first U.S. edition of *New Pathways in Psychology: Maslow and the post-Freudian revolution*. New York: Taplinger Publishing Co., Inc.

References:

Bendau, Clifford P. *Colin Wilson: the Outsider and beyond*. San Bernardino: The Borgo Press, 1979.

Dossor, Howard F. *Colin Wilson: the man and his mind*. Shaftesbury: Element Books, 1990.

Weigel, John A. *Colin Wilson* (Twayne's English Authors Series). Boston: Twayne Publishers, 1975.

Wilson, Colin (1) *Dreaming to Some Purpose*. London: Century, 2003.

Wilson, Colin (2) *Access to Inner Worlds*. London: Rider & Co. Ltd., 1983.

Wilson, Colin (3) *The Essential Colin Wilson*. Wyastone Leys, Monmouth: Nimbus Records Limited, 1986 [NI 5124]

Wilson, Colin (4) *Poetry & Mysticism*. London: Hutchinson & Co., 1970.

The Craft of the Novel (1975)

The Missing Writer's Manual.

Chris Nelson

The essence of creation is a mystery. The *trick* of creation, of engaging the creative forces of the individual, as Colin Wilson points out in *The Craft of the Novel*, is not. It is, in fact, as simple as setting out to solve a problem.

> The writer sets himself a problem – of necessity, something that interests him personally – and attempts to get it on to paper. He may not aim at actually solving it – although that is the ideal – but merely *stating it clearly*... In order to state it clearly, he also has to solve a number of purely technical (or 'artistic') problems: where to begin, what to put in, what to leave out, and so on. Most creative writing courses devote a great deal of time to these technical problems. But that leaves the *real* problem, the problem at the heart of the novel, untouched. And the creative process must begin with this other kind of problem. (Wilson, 1990, p.17)

This is concrete advice for the 'existential' writer, the writer concerned with using the novel as a tool for personal – and ultimately human – evolution.

The Craft of the Novel, like all essential works by Colin Wilson, is an exploration of human consciousness and an absorbing examination of the 'problem' of freedom. It is a natural extension of Wilson's Outsider cycle – particularly *The Strength to Dream* – and a *tour de force* application of the 'existential criticism' that has defined Wilson's approach to literature from *The Outsider* onwards. But it never loses sight of the writer.

The book opens with Wilson describing his experience as a graduate-level writing teacher at Rutgers University. The position was unexpected: he had been planning to teach a course on existentialism, but unbeknownst to him the topic changed to writing before he arrived and there was nothing to be done about it. One cannot help but think that he got his own back by simply teaching existentialism to writers.

The first thing he discovered was that his students were technically satisfactory but 'existentially' lost. That is, they didn't know what to write about. They found themselves in the fundamental existential quandary: all dressed up with no idea of where to go. Like all beginning writers, they were aware of their *freedom* in the sense that they had the *tabula rasa* of the blank page in front of them, but they didn't know what to do with it. For the existential writer, 'What should I write?' is basically the same question as 'How should I live?'

In my experience – and I have perhaps too much of it in this area – the problem with most writing workshops and 'how-to' manuals on writing is that they fail to invite the writer to address this question. Even making allowances for the necessity of teaching technique – and the alleged difficulty of teaching anything else about writing – there is an alarming indifference to what is actually *said* in a writer's work. To compound the matter, the concentration on technique often invites pessimism in through the back door. The writer is typically taught, for example, that characters should have a 'tragic flaw', that plot should hinge on an incident that draws characters inexorably towards some foredoomed conclusion. This advice may be well-meant: it is undeniable that conflict and tragedy are compelling ingredients in a narrative. But the result is that almost to the point of parody modern fiction is permeated by fatalism and inhabited by alcoholics, petty criminals, broken families, and so on. The writer, not knowing what to write about, ends up presenting a slice of life based on *zeitgeist* and formula rather than attempting to answer a problem. For the existential critic this is a cardinal sin, the writer using his or her talents to reinforce the vision of human beings as insubstantial, passive victims of fate, without asking if it really must be so.

The Craft of the Novel, as a work of existential criticism for writers, never lets go of its dogged insistence that the 'serious' novel must grapple with the quintessential existential problems: 'Who am I?' and 'How shall I live my life?' Addressing this first question is a necessary prelude to tackling the latter. Wilson quotes Shaw from *Back to Methuselah*, introducing a theme that runs throughout *The Craft of the Novel*:

> Art is the magic mirror you make to reflect invisible dreams in visible pictures... You use a glass mirror to see your face; you use works of art to see your soul. (1990, p.28)

The novel is first and foremost a tool of self-creation, allowing the writer to both discover and shape himself. Without some idea of who he is, of what he wants and what his values are, the novelist's ambivalence will be reflected in creations that can be technically adept but lacking purpose. Wilson uses Shaw's early novels, written before the latter found success as a playwright, to illustrate this, but most beginning writers are well-acquainted with the problem. A powerful urge to write is by no means synonymous with clarity of purpose, with knowing what to write *about*, any more than it is with mastery of technique. A writer can learn technique by looking outward: through instruction, practice, and reading other writers. He learns what to write about by going within, by studying himself.

In a sense, then, existential criticism demands that the writer be a phenomenologist. Self-awareness, self-understanding, enables the writer to observe his own values and biases as he draws from the well of imagination and constructs a life-world in his novel. It also gives him a stronger sense of his own power and potential. The greater facility the writer has with the mechanisms of consciousness revealed through self-exploration, the greater the work produced, at least by the standards of existential criticism.[1]

Wilson points out that the history of the novel is marked by a descent into pessimism from which it has yet to recover. After the spectacular explosion of the modern novel with Samuel Richardson's *Pamela*, which balanced the inner experience of its titular character with enough plot to keep its massive audience captivated, the novel drifted more and more into subjectivity. Along the way, of course, were the remarkable highs and lows of Romanticism, with its transcendent visions of meaning and subsequent 'morning after' feelings of unremitting despair at being trapped in the mundane world. But too much gazing into the magic mirror of the soul resulted in 'plotless novels all about the hero's feelings', an observation that many writers, beginning and established, would do well to make note of. (Wilson, 1990, p.51) The naturalistic style which followed romanticism as a kind of counter-force, while claiming to be more 'realistic' than romanticism, was in many ways simply subjectivity in disguise. Balzac represents an interesting transition between the romantic mindset and the naturalism that followed it, for although he possessed a vision of man as 'a kind of god', his massive *Comedie Humaine* is permeated by an unrelenting pessimism. So while his work is remarkable for its devotion to detail, it is not necessarily more realistic than the romantic novels that preceded it.

> When you begin to read Balzac, the impact of the realism is overwhelming. But after a few volumes, you begin to notice inconsistencies. People in real life often gamble and win. They choose the right person and make a happy marriage. They strive for something and achieve it...In Balzac, such things seldom happen... We see [here] the

paradox that destroyed romanticism – and started the novel on the long, slow path of decline: the belief that man is a god, allied to a self-destructive pessimism. (Wilson, 1990, pp.50-1)

The general principle that Wilson draws from this – that 'most talk about "artistic detachment" is disingenuous' – is important for both the existential critic and the writer to keep in mind. Striving for realism, for a photographic accuracy in creating a world in the novel, is a legitimate aim, but it is not as simple as it seems. A photographer not only chooses his subject, he also makes any number of decisions about how to capture his image. He sets the lighting and seizes the desired moment to snap the picture. He has a repertoire of lenses and special effects at his disposal with which he can modify the final product in any way he sees fit. Likewise the novelist has broad discretion in picking and choosing what elements of life he wants to focus on. Inevitably, his vision will be influenced by his value system, temperament, personal biases, intelligence, life experiences, and so on. This is another way of repeating that the serious novelist, the one who wants to approach a more universal answer to the problems of human existence, must have something of the phenomenologist in him. He cannot simply report what's going on inside and outside himself. He must endeavor to *understand* it.

Wilson observed of his graduate student writers: 'They had been taught creative writing, but not creative thinking.'(1990, p.16) Can such a thing be taught? Wilson attempts it, first by offering the astonishingly useful suggestion that a writer should learn to be 'his own Socrates', to practice the type of problem-solving discussed at the beginning of this essay. (1990, p.17) What this amounts to is teaching writers how to engage their creative faculties, how to get the ball rolling. View the novel as a thought-experiment allowing you, the writer, to set in motion a chain of events inspired by your individual vision – values, desires, perceptions – and follow it through to the end. Resist fudging the results and your thought-experiment will 'have something of the same value as real scientific experiments in a real laboratory.' (1990, p.77)

The problem with a naturalistic approach like Balzac's was that he cheated. He allowed his temperament to get in the way of his experiments so that the fatalism that inhabits his novels eventually rings false. He left out a part of the equation – that sometimes people *do* win. He is not alone in his pessimism. Referring to Tolstoy's bizarre insertion of lengthy and fatalistic historical essays into the body of *War and Peace*, Wilson comments that 'great creators can be extremely muddled thinkers.' (1990, p.75) It is ironic that the writer often ignores or dismisses the evidence staring back at him from the pages of his own creation. Creating a novel is, after all, an intentional act, a *god-like* act, really, that seems to fly in the face of any kind of determinism. And often the force of creation provides its own answer. From an objective standpoint, for example, while it is arguable that Hemingway may have seen life as essentially meaningless, his best work is so vital that it insists – regardless of what he may have *thought* – that there is something *more* out there. To use a popular illustration I'm sure not even Colin Wilson has come across, there is a song called "Vasoline", by the rock band *Stone Temple Pilots*, whose lyrics seem to imply a relationship between human experience and being a fly stuck in goo – but the taut, propulsive rhythm, soaring guitars and vocal line of the song say something else entirely: that when the reservoirs of energy within humans are concentrated and channeled, we become aware of another dimension of existence, that of *freedom*.

This fudging of the results in favor of pessimism has its roots in the very beginnings of the novel. It permeates both roman-ticism and realism. While realism is dominated by the world of matter, romanticism pays homage to the soul. What they share is an air of resignation, of being trapped in the mundane world, the romantics because their transcendent visions seemed ultimately unattainable, the realists because they dispensed with the visions altogether; their noses are glued to a narrow vision of reality that leaves out the dimension of the soul.

What becomes clear is that in novel writing as in human existence it is essential not to forget the *flexibility* of human consciousness, the ability to zoom in for detail and step back for visions of 'wide-angle consciousness'. The romantics may have been closer to understanding this than the realists, but they could not make that final leap that would have created a more solid bridge between the world of matter and the world of soul, could not quite turn the key that would liberate humankind from the prison of its current perceptions and open new realms of freedom for exploration, new directions for human evolution. Yet this is the ultimate purpose of the novel.

In the fascinating chapter, "Ideas", Wilson writes:

> If a literate Martian came to earth, and was handed novels by Balzac, Dickens, Trollope, Dostoevsky, G. K. Chesterton, Aldous Huxley, Ernest Hemingway, Graham Greene, William Faulkner, Evelyn Waugh – he would ask incredulously: 'Do you mean to say they are all writing about the *same* world?' To which the strictly correct answer would be: No. They are each writing about a world inside their heads – what you might call their individual Life-Worlds. (1990, p.151)

The visions of these writers share elements of the Communal Life-World in which we all have at least one foot. But they are distinguished by the author's unique values, perceptions, thoughts, and so on, to the point where the novels become distinct worlds, sometimes with almost no overlap whatsoever. Can you imagine a blind, tortured 'idiot' from a Faulkner novel strolling through the second part of Goethe's *Faust*, or a G. K. Chesterton story, or something by Hemingway? Or picture Alyosha from *The Brothers Karamazov* transported into an E. M. Forster comedy of manners like *Room with a View*. It is not simply a matter of different settings and literary styles. The works express different emphases, different values – radically different *understandings* of human existence. All these authors may begin with the same 'sense data' of the Communal Life-World, but their interpretations of it are so divergent from one another that we can easily see why our literate Martian would be confused.

Wilson proposes placing literary works on a continuum, with the bottom labeled 'Communal Life-World' and the middle 'Highly Individual Life-World'. Popular fiction will likely be found at or near the bottom because it tends to be about the 'shared world' we are all familiar with. (Wilson makes a point of saying that this doesn't mean such works are necessarily bad.) Further up the ruler, as characters, situations, values become increasingly individualized – as they reflect more and more the author's emerging self-image – we pass through Jane Austen, on to Dickens, then Hemingway and Faulkner. At this point we are near the middle of the ruler. So what lies beyond?

> As we begin to move into the field of great writers – for example, Goethe, Dostoevsky, Tolstoy, Shaw – we are again moving out of the field of Individual Life-Worlds into something more general. As odd as it sounds, they are beginning to write about *the same* world. (Wilson, 1990, p.152)

One is presented with a fascinating vision of writers from Jane Austen to Faulkner digging deeper and deeper into their own *souls* until, finally, in Goethe and the others, they *break through* into another realm. You could say that this place is the transcendent realm of the romantics, of the Imagination (with a capital 'I'), of the mystical revelation. Such works possess a breadth of vision that incorporates 'worm's-eye' and 'bird's-eye' views of consciousness. They connect the dots of human experience, yielding a vision of relationships, of connected-ness, on the plane of the inner world, the unexplored country of the Imagination. When this inner vision informs the outer world, we perceive a more complete view of reality. The novelist's ultimate task is to *bridge the gap* between the inner and outer worlds.

To call this inner world 'unexplored' is, of course, a little disingenuous. Blake and Goethe and countless others have in fact explored it, and their works serve as reports of what they've found. The Austrian mystic Rudolf Steiner explored it and, going one better, spent his life not only describing it, but trying to teach others how to get there themselves. In essence, *all* writers are exploring it whether they know it or not, because the stage on which the 'thought-experiment' of the novel takes place is this inner world.

As opposed to literary technique, existential criticism gauges the success or failure of a novel by the extent to which it success-fully captures the comprehensive vision of the inner and outer worlds and communicates it to the reader. This is why Wilson so appreciates writers like Powys and Romain Gary and even David Lindsay, whose rough-hewn prose in *A Voyage to Arcturus* does not detract from the book's status as a visionary master-piece. These writers, and others – Dostoevsky, Tolstoy, Goethe, and so on – have broken through the wall of personality, stepped out of their Individual Life-Worlds, into a visionary realm, and they have succeeded in transmitting some sense of that other world to the reader.

This is the job of the novel. In a sense, the writer is like a channeler, only instead of channeling angels or aliens, he is channeling this vision of the inner world through himself. (Although, to be fair, and in deference to Blake, angels and aliens might sometimes have a part in the process.) Creation is a kind of communication.[2] And like the channeler's 'messages', the writer's vision must filter through personality, must to a greater or lesser extent be 'contaminated' by personal consciousness. Unlike the channeler, the writer must take what he 'receives' and use it as the raw material of creation, shaping it into a story through the application of technique. The poet Stanley Kunitz, in his introduction to *The Essential Blake*, observes that although Blake wrote that his poetry came to him 'from immediate Dictation… without Premeditation and even against my Will', he still saw fit to rework the words of angels. (Kunitz, 1987, p.5)

The secret here is that it is the act of creation that reveals the inner world. In setting out to solve a problem, we open a dialogue with the Imagination. When Wilson instructs the writer to be his own Socrates, he is providing far more than just a practical bit of writing advice. He is inviting the writer to explore his own soul. So when he writes that the ultimate aim of the novel 'is the exploration of human freedom' (1990, p.87), we can see that the 'freedom' he is talking about is to be found *inside* us, in the realm of the Imagination. As in all his work, Wilson is illuminating this other dimension of ourselves and exhorting us to develop it, because in doing so we will claim the creative power to transform ourselves – and the outer world as well. The novel is one of the most remarkable inventions mankind has created to bridge this gap between worlds.

My most recent unscientific count of 'how-to' manuals for aspiring writers broke off as I was getting uncomfortably close to infinity. How to plot, how to create dynamic characters, memorable settings, tautly-written sentences, compelling dialogue – the list goes on. But there is nothing out there like *The Craft of the Novel*. Technique can be valuable as a means to an end; *The Craft of the Novel* is primarily concerned with *ends*. It is the missing writer's manual, the one that instructs in the art of thinking and casts the writer in the role of midwife to the Imagination. It is at once a panoramic survey of the history of the novel and an inspired blend of psychological and philosophical insights that virtually erupt from the pages, making the reader feel like a participant in the process of discovery. The cumulative power of Wilson's writing lifts the reader into the very state of vision that the best novels themselves aspire to, giving us a glimpse of what we can become. This is one of the more remarkable gifts that Colin Wilson has possessed since page one of *The Outsider*: the ability to induce peak experiences in his readers. His perspective of existential criticism may lead him to cavalierly highlight the failures of many of the 'giants' of literature, but his entire body of work, *The Craft of the Novel* included, is a testament to humankind's tremendous potential, grounded in an understanding of the mental mechanisms that will allow us to harness it.

We may not have cracked the problem of human existence yet, but if Wilson is right – and reading his work one feels certain he is on the right track – we are on the verge of doing so. The novel is one of the most promising tools for the job. What could be more inspiring to the aspiring writer?

References:

Kunitz, Stanley, 1987. (Editor) *The Essential Blake*. New York: Ecco/HarperCollins.

Wilson, Colin, 1990. *The Craft of the Novel*. Bath, UK: Ashgrove Press Limited.

Wilson, Colin, 2009. *Existential Criticism: Selected Book Reviews*. Nottingham, UK: Pauper's Press.

Notes:

1 Critics of *The Craft of the Novel* will charge that the 'purpose' of the novel elaborated upon in its pages is too subjective – that Colin Wilson's vision of what the novel can and should be is far from universally accepted. This misses the essence of the

book as a work of existential criticism, though it must be said that a brief introduction differentiating between the aims of existential and literary criticism would have been helpful up front. For this we must turn to Wilson's essay, "Existential Criticism", first published in 1959, in which he writes:

> Literary criticism has many standards that are based on technique, and a poem or a novel may be judged as a pleasing exercise in words rather than by its sense of purpose. A literary critic turns without embarrassment from Milton to Dostoevsky, from Jane Austen to Shaw... [But] the existential critic... cannot consider Jane Austen in relation to Dostoevsky without asking awkward questions: 'What, fundamentally, was she saying?'; 'How mature was her moral vision of the world?'; 'What concepts of human purpose are concealed in the basic assumptions of her novels?' (2009, p.3)

2   In the essay 'Fantasy and Faculty X', written as his contribution to *How to Write Tales of Horror, Fantasy and Science Fiction*, edited by J. N. Williamson (Cincinnatti: Writer's Digest, 1987), Wilson describes how the opening scene for the *Space Vampires* came into his mind unbidden as he was falling asleep on a friend's couch and, further, how *Spider World* was written with the active cooperation of some other part of himself. All of us have had this experience of ideas coming into our heads from 'elsewhere', and of course Wilson has written about it at length and applied various labels to the phenomenon. I have caught the process in action occasionally, sometimes when lying in bed half awake and 'receiving' – this seems the only appropriate word – a fully formed line for a song lyric, sometimes when writing narrative and finding myself creating a scene I had not 'thought' to create at all.

Mysteries: an Investigation into the Occult, the Paranormal, and the Supernatural (1978)

A retrospective look at *Mysteries* from the perspective of parapsychology.

Stanley Krippner, PhD

When Colin Wilson was a teenager, he was discussing profound questions with a group of friends regarding, for example, where space ends. He was shocked to realize that this question seemed to be unanswerable. Up to that time, he had sensed that the universe looks baffling, but assumed that "somebody, somewhere, knows all the answers" (p. 25). However, he now doubted this assumption, and his 1978 book titled *Mysteries* provides evidence that, even though they may deny it, people are surrounded by uncertainty and insecurity. Yet they "go on living because that's all there is to do" (p. 29), and because they "are far stronger than they suspect" (p. 35).

Wilson has devoted much of his career to asking fundamental questions, hoping that the answers, even if incomplete, will support "aliveness" and "intensity," thus preventing "the collapse of the will," a condition he sees as a predisposition to mental illness. At the same time, Wilson conceives his efforts as supporting "promotion," an ascent up the ladder of consciousness, where one becomes less troubled about "insoluble mysteries" (p. 75).

Wilson's Position and Examples Pose a Question

Wilson starts *Mysteries* by revisiting the material covered in a previous book, *The Occult* (Wilson, 1971). At the end of the 19th century, the Society for Psychical Research was organized in England to construct theories that would serve as a foundation for a "psychic science." Wilson laments that none of the Society's founders "came even remotely near to succeeding," but singles out another Englishman, Tom Lethbridge, as "the only investigator of the 20th century who has produced a comprehensive and convincing theory of the paranormal" (p.46).

Nevertheless, as one reads about Lethbridge's theory (e.g., 1967), one discovers that much of it is based on a hypothetical construct, the "rates of vibration." Exactly how are these "rates of vibration" to be measured? The instrument Lethbridge (1976) used was a pendulum, the same type of pendulum used by dowsers and other practitioners who work with so-called "subtle energies," those "energies" that are not subsumed by electromagnetism, gravity, the weak nuclear force, or the strong nuclear force. Because he proposed to use "one unknown" to measure "another unknown," Lethbridge's work did not attract much attention from research-oriented parapsychologists or from any other group of rigorous researchers.

However, there are other aspects of Lethbridge's theory that, from contemporary perspectives, are better grounded. He wrote that there is some part of the mind that knows the answers to questions of which the ordinary mind is unaware. Lethbridge (1965) made a connection between this notion and Jung's (1968) model of consciousness, but according to Wilson (1978), he had "never taken the trouble to read Jung systematically and find out what he had to say about the collective unconscious" (p. 203). Fortunately, it is this aspect of Lethbridge's theory that stimulates more of Wilson's subsequent material in *Mysteries* than his work with pendulums and "vibrations."

In addition, Lethbridge proposed that there was an intimate, two-way connection between the human psyche and the forces of the earth. Wilson (1978) associated this proposition with several examples, including Henry James's 1844 mental crisis in an area of England "reputed to harbour more ghosts than

Windsor Castle" (p. 479), something unknown to James at the time. Later, Paul Devereux (2001) made a connection between reported hauntings and geographical and geophysical anomalies, giving some foundation to Lethbridge's speculations. In 1989, the Canadian neuroscientist Michael Persinger and I discovered a significant correlation between the accuracy of telepathic impressions of distant material (art prints) during dreams and the surrounding geomagnetic field at the time the experiment was in process. Each of these examples supports Lethbridge's assertion that the human psyche and Nature are inevitably entangled.

The rest of *Mysteries* provides its readers with fascinating material, all presented within the Lethbridge framework, as well as the conjectures of better-known writers such as Eric Dingwall, Celia Green, Thomas Kuhn, Abraham Maslow, and Charles Tart. One discovers, for example, that the French diplomat Benoit de Malliet proposed a remarkably accurate view of evolution in about 1715, claiming that, over vast spans of time, earlier species evolved into later species and became extinct if they lost the battle of survival. This proposal was almost unanimously rejected by members of both the scientific and ecclesiastical establishments (pp. 189-190). There are dozens of similar examples, some of which will enlighten and some of which will irritate readers; however, *Mysteries* is a book that is never boring.

For me, one of the most riveting sections of the book was Wilson's discussion of "the powers of evil," a topic that is especially timely in the current era of war and terrorism. For Wilson, the tendency to reduce all the horrors of our times to their psychological components has swung too far in a direction opposite to that of the days when unspeakable acts were attributed to demons and devils that "possessed" a vulnerable human or group of humans. This section of *Mysteries* is filled with historical examples and contemporary case histories of curses, jinxes, and spells that purportedly have resulted in murders, suicides, and even shipwrecks. The current parapsychological explanation of poltergeist phenomena (which are usually mischievous but occasionally destructive and life-threatening) is that of a dissociative part of the psyche that is "acting out" resentment, frustration, or repressed emotion. However, not all cases provide a neat fit with this model; there are some instances where "discarnate entities" (p. 461) and "other realms of being" (p. 473) are persuasive, at least to Wilson. One might add that, in view of the 21st century's spate of genocides, suicide bombings, torture, and assassinations, every hypothesis that might lead to or provide a clue to prevention needs to be entertained.

Wilson's education included considerable training in scientific thinking and logical analysis. The question might be asked why *Mysteries* leans so heavily on anecdotal and historical data, and so lightly on laboratory experiments. When Wilson does cite an experiment, he does not stress the importance of replication or assure the reader that all ordinary explanations had been ruled out thanks to a scrupulous experimental design. An example is his citation of Gertrude Schmeidler's well-known parapsychological experiment in which "sheep" (research participants who believed in the possibility of extrasensory perception or ESP) made higher scores on ESP tests than "goats," research participants who did not accept the possibility. Indeed, the former group scored significantly above chance, and the latter significantly below chance. The experiment is correctly reported, but Wilson did not tell his readers that this effect does not occur every time the experiment is attempted, and that its interpretation "is not as simple and straightforward as one might expect" (Palmer, 1978, p. 153).

Mitroff and Kilmann Provide the Answer

I was perplexed by Wilson's mixture of skepticism and credulity, until I recalled that I. I. Mitroff and R. H. Kilmann (1978) had developed a systems-oriented typology of social scientists. According to the psychoanalyst C. G. Jung (1921/1971), people can assimilate data from their inner or outer world by either sensation or intuition, but not by both processes simultaneously. The sensation category includes individuals who typically perceive information by means of the senses. They are most comfortable when attending to details of any situation and prefer basic facts when engaging in problem solving. Sensation types are realists who take a hard, objective stance; they are practical and are oriented to what is feasible in the immediate present, not the past or the future.

In contrast, intuitive individuals take in data by means of their imagination. Intuition involves an awareness of the whole configuration, regardless of whether it pertains to inner or outer phenomena. Unlike sensing types, who prefer to divide a problem into its parts, gathering hard information and comprehending details, intuitive types prefer to perceive the whole picture. They like to focus on the hypothetical possibilities of a situation, often more so than the facts-at-hand. They may conjecture "what might be" rather than "what is." As a result, they might create novel situations that allow them to innovate. The sensation type cannot see the forest for the trees; the intuitive type cannot see the trees for the forest.

Sensation and intuition are non-rational functions, not because they are contrary to reason but because they are outside the province of reason and therefore not bound by it. Thinking and feeling, however, are two functions used in an assessing or judging capacity. They are termed rational functions and are antithetical to one another. Jung described the thinking individual as one whose every important action proceeds from intellectually considered motives. Thinking is the process of reaching a decision based on impersonal, formal, or theoretical modes of reasoning. It seeks to explain inner or outer phenomena in technical, logical, or theoretical terms independent of human purposes, needs, and concerns. Thinking classifies, clarifies, and categorizes. It is concerned with content; it is not unduly concerned with moral, ethical, or aesthetic values.

Feeling, in contrast, is the process of reaching a decision based on value judgments that may be unique to the particular individual. It imparts a definite value to the content, asking whether it is pleasing or unpleasing, moral or immoral, likeable or unlikeable, life-giving or life-denying—in regard to a particular individual at a specific place and time. Given two or more inner or outer phenomena, the feeling person seeks to find what is unique about each of them.

On the basis of these descriptive terms of personality functions, Mitroff and Kilmann described the "sensing-thinking" type or "analytical scientist" as one who is characterized by precision, accuracy, reliability, exactness, and skepticism. In contrast, the "intuition-thinking" type or "conceptual theorist" is speculative, holistic, and imaginative, and values the creation of novel conceptual possibilities. The "intuition-feeling" type or "conceptual humanist" admits to being interested rather than "disinterested," personal instead of "impersonal," aware of personal biases rather than claiming to be "unbiased" when engaged in scientific activity. The "sensing-feeling" type or "particular humanist" holds that science does not necessarily occupy a privileged position but may be subordinate to literature, art, music, or even mysticism in approaching certain questions, a position also taken by many so-called "postmodern" thinkers.

Applications to Creativity Research

In an article applying this system to creativity research (Krippner, 1983), I cited Paul Torrance (e.g., 1971) as an "analytical scientist"; his *Tests of Creative Thinking* were break-through instruments in identifying and cultivating creative behavior. For my example of a "conceptual theorist" I selected J. P. Guilford (e.g., 1977), whose "Structure of Intellect" model (and its differentiation between "convergent" and "divergent" thinking) lent itself as an aid in developing curricular plans as well as serving as a diagnostic tool for individuals and groups. Rollo May (e.g., 1975) was my example of a "conceptual humanist," because he used his background as a depth psychologist to portray the nature of human creativity, and his convictions as an existential psychotherapist to describe the "courage to create." For the "particular humanist," I chose Mildred Goertzel (1978), whose case studies of 300 eminent creative personalities contained insights into their early life experiences and why, for example, they typically loved learning but often disliked school. Finally, I proposed a systems model in which all four of these types could play an important role in identifying a problem, proposing alternative solutions, and implementing and/or evaluating the solution once it had been selected.

Applications to Parapsychological Research

I had the opportunity to use Mitroff's typology again when I gave my presidential address to the Parapsychological Association in 1983 (Krippner, 2002). On this occasion, I used J. B. Rhine (e.g., 1938), who brought quantitative, experimental, and statistical approaches into the field, as my example of the "analytical scientist." The "conceptual theorist" I selected was E. H. Walker (e.g., 2000), who applied his work in quantum physics to the "hidden variables" that he posited were present in parapsychological interactions. My choice of a "conceptual humanist" was Lawrence LeShan (e.g., 1976), the psychologist who posited several "alternate realities" on the basis of his work with noted claimants such as mediums and "psychic healers."

My example of the "particular humanist" was Hans Bender
(e.g., 1974), the German psychologist and physician who placed
art, philosophy, and mystical insights on an equal footing with
science, especially when he took an interest in the effect that his
investigations would have on his research participants. In fact,
Wilson (1978) demonstrated considerable affinity for Bender,
citing his work several times in *Mysteries*, most notably in his
discussion of Bender's in-depth investigation of a poltergeist
("noisy ghost") case in Rosenheim, Germany (pp. 466-470).

In my remarks, I pointed out the contribution that each type
of parapsychologist could make to the advancement of the field.
I noted that, when psychical research originated, particular
humanists were in the forefront of the movement; they gave way
to analytical scientists when parapsychology began to utilize
controlled settings and laboratory equipment. However, all four
types are needed, and each has something to offer. In fact, I
made the case that particular humanists represent the greatest
challenge to contemporary ideas regarding science. They hold
that a basic aim of science is to help people to know themselves,
and they do this through "a logic of the unique and singular" in
which the case study is the preferred mode of inquiry (Krippner,
2002, pp. 109-110).

Finding A Place for Colin Wilson

By putting Wilson in the "particular humanist" camp, one can
appreciate his contributions and forgive his lapses.
Parapsychologists in the United Kingdom have told me that
Wilson provides more credibility to Uri Geller than would be
granted by most parapsychologists (e.g., Wilson, 1978, pp. 447-
448), that he tends to gloss over or provide an "unproven"
verdict on some of the alleged fraudulent behaviors of mediums
and other psychic claimants (e.g., p. 613), and that he writes
about such hypothetical constructs as "ley lines" as if they were

established phenomena (e.g., p. 132). They tell me that he is most open to criticism by his use of the term "supernatural" as a synonym for "paranormal" (e.g., pp. 355, 471). By and large, contemporary parapsychologists take the position that anything "supernatural" (i.e., a reported phenomenon that violates the laws of Nature) cannot be empirically verified. Furthermore, if one accepts the premise that "supernatural" forces are actively involved in the world's daily affairs, scientific investigation of anomalous phenomena might well be impossible (Alcock, in Clay, 2010).

In response to the above, I would suggest that Wilson has made outstanding contributions in many ways, most notably by conceptualizing reported psychic experiences as examples of unexplored human potentialities. In fact, in a 1995 essay, Wilson made an explicit connection between his breakthrough book, *The Outsider*, and his later interest in anomalous phenomena. He recalled that, at that time, "I was concerned with romantic art and literature for the liberation of the human imagination.... Compared with this liberation, the question of spirits and ectoplasm and floating trumpets seemed trivial.... [Later] I had recognized the nature of my error. If telepathy, clairvoyance, precognition, and psychokinesis existed—as I was now certain that they did—then they bore witness to the unrecognized potentialities of the human psyche just as much as the genius of Shakespeare and Mozart" (p. xx).

In these few phrases, the stance of the particular humanist is echoed, a stance that includes literature, art, music, and even mysticism as disciplines that hold explanatory possibilities for human potentialities. In *Mysteries*, Wilson draws heavily upon the humanities, for example using Dostoyevsky's description of Alyosha Karamazov's "moments of intensity" under the stars to portray times when one's inner being "expands from the size of a small room to the size of a cathedral," accompanied by "a strange feeling of inner *connections* as if the vibrations of one part of [a person's] being could cause another to vibrate" (p. 354, italics in the original). On the one hand, this use of the word "vibrations" has more explanatory power than Lethbridge's pendulum-derived numerical "vibrations." On the other hand, most general readers will find it easier to resonate with Dostoyevsky's description (even in translation) than that of most research participants who attempt to articulate their extraordinary experiences. It will come as no surprise that Wilson (1972) has been a champion of humanistic psychology, the perspective that—more than any of its competitors—has drawn upon novels, poetry, and other products of humankind's creative spark to elucidate its principles and speculations.

There is yet another way in which Wilson follows the path of the particular humanist. For these scientists the case study is the preferred mode of inquiry, as specific examples, related in some depth, hold the promise of helping people to follow Socrates' adage to "know thyself." It is here where Wilson shines; some of his case examples require an entire book, while others serve their purpose in a few paragraphs.

Wilson is especially adept at resurrecting nearly-forgotten individuals who have, nonetheless, made contributions to knowledge that can be better appreciated now than when their creators were alive. He tells the story of the bookkeeper-turned-writer George Russell, who formulated the idea of the "collective unconscious" and the practice of "active imagination" at least a quarter-century before Jung. He joined the Theosophical Society and was successful in inducing "kundalini energy" during meditation. Wilson considers him "perhaps the greatest natural mystic of the twentieth century" (p. 318).

Few people recall the name of Mary Anne South, an English writer whose father was a classical scholar and conveyed his enthusiasm to his daughter. South also performed home-grown experiments in hypnotism and spirit mediumship; again, Mary Anne followed the paternal example. She used her knowledge of classical Latin and Greek to translate early treatises of alchemy into English; she and her father rejected the then-fashionable notion that alchemical writings were complex analogies. Rather, the South team felt that they enshrined the ancient mystery schools in symbolic form. Mary Anne also saw connections between these mystery schools and the early experiments she and her father had done with spiritualism and hypnosis; she put all of these insights into a massive book that was immediately published. But Mary Anne had not run her treatise by her father; once he read the book, he called in all copies that had been sent out and burned them in a massive bonfire. The book was not reprinted until a decade after Mary Anne's death, and its destruction devastated her literary ambitions. Wilson considers that Mary Anne is a forerunner of Jungian thought (yes, another one), but that the essence of her book was her conviction that, with the appropriate mental state, an alchemist could actually transmute base metals into gold (p. 409).

Wilson is a master storyteller, and his inquiries into alchemy take the better part of two chapters in *Mysteries*. If readers persist, and Wilson's prose is so masterful that this is an easy task, they will learn half a dozen interpretations of alchemical texts, how Jung became interested in the topic and what he wrote about alchemy, and even that some anecdotal fragments indicate that a few alchemists whose "concentrative powers" (as Mary Anne South put it) were well focused actually engineered this physical transformation.

In his autobiography, Wilson (2004) noted that, when he signed the contract to write a book titled *The Occult* (because "I needed the money," p. 278), he expected he would be pressured into writing about ghosts and banshees, even though "I am as naturally skeptical about such tales as any scientist" (p. 287). But his emphasis began to change when he found himself "stumbling on examples of unusual powers of certain individuals" (p. 287). As a particular humanist, he reveled in these stories, which became the case studies he passes on to his fortunate readers.

The Occult received favorable reviews and sold well. If scientifically-oriented readers can accept the orientation of *Mysteries* as that of a particular humanist, they can take issue with specific parts of the book where the evidence is less than what they might find persuasive. But at the same time they can derive both enjoyment and insight from what the rest of this incredible treatise has to offer regarding human potential and its manifestations.

References:

Bender, H. (1974). Modern poltergeist research. In J. Beloff (Ed.), *New directions in parapsychology* (pp. 122-143). London: Elek Science.

Clay, R. A. (2010, May). Theism vs. naturalism: Psychologists debate their discipline's stance toward God. *Monitor on Psychology,* p. 16.

Devereux, P. (2001). *Haunted land: Investigations into ancient mysteries and modern day phenomena.* London: Piatkus.

Goertzel, M. G. et al. (1978). *Three hundred eminent personalities.* San Francisco: Jossey-Bass.

Guilford, J. P. (1977). *Way beyond the IQ.* Buffalo, NY: Creative Education Foundation.

Jung, C. G. (1968). *Analytical psychology: Its theory and practice.* London: Routledge and Kegan Paul.

Jung, C. G. (1971). *Psychological types. Collected works* (vol. 6). Princeton, NJ: Princeton University Press. (Original work published 1921.)

Krippner, S. (1983). A systems approach to creativity based on Jungian typology. *International Journal of Systems Science, 27,* 86-89.

Krippner, S. (2002). A systems approach to psi research based on Jungian typology. *Journal of the American Society for Psychical Research, 96,* 106-120.

LeShan, L. (1976). *Alternate realities: The search for the full human being.* New York: M. Evans.

Lethbridge, T. C. (1965). *ESP: Beyond time and distance.* London: Routledge and Kegan Paul.

Lethbridge, T. C. (1967). *A step in the dark.* London: Routledge and Kegan Paul.

Lethbridge, T. C. (1976). *The power of the pendulum.* London: Routledge and Kegan Paul.

May, R. (1975). *The courage to create.* New York: W. W. Norton

Mitroff, I. I., & Kilmann, R. H. (1978). *Methodological approaches to social science.* San Francisco: Jossey Bass.

Palmer, J. (1978). Extrasensory perception: Research findings. In S. Krippner (Ed.), *Advances in parapsychological research* (Vol. 2, pp. 59-243). Jefferson, NC: McFarland.

Persinger, M. A., & Krippner, S. (1989). Dream ESP experiments and geomagnetic activity. *Journal of the American Society for Psychical Research, 83,* 101-116.

Rhine, J. B. (1938). Experiments bearing on the precognition hypothesis. *Journal of Parapsychology, 2,* 38-54.

Torrance, E. P. (1971). Are the Torrance Tests of Creative Thinking biased against disadvantaged groups? *Gifted Child Quarterly, 15,* 75-80.

Walker, E. H. (2000). *The physics of consciousness.* New York: Perseus Books.

Wilson, C. (1956). *The Outsider.* London: Gollancz.

Wilson, C. (1971). *The Occult.* London: Hodder.

Wilson, C. (1972). *New pathways in psychology: Maslow and the post-Freudian revolution.* London: Gollancz.

Wilson, C. (1978). *Mysteries: An investigation into the occult, the paranormal & the supernatural.* New York: Perigee/G.P. Putnam's Sons.

Wilson, C. (1995). Preface. In A. Imich (Ed.), *Incredible tales of the paranormal* (pp. ix-xxi). New York: Bramble Books.
Wilson, C. (2004). *Dreaming to some purpose: An autobiography.* London: Century.

The author acknowledges Saybrook University's Chair for the Study of Consciousness for supporting the preparation of this essay.

The Haunted Man: the strange genius of David Lindsay (1979)

The Haunted Man

Murray Ewing

When Colin Wilson's study of David Lindsay, *The Haunted Man*, came out in 1979, something of a Lindsay revival was underway. This was remarkable because, ever since the publication of his debut novel, *A Voyage to Arcturus*, in 1920, Lindsay's publishing career had been on something of a downhill slide.

Arcturus was a work out of step with its time. Lindsay's original title, *Nightspore on Tormance*, was immediately changed by the publisher to make it sound more in the Verne and Wells tradition, something more likely to "capture public interest" (Sellin, 1986, p. 22). On its release, a contemporary reviewer struggled to compare the novel with "Baudelaire, or Poe in his most grisly vein" (Wilson et al. 1970, p. 3), mistaking Lindsay's intent for a desire "to make the gorge rise". Even within the burgeoning but as-yet-unnamed genre of science fiction, *Arcturus* was an anomaly. It had a voyage to an alien world, meetings with nonhuman beings, the transformation of the body with new limbs and sensory organs, and this was innovation enough; but these were just the background Lindsay needed to get started saying what he wanted to say. The trouble was, the critics and public of his day were too bewildered by that background to even begin to understand the message. No, to find the time when Lindsay should have published, we need to either go back to the days when the likes of Bishop Francis Godwin (in his *Man in the Moone: or a Discourse of a Voyage Thither by Domingo Gonsales* (1638)), John Wilkins (in his *Discovery of a New World in the Moone* (1638)), or Margaret Cavendish (in her *Description of a New World, called The Blazing World* (1668)) used the fanciful idea of a voyage to the Moon, or the Sun, or some other, unknown world as a vehicle for Utopian philosophical speculation (Aldiss and Wingrove, 1986, p. 71–3); or we need to come forward forty-odd years to the 1960s, when writers like Ursula Le Guin and Robert Silverberg began incorporating the so-called "softer" sciences of sociology, ethnology, biology and psychology into their SF (now the trappings of the genre were well enough established not to be themselves the centre of attention), and sometimes a little mysticism, too.

Lindsay's subsequent novels, though more earthbound and restrained in their use of the fantastic, met with no greater success. An ad run by publisher John Long in the *Times* of 30th November 1923 announced Lindsay's *Sphinx* with the words: "A refreshing originality pervades this charmingly whimsical novel." Calling *Sphinx* — a novel about the tragic death of a creatively bankrupt composer, and a young man's philosophical inquiries into the nature of deep-sleep dreams — "charming" and "whimsical" is as much off target as comparing *Arcturus* to Baudelaire and Poe. Lindsay, I can't help thinking, would have felt those words like a slap in the face, and it certainly can't have done anything to sell the book.

How much his decision to make his post-*Arcturus* novels earthbound was a commercial one, or whether it was part of the need, as stated by Krag at the end of *A Voyage to Arcturus*, to "return to the struggle" (Lindsay, 1920, p. 242) and take the fight against Crystalman — against the falseness of reality itself — back to Earth, we cannot say. Certainly, in retrospect, it seems Wilson had it more than a little right when he says Lindsay "undoubtedly misunderstood his talents when he decided to become a novelist, for the novel for Lindsay meant people; people wrangling and interacting and quarrelling. And he was not really interested in people." (Wilson, 1979, p. 61–2) The writing of *Arcturus* had been powered by Lindsay's long pent-up imagination; the later novels suffered from a self-consciousness of style he was never to overcome.

The rest of Lindsay's life is, sadly, a well-rehearsed tale. As he found it more difficult to get published, he found it more difficult to write. He retreated further and further into his own ideas, and his last two novels are his most inaccessible: *Devil's Tor* — his "monster", as he called it (Wilson et al. 1970, p.116), or "that immense, ponderous block of German metaphysics and pagan mysticism" as Wilson has called it (Wilson, 1979, p. 46) — was his largest novel yet, as weighty, in both heft of pages and density of prose, as the Tor itself, followed by *The Witch*, whose final (still unpublished) chapter is almost as long as the preceding nineteen, and whose language becomes as uncompromising and impenetrable in its prophetic tone as anything Lindsay ever wrote.

Finally, he retreated from the world itself. Isolating himself in his room at the top of the boarding house in Hove that his wife had taken on to provide them with a living, he left a dental abscess untreated till it turned to cancer and blood poisoning killed him. Wilson has called it "one of the saddest stories in 20th century literature" (Wilson, 2002, p. 399), made all the more poignant by the fact that Victor Gollancz republished *A Voyage to Arcturus*, due to a growing demand, the very next year.

But even that republication was not enough to start the Lindsay revival. It simply wasn't sufficient for *Arcturus* to be republished in hardback, in the United Kingdom, every few years (Gollancz issued it again in 1963 and 1978). *Arcturus* was still a rare seed scattered on stony ground. It needed to be propagated far and plentifully to find the few cracks of fertile soil in which it would grow. That meant, preferably, that it be published in paperback, preferably in America, and preferably — if by lucky chance it could be arranged — on the back of some major new craze for the fantastic.

Two decades after Lindsay's death, the stars were right. In the late sixties, Tolkien's *Lord of the Rings* was taking the college campuses of America by storm, thanks in part to two rival paperback versions (one authorised, one not) being issued at the same time, and the resultant brouhaha raising a publisher's legal wrangle into something of a hippie cause (see Lachman, 2010, p. 72–9). Suddenly there was a whole new generation of readers who wanted their minds expanded, and their ideals of Arcadian, pre-technological quests of self-discovery reflected in their reading, and it so happened that the fantasy and science fiction of the day had matured enough to meet the demand. Ballantine Books (publisher of the legitimate edition of *The Lord of the Rings* in America) were looking for other works in a similar vein to feed this new readership's Hobbit habit, and one of the titles they chose was *A Voyage to Arcturus*.

This was the true start of the Lindsay revival. Ballantine's paperback of *A Voyage to Arcturus* came out in 1968, and remained in print well into the following decade. Thanks to it, many new readers discovered Lindsay's work. Thanks to it, *A Voyage to Arcturus* was soon translated into French, German, Spanish, and Japanese. Thanks to it, within two decades, all of Lindsay's other works (except his least characteristic novel, *The Adventures of Monsieur de Mailly*) were made available for a whole new generation of readers. Thanks to it, *A Voyage to Arcturus* would become "a staple of college courses in fantastic literature" (Wolfe, 1982, p. 8). And thanks to it, Lindsay's pronouncement that "as long as our civilisation lasts one person a year will read me" (Lewis, 1982, p. 145–6) no longer relied on Gollancz's willingness to reissue it as a "Rare Work of Imaginative Fiction" every few years. It was out there, it was known, and has remained so to this day.

All this, then, was thanks to Ballantine issuing *A Voyage to Arcturus* in paperback.

And Ballantine issuing *A Voyage to Arcturus* in paperback was thanks to Colin Wilson.

Wilson first read *A Voyage to Arcturus* in 1963, and first wrote about Lindsay in his 1965 collection of literary essays, *Eagle and Earwig*. (This was the first study of Lindsay to appear between hard covers.) It begins: "David Lindsay's *A Voyage to Arcturus* is one of the strangest, and most certainly one of the greatest books of the twentieth century. Yet its greatness is of such a curious order that it is still almost unknown today, nearly half a century after it was first published." (Wilson, 1965, p. 128)

The essay goes on to mention that reading *Arcturus* led Wilson to begin a correspondence with E. H. Visiak, author of another of Gollancz's "Rare Works of Imaginative Fiction", *Medusa* (originally published in 1929), and one of Lindsay's few literary friends. And while the correspondence was mostly unilluminating on the subject of decoding Lindsay's novel, it bore other fruit. Visiak, at the time, seemed to regard himself as dwelling in the long fade-out to a largely undistinguished literary career, and was apparently quite prepared to die of boredom in the nursing home he had recently moved into. In response to a particularly miserable letter from Visiak in 1967, Wilson suggested a work cure: they would collaborate on a book about David Lindsay. Hearing that J. B. Pick (the only other person, at the time, to have written to any extent on Lindsay, in an essay for the January 1964 issue of *Studies in Scottish Literature*), might be planning something similar, Wilson wrote to him, with the happy outcome that the duo of authors became a trio.

The Strange Genius of David Lindsay: An Appreciation was published by John Baker in 1970. Wilson had written his contribution to the book, a lengthy essay providing an in-depth analysis of Lindsay's themes throughout his major novels, in 1968. It was in this year, too, that Wilson heard of Ballantine's search for works to reprint as part of what would become their influential "Adult Fantasy" series, and wrote to them, suggesting *Arcturus*. Ballantine took up Wilson's idea, though not his offer to write the introduction (as, it seems, Loren Eiseley's came with the rights Ballantine bought from *Arcturus*'s first US publisher, Macmillan).

It's curious to think that, despite Wilson's extensive involvement with Lindsay, and the many books he's written introductions to as a result, he has never written an introduction to *A Voyage to Arcturus*. But this hardly matters, considering what we do have. Aside from the long essays ("Lindsay" in *Eagle and Earwig* (1965), "Lindsay as novelist and mystic" in *The Strange Genius of David Lindsay* (1970), "David Lindsay and *A Voyage to Arcturus*" in *The Books in My Life* (1998)), we have introductions to other Lindsay novels (*The Violet Apple and The Witch* (1976), *Sphinx* (1988)), introductions to books about Lindsay (Bernard Sellin's *The Life and Works of David Lindsay* (1981), David Powers' *David Lindsay's Vision* (1991)), and an extensive examination of Lindsay's works as part of *The Craft of the Novel* (1975). Of these writings — none of which is wholly replaceable by any other — it is "Lindsay as novelist and mystic" that has had the longest life. Republished (with slight expansion) as a standalone book, *The Haunted Man: The Strange Genius of David Lindsay*, by the Borgo Press in 1979, it was republished again as part of Savoy Books's beautiful hardback edition of *A Voyage to Arcturus* in 2002, to which Wilson also provided a brief afterword.

For me, one of the most admirable aspects of Colin Wilson's work has always been its inclusiveness, its willingness to treat every area of life as a possible source of answers and ideas. Day-to-day consciousness, including the dull moments like hanging out the laundry or peeling the potatoes, gets the same focus of interest as peak experiences (and always with the question, "Why can't the one be like the other?"). The same goes for those areas that some writers wouldn't touch with a bargepole — poltergeists, UFOs, the occult, for example — simply for fear that the grime of the credulous might sully their own writings through association.

There's none of this squeamishness with Wilson. And the reason is obvious. He's too focused on the truth to be cowed by proprieties. It's the *whole* of the human picture that matters, the entirety of lived experience, not the carefully selected "acceptable" bits. The answer, after all, could lie anywhere. Petty crime can reveal as important truths about the criminal mind as murder; boredom is as important a factor in understanding the human condition as the triumph of great achievements. There's a wonderful muddy-handedness about Wilson's willingness to examine any subject that interests him.

The same goes for his attitude to the literature of the fantastic. Fantasy and science fiction have always been treated with a certain contempt by the literary establishment. At first they simply ignored them, but when the boom of the sixties made this increasingly difficult, academia responded by ring-fencing the fantastic into specialist studies, and only regarding these genres formalistically, as literary conventions. But this is to seriously miss the point, because many of the writers who write these genres, and many of the readers who read them, do so because of the ideas, the content, not the form. Nowadays, academic treatment of the fantastic, though more widespread, is often even more debased. Fantasy and science fiction are regarded from a pop-culture perspective, under which every work, whatever its quality or content, is considered equally valid, and the ideas of no consequence at all. (Oddly enough, the only critics consistently interrogating the *ideas* in fantasy fiction at the moment seem to be a certain section of conservative Christians, who have developed a mini-industry of titles to help parents decide whether letting their kids read J. K. Rowling or Philip Pullman is the start of a downslide into Satanism.)

Wilson, though, is one of the few writers willing (and able) not only to treat imaginative literature seriously, but to move without difficultly or embarrassment from talking of Joyce and Eliot to Tolkien or Lovecraft, and to consider all these works with the same rigour and seriousness.

A key book here is *The Craft of the Novel*. In the penultimate chapter, "Fantasy and New Directions", Wilson says that the age of the "great experimenters" in the novel came to an end with the death of Joyce in 1941, and that, ever since, there's been a gap between the writers of bestsellers and serious novelists, something that simply wasn't true in the days of Defoe, Scott, and Dickens. The implication is that the novel may be on its last legs as a serious form. But he goes on to cite the "revival of interest in fantasy" (Wilson, 1975, p. 208) as a potentially important change. Quickly dismissing the idea that fantasy is just about escapism, he points to Maslow's hierarchy of values for an alternative explanation: "By the second decade of the twentieth century... The majority of people in the civilised countries had more security than ever before... Which meant that most people were in the position... to explore the realm of imagination." (Wilson, 1975, p. 210) Thus, "The swing back to romanticism and mysticism may be more than an 'escapist' reaction; this time it could be the next step forward." (Wilson, 1975, p. 211) Wilson, always interested in "the next step forward", presciently calls *The Lord of the Rings* "one of the most successful works of art of the twentieth century" (Wilson, 1975, p. 212), a view amply corroborated when it was voted (to many critics' disgust) the best-loved novel of the 20th century, in several country-wide polls that were carried out in the late 1990s.

David Lindsay is the last writer treated in *The Craft of the Novel*, and his novels are used to demonstrate Wilson's faith in the potential of the literature of the imagination: "One thing emerges clearly from the study of Lindsay's work; fantasy is not another name for free-floating imagination. It is a highly disciplined faculty that uses imagination to explore ideas; and its laws are as rigorous as the laws of mathematics." (Wilson, 1975, p. 219–220).

It's easy to see why Lindsay appealed to Wilson. Lindsay was, Wilson says, a writer who was "deliberately inventing a mythology to explain his ideas of the world's inner nature" (Wilson, 1965, p. 128–9). And it is this "inner nature" that interests Wilson, too. Both, as writers, are "high flyers", to use Wilson's term (Wilson, 1979, p. 6–7) (which was itself inspired by Lindsay's division of imaginative writers into "those who describe the world and those who explain it" (Wilson et al. 1970, p. 27–8)). And, as explainers, as "high flyers", Wilson and Lindsay share the same areas of concern, the big questions about life and meaningfulness, about thought and human will. At one point in *Eagle and Earwig* Wilson says: "in a single sentence Lindsay states the essence of phenomenology: 'We are each of us living in a false private world of our own, a world of dreams and appetites and distorted perceptions.'" (Wilson, 1965, p. 138)

There are some happy parallels between the writers' work. For instance, a key idea in Wilson's writing is that perception is intentional — you don't just passively see the world around you, but reach out and *grasp* its meaning — and this is perfectly embodied in the multiplicity of new sensory organs Maskull gains in his journey across Tormance, each of which has the effect of changing his way of understanding the world around him. Chief among these is the eye-like "sorb", an organ through which Maskull sees everything "as an object of importance or non-importance to his own needs" (Lindsay, 1920, p. 77), and which can be used to effectively project one's will, and impose it on others, even to the point of absorbing their essence into oneself. (And this notion proved to be the key to a breakthrough in Wilson's own thinking on a problem that had been dogging him for some time. In Lindsay's depiction of one person "sorbing" another, Wilson found "the root of the male sexual impulse; it satisfies the hunger of the *will* as food satisfies the hunger of the body." (Wilson, 1979, p. 22.))

The most obvious point to make linking Lindsay's fiction

with Wilson's thought is, of course, that Lindsay was quite evidently an Outsider, as an anecdote from E. H. Visiak makes clear. The two were on a countryside walk one night, when Visiak paused to remark on how strange the moon looked:

> [Lindsay] was already looking up at it. 'White,' he murmured. 'White, *empty*.' His face looked wild and tragic, and he cried with startling emphasis, 'I ought *never* to have been born in this world!'
>
> I was amazed, but I said mechanically, 'In what world, then, ought you to have been born?'
>
> 'In *no* world!' (Wilson et al. 1970, p. 100)

Outsiders are spontaneous self-initiates into a Mystery cult which no longer exists, a Mystery cult of one. Forced to enact their own rites, it's no surprise so many of them become artists, where the tricksterish dramas they produce are all too often unconscious attempts to initiate or awaken others — not so much to end their own Outsiderism, as create a new kind of Insiderism, of the awakened, the initiated. In *A Voyage to Arcturus* this is evident in the constantly repeated mini-drama of Maskull having his beliefs (in a philosophical system, a religious idea, or the true nature of the world) built up, then swept out from under his feet by the annulling appearance of the Crystalman grin, which becomes a sort of trademark of the illusory nature of the world. This is the form of *Arcturus* on the episodic level; its ultimate message, and the real power of the novel's ending, is that truth itself is endangered. Muspel, our "real" home, is fighting a desperate battle with falseness, with illusion, with (in Lindsay's belief) worldly pleasure. But Lindsay's Outsiderism was, after *Arcturus*, confounded by a desperate need to become an Insider, to be taken seriously as a writer and thinker, which he could only think of doing on *their* terms. He wavered, and compromised, and that is always fatal for an Outsider.

What went wrong?

I've already quoted Wilson's remark that, for Lindsay, the novel "meant people", and the trouble with this was that Lindsay "was not really interested in people" (Wilson, 1979, p. 61–2). Yet earlier in the same essay, Wilson says "Lindsay is probably the most acute psychologist since Nietzsche." (Wilson, 1979, p. 23) Not interested in people, yet an acute psychologist? Surely there is a contradiction here?

If so, it's easily resolved. Wilson himself sums it up in the remark: "All artists are planets of a double star" (Wilson, 1979, p. 9). And this is perhaps true of Lindsay more than most. Lindsay's social self was stiff and formal. In essence it was, like his false god Faceny, "all face; and this face is his shape" (Lindsay, 1920, p. 177), with nothing but hollowness and sham within. *A Voyage to Arcturus* is a direct expression of this condition: attraction to worldly pleasure, followed by a sudden revulsion when that pleasure is found to be superficial, empty and meaningless. And why this hollowness of response? Because ultimately meaning, substance, and the ability to feel lasting pleasure come from one's deepest responses, one's authentic self. But Lindsay's other self — his "second star" — was so starkly in contrast to his social face that when he felt the influence of the two, just as when Maskull feels the influence of the twin suns Branchspell and Alppain, the result is pain, and even (in the novel) death. But the death suffered in *Arcturus* is only the death of Maskull — the mask, the social face, the false self — which serves to release the spiritually toughened, bleak-souled Nightspore. This is Lindsay's problem, as dramatised in *A Voyage to Arcturus*: how to free Nightspore from the delusion that he is Maskull.

(It's quite easy to see why Lindsay had such a sharp divide between his social and inner selves. An intelligent, contemplative young man, he was immediately denied the chance to follow his natural path into the life of the mind when the family's financial situation forced him to do his duty and earn a living. And with the start of the First World War, he was disgusted to find that even *this* concession to the world was no longer enough, when he was conscripted into that even more depersonalising institution, the army.)

The artist's task, then, is self-integration — the Outsider's problem of how to live authentically, to be true to oneself while existing in a shared world of "other people". As Wilson points out in *The Craft of the Novel*, a writer, in creating a hero for his novels, sets out to create a self-image that solves this problem of authenticity: "An effective hero should spring from the writer's own self-image. He should reflect the writer's own striving, his own sense of purpose and identity." (Wilson, 1975, p. 26) This is done by a series of novelistic "thought-experiments" (Wilson, 1975, p. 70). Lindsay's Arcturan attempt at such a thought experiment was certainly not of the test-tubes and bunsen-burners kind; it was a Hadron collider of the imagination, trying to split the fundamental particle of the Self.

And I think Lindsay did come up with an answer in *Arcturus*, though one so strange he perhaps didn't see it, or simply couldn't accept its boldness. The only truly vital personality in *A Voyage to Arcturus* is Krag, the guardian and representative of the "true world" Muspel. Krag has humour, insight, a weird *joie-de-vivre*, and above all he has freedom ("from the beginning, the basic aim of the novel was bound up with this sense of freedom, and the problem of freedom became one of its main themes" (Wilson, 1975, p. 71)).

But after *Arcturus*, where is that Krag-like spirit of freedom in Lindsay's writing? Where is Krag the impulsive mixture of "sagacity, brutality, and humour" (Lindsay, 1920, p. 23) who can so freely speak his mind, even within the dreaded confines of an upper-middle-class drawing room? It can be glimpsed, in echoes, but is never strong. Most evidently, I find it in Haidee

Croyland's impulsive decision to eat one of the fruit descended from the Biblical Tree of the Knowledge of Good and Evil in *The Violet Apple*. But elsewhere, that spark of freedom has been forced into almost total retreat before the demands of the social world. For Lindsay, the social world is too cloying, too restrictive, yet he feels that, as a novelist, it is his duty to fit in with it — not realising that being a novelist was the only way he could truly be free of it.

By taking Maskull to Tormance, Krag seeks to awaken him to his true nature as Nightspore. And when that is done, the next step is to return to Earth and save more souls from Crystalman's clutches, to proclaim the vision of the path to freedom — and this is a task that the subsequent earthbound novels could be said to be trying to put into practice. Only, what happens instead is what happens to Isbel Loment and Henry Judge when they descend from the sublimity of the "upper rooms" in *The Haunted Woman* — they forget their true purpose, they forget their true selves. Lindsay's later novels take this situation as their subject, and all too often end up more concerned with bemoaning the condition of man mired in the restrictive social world than in saving him from it.

It should be clear from this examination how Colin Wilson has provided vital keys to understanding both David Lindsay's work and his life. At the end of his afterword to the Savoy edition of *Arcturus*, Wilson writes: "Will Lindsay ever become a 'classic'? The answer is obviously no. But his masterpiece, *Arcturus*, will always have enthusiastic readers." (Wilson, 2002, p. 401) But Lindsay was never destined to sit alongside the likes of Dickens or Austen; there will never be a BBC costume drama of *The Haunted Woman* or *The Violet Apple*. Yet I think *Arcturus* has nevertheless gained the exposure it needed to find further recruits for Krag's — and Lindsay's — mission to awaken a world mired in illusions. Ninety years after its first publication, *A Voyage to Arcturus* is still in print, still read, and still talked about, and will be for the foreseeable future. Colin Wilson's role in this has been vital, and his writings are, and should remain, an essential guide to understanding David Lindsay's work.

References:

Aldiss, Brian & Wingrove, David. 1986. *Trillion Year Spree: The History of Science Fiction*. London: Gollancz.

Lachman, Gary. 2010. *The Dedalus Book of the 1960s*. Sawtry: Dedalus.

Lewis, C. S. 1982. *On Stories and Other Essays on Literature*. New York: Harcourt.

Lindsay, David. 1920. *A Voyage to Arcturus*. London: Methuen. (Actual edition used: 1963. London: Gollancz.)

Sellin, Bernard. 1981. *The Life and Works of David Lindsay*. Cambridge: Cambridge University Press. (Actual edition used: 2006. Cambridge: Cambridge University Press.)

Wilson, Colin. 1965. *Eagle and Earwig*. London: John Baker.

Wilson, Colin, 1975. *The Craft of the Novel*. London: Gollancz. (Actual edition used: 1990. Bath: Ashgrove Press.)

Wilson, Colin. 1979. *The Haunted Man: The Strange Genius of David Lindsay*. San Bernardino: The Borgo Press.

Wilson, Colin. 2002. "Afterword" to Lindsay, David. *A Voyage to Arcturus*. Manchester: Savoy Books.

Wilson, Colin, Pick, J. B, and Visiak, E. H. 1970. *The Strange Genius of David Lindsay*. London: John Baker.

Wolfe, Gary K. 1982. *David Lindsay (Starmont Reader's Guide 9)*. Washington: Starmont.

Access to Inner Worlds (1983)

Colin Wilson's *Access to Inner Worlds*

David Power

In the spring of 1981, Colin Wilson was a man under pressure. He had been commissioned to write no less than three books in four months. This situation came about because, as Wilson himself acknowledges, writers are habitually short of cash and the terms of the three commissions were enticing. He didn't feel he could refuse any of them. Moreover, he felt sure that the commissioner of the first book, *Poltergeist* could be persuaded to give him an extension so that he could complete the other two. When it became clear that this extension would not be forthcoming, the heat was really on:

> The very thought of all that non-stop typing, without time for relaxation, made me feel trapped. In 1973, I had been under similar pressure, and had begun to experience 'panic attacks' – bouts of sudden fear and intense depression. I had struggled my way out of these with common sense and a certain amount of self-analysis. Now the old sensation of unease began to return. (Wilson 1983, p.28)

However, unlike the panic attacks of 1973 – comprehensively discussed in Wilson's book *Mysteries* – the panic attacks of 1981 ran alongside actual physical health problems. At this point, Wilson was diagnosed with high blood pressure and told he needed to lose two stone in weight immediately. He was also referred to a specialist 'about a problem of internal bleeding that sounded ominously like cancer.'(p.28) In a number of ways, these four months sounds like amongst the worst of Wilson's professional life. Nevertheless, the whole episode yielded some very important insights:

> When I got back from the doctor's, I went to my desk to write about the burning and torture of the Bamberg Witches; as I wrote I began to experience a 'sinking' sensation, accompanied by the old feeling of panic. . . . There is a feeling of energy draining away, and a suspicion that life is a battle that has been lost in advance. I forced myself to go and look for a reference book that I needed . . . Then I went back to my typewriter, gritted my teeth against the sense of misery and futility, and went on writing. . . . Quite suddenly, the oppression vanished – as abruptly as the sun coming out from behind a cloud. With an almost dizzy feeling of astonishment and triumph, I realized that my emotions had been 'trying it on', having a tantrum, and that they had suddenly decided to give it up. And at once I saw with great clarity that human beings possess *two bodies*. One is the physical body, the other – just as real, just as self-contained – is the emotional body. Like the physical body, the emotional body reaches a certain level of growth, and then stops. But it stops rather sooner than the physical body. So most of us possess the emotional body of a retarded adolescent. And as soon as we find ourselves under pressure, as soon as life begins to look difficult, the emotional body bursts into tears and tries to run away.' (p.29)

As Wilson himself says, this insight was a turning point. However, he still had all the work to do and still had the anxieties about his physical condition to contend with. He pressed on with sheer will power. Some days he felt so low, he could only eat a few biscuits. Some nights he lay awake for hours trying to stop the pounding of his heart and resisting negative thoughts. However, he continued to press on and, gradually everything began to fall into place. He finished the first book on time and the publisher of the third book relented and gave him an extension after all. Not only that, the internal bleeding turned out to be nothing worse than a broken vein. Wilson was on a high now:

> I began to experience a sort of grim exhilaration as I forced myself into the final gallop. I finished the [third] book with several days to spare . . . At the end of the four months, I had the satisfaction of calculating that I had written a quarter of a million words, the length of Joyce's *Ulysses*. (p.30)

And when he came to analyse the previous four months, he concluded that the most important thing was the recognition that 'if I could drag myself out of a state of fatigue and depression into 'normality', then there was no reason why I should not drag myself out of normality into a state of far higher energy and intensity.' (p.30). At this point Wilson left England to attend a ten day seminar in Viittakivi where he would meet a man 'who stumbled accidentally on the 'trick' and whose life had been totally transformed by it.' (p.26). This man was Brad Absetz – the subject of Wilson's book *Access to Inner Worlds*. However, before we look at his story, I would like to step back a bit and summarise Wilson's underlying philosophy.

Central to this philosophy are 'those strange moments of delight when we feel *all is well*. Ever since I was a child, I have experienced the same profound sense of the *authenticity* of these moments.' (Wilson 1988, p.1) Wilson's central questions are why we can't currently achieve these moments at will and what do we need to do to acquire the ability to achieve them at will. As Wilson himself has said, this is his life work and he has achieved a great deal of information about it. However, there are two of his insights that seem central to me.

First, in a phrase borrowed from the philosopher Edmund Husserl, Wilson has noted that all perception is intentional. What does this mean? To illustrate it, here is an example that Wilson himself uses many times: if you look at your watch but aren't paying attention, you will fail to see what time it is. To see the time — to perceive it — you have to direct attention at your watch. The meaning – i.e. what time it is – is there whether you notice it or not. What determines whether you notice the time or not is the attention you put into it. This is what all perception being intentional means.

As with the watch, so it is with life. There is plenty of meaning out there but how much of it we perceive depends on how much energy and effort we put into our acts of perception. On the face of it then, the solution would seem to be simple. Put more effort into your perceptions. However, to see the problem here, consider this. Imagine you are bored and trying to 'unbore' yourself simply by looking with more interest and attention at your surroundings. You will note – perhaps with surprise – that it is very hard indeed to cause much of an improvement this way. Why is this?

Wilson believes there are two reasons. First, the parts of our minds that determine how much energy we put into our perceptions are not under our conscious control. It is done by a complicated mechanism of feedbacks and suggestions between the two hemispheres of the human brain the details of which I don't have the space to go into here. This is Wilson's Laurel and Hardy theory of consciousness, (see: Wilson 1985(2), pp.154-163.)

The second reason is what Wilson calls the 'Robot'. This is the part of us that does things automatically. Here the example Wilson often gives is of learning to type. When he first started, he had to make a conscious effort to hit the right keys. Now he can do this automatically. This is thanks to the 'Robot'. The 'Robot' is very useful, Wilson believes (how many fewer books would he have written if he had spent his whole life needing to think consciously about the act of typing rather than the meanings he wanted to convey in his writings?) However, Wilson points out that the 'Robot' has an enormous disadvantage. It also takes over when we are doing pleasurable things like listening to music. The record can be over and we have barely noticed the music because the 'Robot' has been listening for him. The 'Robot' makes our perception of the music less intentional so we consciously get less out of the music, we perceive less of it.

So there are two enormous hurdles for us to overcome to get to the point where we can experience those strange moments of delight at will. As for those moments themselves, what does Wilson tell us about these? In my view, one of Wilson's most important theories about this aspect of the question is his view that all consciousness is relational.

By relational, Wilson means that you cannot see things in isolation. A finger, for example, cannot be seen in isolation in the sense that you cannot think of a finger without knowing what it is for, that it is part of the hand and so forth. To go back to the watch example, if you look at the watch without paying attention, you do not see the time. However, as Wilson writes in an essay entitled 'Love as an Adventure in Mutual Freedom' (1972): 'But "seeing the time" involves a lot more than saying "half past two". It involves a more complex thought: "Half past two in the afternoon – an hour since lunch, two hours before teatime." To see the time is to place it in relation to the rest of the day.' (Wilson 1985, p.58)

'But now, here, for me, is the decisive leap in the argument. I am reading Eliot's *The Wasteland*, and I read the quotation from the beginning of [Wagner's opera] *Tristan and Isolde*, "Frisch weht der wind ..." I experience the tingling sensation that A. E. Housman declares to be the test of poetry. Why? What has happened?

Only this: I have been reminded of a work with which I am familiar, and which has often moved me deeply. It is rather like a place in which I have been happy; it has established its own separate reality in my mind.' (*Ibid.*, p.58-9)

Wilson adds that 'To see a thing truly is to see it in the widest possible field of relations.' The 'nausea' of Sartre's novel with that title is seeing an object with very little relationality. Ordinary consciousness involves seeing things with more relationality but moments of intense consciousness involve seeing things in a far larger 'web' of relationality than normal.

Let us summarise the argument so far. Since childhood, Wilson has had experiences of a much more intense consciousness than normal and the world he has perceived in these moments has seemed to him to be self evidently broader and more true than how he perceives it normally. He has devoted his life to this question and has discovered many things about it. His central discoveries that are pertinent to his book *Access to Inner Worlds* are these. First: perception is intentional. Second: the more effort we put into our perceptions, the more meaning we perceive. Third: consciousness is relational and finally: the more effort we put into our perceptions, the wider a field of relations that things are perceived in, the more broadly and truly they are perceived and the more intensely conscious we are. The reasons we cannot achieve these moments at will are that the energies that we put into our perceptions are not under our conscious control. If we could learn how to control these energies consciously – to turn them on at will, so to speak, we would transform our lives. Wilson's central reason for writing books is to covey this message and his own progress in trying to learn how to do this.

However, there is one more important piece of the jigsaw to

add. In the 1970s Wilson became interested in the subject of split brain research. To keep the matter simple, the human brain has two hemispheres and each hemisphere functions differently:

> The left [hemisphere] is obsessed by time; the right seems to have little sense of time. This seems reasonable since, since logic and language have a lineal and serial structure – like a chain – while patterns spread out sideways so to speak. The left brain tends to hurry forward, its eyes fixed on the future, while the right strolls along (Wilson 1983, p.20).

The challenge is to *either* slow down the left brain *or speed up* the right brain to bring them into alignment and achieve a much more intense consciousness:

> Hesse expresses [this] with beautiful clarity in *Steppenwolf*.
> . . At the end of a long and frustrating day he goes to a tavern to eat and drink; the wine causes a sudden relaxation into right brain consciousness: 'a refreshing laughter rose in me . . . it soared aloft like a soap bubble . . . The golden trail was blazed, and I was reminded of the eternal, of Mozart and the stars'

> The laughter is the equivalent of the 'of course' feeling. . . But what is important here is the phrase *'reminded* me of the eternal, and of Mozart and the stars'. There was nothing to stop him *thinking* about Mozart and the stars at any time of the day. But he is referring not to thinking , but to a feeling of the *reality* of Mozart and the stars. It is as if an inner trapdoor had opened, leading to an immense Aladdin's cave.
> What, then, has happened? In effect, Steppenwolf has brought his right and left hemispheres into alignment. He has relaxed *into* right-brain consciousness. (p.20)

This brings us back to Brad Absetz and *Access to Inner Worlds* since Absetz is a man who accidentally discovered the secret of how to get into this Aladdin's Cave, of how to achieve right-brain consciousness. Here is his story.

In 1961, Brad and his wife adopted a baby. In the earliest stages of its life this baby had been left alone a great deal. By the time Brad and his wife adopted it, the baby was clearly damaged. Not only that, when the baby was five he was diagnosed with terminal cancer. Brad and his wife did their best to make the last months of his life as complete and rewarding as possible. When he eventually died, it was a shattering experience for them.

Brad's wife became very depressed and lost in an inner world of guilt and hallucinations. Brad would lie on the bed next to her for many hours every day, waiting until she came out of this inner world so he could support and comfort her. While doing this he learned to relax while remaining inwardly alert for changes in his wife's condition. On one of these days, he felt an impulse to move his arm:

> 'One day I was lying on my back on the bed beside my wife during one of these long periods of relaxed but concentrated sensitivity, when I noticed a clear but puzzling impulse in the muscles of my upper right arm, near the shoulder. What was clear about it was that the impulse was a movement impulse, i.e. the muscle was indicating a readiness to move. What was puzzling was that I had no thought or intention of moving my arm . . . However, being relaxed . . . I was not alarmed, but I was rather curious.' (p.45)

Brad 'let' the arm move. 'It waited for a moment during which the impulse got stronger, and my arm really did rise slowly from the bed and stopped in mid-air as the movement impulse ceased. (p.45). As time went by, the movement-impulses became more complex and started to involve his whole body and his breathing:

'These movements formed series and patterns involving my whole body and my breathing too. These were not repetitive routines in which the same series and patterns would occur time after time. Basic movements occurred in different patterns, and in different series, lasting different lengths of time, and with differing degrees of muscle strain and intensity each time.' (p.45-46)

The next development occurred when he was queuing for lunch at work. He felt the familiar impulse to move his arm. He allowed it to happen and this time, found himself selecting various foods from the buffet for his lunch. Again he had no conscious control over the movements. The choice of foods surprised him in that they included foods he had not eaten for years. This continued day after day with the arm movements sometimes selecting large meals for him, sometimes small ones and occasionally no dinner at all. Over the next few weeks he lost about ten kilograms in weight and this extra weight never returned.

The same thing happened in a number of other areas in his life. He went through a tea ceremony phase, a writing poetry phase and a drawing and painting phase. Here is one of the poems, or 'concentrates' as Brad himself called them:

The world is full of promise
When I am empty of threat
When the world is empty of threat
I am full of the world. (p.39)

Others had what Wilson describes as a 'romantic melancholy'

about them as shown in this extract from another untitled
concentrate:

> The morning tide is out,
> the beach washed clean and smooth
> of even the sharply etched stepping of early birds;
> the far water line
> is undulating ever so slowly:
> perfectly reflecting an inner seascape. (p.40)

It was the longest of the concentrates that first persuaded
Wilson to consider writing a book about Brad Absetz. It is too
long to quote in full and quoting extracts won't really help so I
will simply give Wilson's reaction to it. 'This concentrate excited
me because it was such a striking example of Jung's "active
imagination", or of the kabbalistic technique of inner travel.'
(p.63) Wilson adds that he has no doubt that Brad made contact
with that same 'wise old man' part of the brain that Jung did
during his phase of active imagination.

During the writing phase, an interesting – if disturbing –
thing happened. Here is Absetz's own account of it:

> 'One morning, in my study, movement-impulse writing
> began, but the handwriting that took form on the page
> was completely foreign to me – it was not like my
> handwriting at all. I do not remember the sentence word
> for word, but it was a sentence in which a person, who
> named herself, briefly introduced herself. I looked at the
> sentence in amazement. Always, up to now, I had felt
> quite clearly that my movement-impulse writing was
> expressing various levels of myself. Strong rejecting
> feelings filled me completely. I put the pencil down,
> pushed the paper away and found myself saying with a
> tone of uncompromising determination "I . . . will . . . not

... be ... a ... mouthpiece ... for ... anyone ...but ...
myself!"' (p.59 – the leader dots are in the original quote)

Wilson makes the following comment on this:

'This is important, because it makes clear that Brad recognized "movement-impulses" as part of himself. [. . .]
Many modern investigators in the field of psychical
research are inclined to believe that all 'automatic writing'
is simply an expression of the unconscious mind of the
writer. Brad's experience clearly contradicts this view. On
this one occasion, he recognized the entity as *another
person* who wanted to join in the dialogue. He concludes
that there was never a repetition of this kind of
experience.' (p.59-60)

As for the drawings, here are Wilson's comments on them:

'I found them fascinating. . . . Each one is a beautiful,
elaborate and complete pattern, virtually a complete
painting. Two of them resemble Paul Klee . . . I imagine
that Klee was giving expression to the same deep pattern-
making impulses of the subconscious. They are all very
elaborate, and deeply satisfying to look at. A good
painting has some satisfying complexity that makes it
resemble life. Brad's colour drawings all have this
complexity. Although they all look like small fragments of
various – and totally different – patterns, they are quite
unlike, say, the design of a carpet, which is repetitive.
These seem to be designs caught in flight as they rush
through the mind, expanding into other designs with the
infinite variety of the unconscious. Some look like
glimpses of space with exploding stars, some like a
shower of multi-coloured eyeballs, some like strange,

angular birds, some like Douanier Rousseau flowers, some like creatures seen under a microscope, some like curious abstract paintings. To my mind, they are the most striking of the products of his "impulses", for they could not be faked. They leave no doubt that the subconscious self knew precisely what it was doing. They are instant, visual evidence that something very strange took place.' (p.55)

Brad Absetz's story certainly makes interesting reading. However, what is *as* interesting is *how* Wilson tells the story. He top and tails the book with chapters about his own central philosophy. Wilson then tells us about his health issues and his overwork writing the three books in four months which we have already looked at. The telling of this is very effective as Wilson brings all his novelist skills to the task along with a total absence of self pity. However, it is the contrast with the next chapter that is really interesting and, in a way, the whole point.

The next chapter tells the story of Wilson's journey to Viittakivi in Finland where he has been engaged to deliver workshops in a ten day seminar. This came immediately after the four months of overwork. Again Wilson's skills as a novelist come into play. We get quite a vivid and evocative description of an old fashioned tea shop in Helsinki. Just a few sentences but, like a few effective brushstrokes on a painting – enough to bring the tea shop vividly to life. Wilson ends his description by saying that he imagines this place looked the same in the days of Ibsen and Strindberg.

Next we meet Brad Absetz himself:

'The main thing that struck me about him was that he seemed to be at ease and at peace, like a man sitting in front of his own fireside. He made me think of that earlier generation of Americans, like Henry James and Henry

Adams, who had come to Europe looking for a sense of the historical past. If that was what Brad was looking for, he seemed to have found it. (p.32)

Then we get a description of the landscape through the windows of the train as Wilson travels to Viittakivi itself with Brad:

'The train pulled out of the station, past the harbour, and we were soon in the open countryside. There is something very soothing in the green, flat, Finnish landscape, with its wooden houses and glimpses of water between the trees. I experienced suddenly that curious sense of satisfaction that can only be described in the words 'being where you are'. That sounds absurd only until we reflect that for most of our lives we are *not* where we are. I am walking down a lane in Cornwall, but only my body is there; my mind is "elsewhere." It is not in a particular place; it is just 'not all there' . . . And then, beyond a certain point of relaxation, it happens. The left brain slows down; suddenly, it is walking in step with the right [brain]. And you are there, in the present moment, wholly and completely.' (p.32)

The first time I read *Access to Inner Worlds*, I read from the beginning up to this point in a single sitting. I found that these vivid descriptions of Finland following immediately after the equally vivid descriptions of Wilson's overwork and health issues induced in me – as a reader – that very same sense of being wholly and completely in the present moment that Wilson was talking about at this point of the book. I was very struck by this. I realized that Wilson's books are, in places, as much about *inducing* these states of consciousness as being vehicles for talking about them. Earlier we saw Wilson comment on the effectiveness of Eliot's quotation from Wagner in *The Wasteland* and how it opened up a much wider relationality in his consciousness. Wilson is doing the same here, choosing and structuring his material to create this effect.

One of the most common criticisms leveled at Wilson's work is that he simply borrows other peoples' ideas, lumps them together and then mistakes the results for a logical argument.

First, it should be noted that logical argument is usually employed to prove something that was hitherto in doubt. However, Wilson does not doubt his central thesis. Not only that, it was his actual experience rather than logical argument that convinced him of the truth of his central thesis. This makes him aware that it is experience as much as logic that will convince the readers and this, in turn, informs the methodology he employs in his books. Yes there is logical argument. However, there is also a 'mapping' of actual examples from other peoples' experience of these states of consciousness, an ongoing record from book to book of his own progress in the search for these states of consciousness and attempts to actually induce these states of consciousness in his readers by the way he uses his material. The quotes etc are contributing to *all* these tasks, not just the parts of his work that are logical arguments.

This may seem an unusual methodology but I think it is the right one for the job in hand. A comparison with Nietzsche may help. Until near the end of his sane life, Nietzsche vehemently opposed philosophical systems – i.e. attempts by philosophers to explain everything. Some of Nietzsche's own books are made up of either separate, numbered paragraphs or even just series of maxims or aphorisms etc. Immediately, they create a visual impression of shards or fragments and that is deliberate. Not only that, the aphorisms in particular often leap about from subject to subject in a bewildering way and they sometimes cover topics not usually dealt with by philosophers. Nietzsche is doing all this so that the structure as well as the content of his books attacks and undermines the very notion of an over-arching philosophical system. Again an unusual methodology;

again the right one for the job in hand.

Colin Wilson is eighty this year but remains neglected by many who accept the criticisms that seem to be leveled against him so often. I hope my close study of *Access to Inner Worlds* has thrown doubt on these criticisms. However, if all I have done is to encourage more people to read *Access to Inner Worlds* itself – a somewhat neglected gem in Wilson's overall output – I shall be happy enough.

References:

Wilson, Colin (1983) *Access to Inner Worlds*. Rider.

Wilson, Colin (1985) *The Bicameral Critic*. Salem House.

Wilson, Colin (1985(2)) *The Essential Colin Wilson*. Harrap.

Wilson, Colin (1988) *Autobiographical Reflections*. Paupers' Press.

A Criminal History of Mankind (1984)

Brockengespenst Horror

Philip Coulthard

Nietzsche suggested that anyone wanting to study moral matters "opens up for himself an immense field of work. All kinds of passions have to be thought through separately, pursued separately through ages, peoples, great and small individuals; their entire reason and all their evaluations and modes of illuminating things must be revealed! So far, all that has given colour to existence still lacks a history: where could you find a history of love, of avarice, of envy, of conscience, of piety, of cruelty?" (Nietzsche 2001, p.34) By writing a vast history of human cruelty, it could be said that Colin Wilson has taken up Nietzsche's challenge. Twenty-seven years after its initial publication, *A Criminal History of Mankind* remains an extremely relevant book, with an expanded edition appearing in 2005 covering global horrors since the mid-eighties (London: Mercury Books). The juxtaposition of violence and evolution through the book is particularly stunning, with the section describing the 'rape of Nanking' and the discovery of Peking Man being one of my personal 'favourites'. And best of all, this being Wilson, none of it is depressing.

The book continues the researches of his original "criminal trilogy"[1] utilising the perceptual and philosophical developments made during his prolific period in the seventies and early eighties. Although the bulk of the text can be read as much as a storehouse of criminal cases as well as an excellent history book, it concerns itself mostly with the development of human consciousness. As with most of Wilson's output, the subject is really used as a narrative to develop philosophical disciplines. *Criminal History* charts the development of rational consciousness, noting its obvious scientific, social and cultural achievements, but mainly concentrating on its 'waste' —the seemingly inexhaustible supply of unnecessary violent human activity since antiquity. For Wilson, studying crime is a forensic method which demonstrates the flaws in human perception with a visceral dynamism which is usually absent from philosophy. "Murder interests me because it is the most extreme form of the denial of this human potentiality. Life-devaluation has become a commonplace of our century." (Wilson 1969, p.22) Wilson's reason for investigating this type of extremity is neither sensationalist nor morbid, as some critics have suggested. To understand this, we will have to take a brief look at his philosophical position.

Wilson's first book, *The Outsider*, was concerned with this problem of life devaluation, which mostly found its expression in the canon of Western literature. (A fragment intended for the book concerned with the 'criminal outsider' was eventually included in *The Encyclopedia of Murder*). His dissection of pessimism in literature and philosophy is highly relevant to understanding the negatively repugnant behaviour of criminals. When Sartre declares that "man is a useless passion" he is inadvertently giving intellectual credence to the indulgences of the modern murderer, who will be able to 'justify' his crimes by perhaps gesturing in Sartre's direction. Ian Brady 'justified' the killing of working-class innocents with reference to de Sade's attempted philosophy. Wilson dubs de Sade 'the Patron Saint of Serial Killers', and maintains that his materialism is identical to many modern scientists and philosophers. The killer Carl Panzram felt comfortable in his trough of pessimism through his vanity reading of Schopenhauer, and—unlike Nietzsche, whose healthy intellect ultimately rejected him—was deadly serious in his ludicrous fantasy that he'd "like to kill the whole human race." [2]

Further volumes in the "Outsider Cycle"[3] addressed the

spiritual, sociological, imaginative, sexual and philosophical implications of this 'life failure' yet also developed Wilson's main weapon against it: the New Existentialism. A seventh volume, *Introduction to the New Existentialism* (Hutchinson, 1966) outlines the techniques and implications of this new method. In this book, he notes that hardly *any* of us outgrow a "certain pleasure in destruction" (Wilson 1966, p.51) as it remains associated with freedom, freedom from the apparently impersonal nature of the world.[4] The problem of this alienated attitude, its genesis, and its unfortunate (and unnecessary) feedback via culture and crime is the backbone of *Criminal History*.

The 'New' Existentialism actually went back to the founding fathers of Existentialism—Franz Brentano [1838-1917] and Edmund Husserl [1859-1938]. It was Brentano who suggested that consciousness is 'directional'—that is, it encloses an object in the same way that a fruit encloses its stone. But it was his pupil who took it further and devised a rigorous method of analyzing the architecture of consciousness known as phenomenology. Wilson has a typically ingenious image of Husserl's method in action. Before Husserl, philosophers took it for granted that they were merely mirrors reflecting reality—Descartes' "I think, therefore I am." The Cartesian philosopher is rather like a detective questioning a roomful of suspects and doubting all of their statements. "Now Husserl has suggested a new and most disturbing possibility. *Suppose the detective himself is the murderer?*" (Wilson 1966, p.38-39) The sleuth has doubted everything except his own innocence, his own passivity. Consciousness must be studied as something *active*. Husserl defined phenomenology as 'the study of the structure of consciousness' and Wilson has summarized Husserl's insight in his often repeated assertion that perception is intentional. "Consciousness participates in perception; it reaches out and *attacks* reality, as the teeth of a mechanical digger tears up the earth." (Wilson 1984, p.658)

It all sounds abstract enough, but this is of fundamental importance in understanding the criminal mentality. Because Husserl has demonstrated that consciousness is selective, that is to say *prejudiced*, it follows that 'the crime explosion' is one unfortunate effect of this development. The criminal 'brackets out' as much complexity as possible and sees his 'victims' as mere objects to be moved out of the way, like chessmen on a board. Yet the strange paradox of this prejudiced consciousness is that while it could be argued that it is the cause of the often reported prejudices in society such as racism and sexism[5], as well as criminal acts, it is also responsible for the construction of society itself. It is the development of this mentality which Wilson traces in *A Criminal History of Mankind*.

Wilson seems to have been inspired to write the book as a response to H.G. Wells' *Mind at the End of Its Tether*, a postscript to his condensed edition of *Outline of History*. Wilson found Wells's pessimism frustrating; Wells writes that "the human story has already come to an end and that *Homo sapiens*, as he has been pleased to call himself, is in his present form played out." (p.3) This would have been understandable had it been published at the beginning of World War II, but was actually written after Hitler's defeat. Wilson takes issue with Wells's 'pragmatism'—his late Victorian optimism left him unaware that the unfortunate by-product of human intelligence has been the crime explosion. Certainly, the types of crimes which have become a commonplace since Wells's era—serial killing, mass terrorism—would have drove Wells to an even deeper despair (if that was possible).

This 'pragmatic' attitude is still a commonplace reaction to serious crimes, as a glance at the tabloids or an open ear on public transport will verify. But if Wilson's book proves anything it is that the criminal mentality is gradually becoming less and less of a commonplace as history develops. Crime studies and

crime statistics appear to bear this out.[6] But what is truly fascinating and important about his hypothesis is that it is with a
simple change in attitudes, engineered by a healthy culture—
which helps cause this change.

The sense of bewilderment after any horrific crime is understandable, but not conducive to the kind of clear thinking which
is needed to start a process to help solve such a seemingly
complex social and psychological problem. Studying the worst
excesses of humankind with the clinical precision of Husserl's
unemotional method, as Wilson does here, is a better way. That
this method is developed inside the fascinating narrative of
human history and its deviations is what makes *Criminal History*
such an essential Wilson book; for all its perceptual concerns, it
is fundamentally a "page turner". So rather than take the
'pragmatic' attitude of resigned misanthropy when confronted
with disturbing new trends of violence in society, Wilson is
optimistic enough to see unusual and revealing parallels and
solutions in philosophy and psychology. Confronted with so
called 'motiveless' murders—the term itself implies a lack of
meaning—Wilson saw a correspondence with Maslow's
'Hierarchy of Needs'. Food, shelter, relationships and self
esteem must be satisfied before the possibility of 'self-actualisation' emerges. Corresponding to these needs, Wilson noticed,
were the social strata of historical criminal cases. The changing
pattern in crime can be seen as a barometer of social development in negative. "Until the first part of the nineteenth
century, most crimes were committed out of the simple need for
survival—Maslow's first level." (p.15) The Edinburgh body-
snatchers, Burke and Hare are a perfect example of this type of
'basic' crime. By the mid-nineteenth century, with increased
wealth due to the industrial revolution, murderers such as Dr.
Palmer, Dr. Pritchard and Lizzie Borden were all committing
crimes to safeguard their domestic security. This corresponds to
the second hierarchy of Maslow's pyramid. The Jack the Ripper

murders in 1888 represent such a huge change from the domestic crimes to sex crime that contemporary analysis thought the killer 'morally insane' - "as if his actions could only be explained by a combination of wickedness and madness." (p.15) What is unusual about the Ripper murders is that they contain not only the sexual element which makes them a shadow of Maslow's third level; they also contain a destructive attempt at reaching the higher level of self esteem. Wilson suggests that this pattern becomes increasingly common in the twentieth century with the rise of the serial killer. "From then on, there was an increasing number of crimes in which the criminal seemed to feel, in a muddled sort of way, that society was somehow to blame for not granting him dignity, justice and recognition of his individuality, and to regard his crime as a legitimate protest."(p.15-16) The criminal is someone who feels that they must be noticed at any cost, but find the long and complex effort of any kind of creative ideal too taxing, so choose to take a short cut through criminal activity to achieve 'recognition'.

But this muddled thinking—'magical thinking', as Sartre called it [7]—has ravaging effects on the fabric of society. When labourer Patrick Byrne decapitated a woman at a Birmingham hostel in 1960 and it was explained later that he did so to 'get his revenge on women for causing him sexual tension', this is an example of magical thinking. "This tendency to allow our emotions to reinforce our sense of being justified is a basic part of the psychology of violence, and therefore of crime." (p.70) This sense of justification, of being *right*, is the essence of the criminal mentality, but it is also a common human trait, even in 'objective' circumstances. In *Mysteries*, Wilson takes the Kuhnian line on the 'objectivity' of scientists and remarks that the revolutionary spat between Galileo and The Pope was more to do with either party believing that each was 'right' as much as any type of objective truth (Wilson 1978, Part two, chapter one). The science fiction writer A. E. Van Vogt coined the term 'Right Man' for an individual who considers him/herself to be always right (there are also examples of Right Women, notably the mother of the novelist Turgenev, who had many of her serfs flogged to death). This type of individual constructs a fantasy environment where, against all appearances they are correct on every level. And it need not be obvious examples such as Hitler or Stalin, it could be in an apparently cosy domestic setting in your locality; for as Van Vogt notes, the classic example of Right Man behaviour is the authoritarian male.

In other words, the all too depressing spectacle of domestic violence reported in the news. But Van Vogt writes that the Right Man is actually an 'idealist' — "that is, he lives in his own mental world and does his best to ignore aspects of reality that conflict with it." (Wilson 1984, p.66) This is an important point, and illustrates the prejudiced nature of consciousness, the unfortunate drawback of our mental evolution. Of course, consciousness *has* to be prejudiced — without filters, we would be driven insane by sensations. But again, it is essential to understanding the origin not only of perception, creativity, but its shadow, its Mr Hyde, 'the crime explosion'.

Armed with the tools of phenomenology, Maslovian psychology, and his own synthesis of the New Existentialism — all *optimistic* disciplines — Wilson spreads out the map of history to demonstrate how crime will always be outweighed by creativity and intelligence. Interestingly, he adds: "This book is an attempt to tell the story of the human race in terms of that counterpoint between crime and creativity, and to use the insights it brings to try to discern the next stage in human evolution." (p.7) Of course, the latter concern is a strong undercurrent surfacing in all of Wilson's books, and the utility of the human will is central to understanding his attitude towards things. For Wilson, crime is a *particular way of seeing the world*. The 'acid bath murderer' John Haigh was brought up by a loving family and was a talented musician, yet his extremely grim criminal actions earned him a paltry £15,000 over fifteen years, a miscalculation of almost comic proportions. And time after time, criminal cases illustrate this laughable anti-logic in operation. In the text, Wilson goes on to suggest that the discoveries of split-brain research could help us understand this type of calculated absurdity.[8] Wilson believes that it is the left hemisphere, with its self-consciousness, that is partly responsible for criminality. He draws attention to Julian Jaynes' controversial yet highly plausible theory of bicameral consciousness to support this. Jaynes thinks that early man had no self awareness in the contemporary sense; a cursory reading of *Gilgamesh*, *The Illiad* or *The Odyssey* reveals no interior monologue of a narrator—instead 'the Gods' are forever instructing individuals with extreme authority. (Thousands of years later, Peter Sutcliffe, the 'Yorkshire Ripper', would attempt to abrogate responsibility for his crimes by laying the blame on authoritarian voices in his head.) Jaynes believes that these 'voices' were auditory hallucinations from the right brain. But slowly, Jaynes suggests, consciousness or self-awareness began to develop, with the invention of writing playing a major part in this new development. Marshall McLuhan [1911-1980] also described this change. "When the perverse ingenuity of man has outered some part of his being in material technology, his entire sense ratio is altered." (McLuhan 1962, p.265) The creation of linear, fragmented analysis "with its remorseless power of homogenization" pulled human consciousness out of the primeval swamp of collective or tribal consciousness ('acoustic space' – *hearing* rather than *seeing*) and as the linear left brain became dominant over the right, the rational ego began to develop.

Wilson does not necessarily support Jaynes' theory all the way. Jaynes suggests that the invention of 'the Gods' is a recent invention—about 10,000 BCE—yet Wilson counters with evidence of religious artifacts from the Neanderthal era which are obviously much earlier. He also suggests that early peoples were 'unicameral' rather than bicameral; with the intuitive sense being the only sense, and the left hemisphere becoming dominant only with the invention of new technologies such as writing, and McLuhan would concur. But he maintains that Jaynes' real achievement is the idea that our present form of 'alienated' consciousness is a fairly recent development. The standard Western rational consciousness is 'desynchronized' with most activity happening on the left side of the brain. In deep modes of relaxation, both left and right hemispheres are synchronized, and Wilson's work is of course crammed full of examples of this 'other mode' such as Proust's epiphany, Steppenwolf's "Mozart and the stars" and many other 'peak experiences' from literature, history and anecdote. Despite the fleeting nature of these moments, despite the fact that the sheer complexity of our environment forces us to live more or less permanently in the 'prison' of the left brain, Wilson still considers 'desynchronization' as a "considerable evolutionary achievement". For all their permanent intuitive feeling of well-being and synchronization, these 'unicameral' peoples were probably incapable of the type of extreme 'egocentric' criminality detailed in Wilson's book. But they were also incapable of the kind of intellectual detachment which we take for granted. So although humans developed bicameral consciousness as a means of survival—it would have been easier to stay in unicameral simplicity—and its unfortunate side effect has been 'the crime explosion', self-awareness has also developed. Divided consciousness produced democracy as well as crime. Crime, Wilson says, can only be understood as part of the evolutionary pattern. To *know* this is to be free from the kind of moral 'pragmatism' which tormented H. G. Wells and continues to mystify society whenever a serious crime is reported.

Although *Criminal History* is over 700 pages—longer in the updated edition—and has page after page of stomach-churning details, it is as typically uplifting as any Wilson book; he has the ability to take the worst excesses of human narrowness and stupidity and make them illustrate a fundamentally optimistic method of reading the world. After describing the sadistic brutality of the "Assyrian war machine" he wonders why they disappeared from history so quickly. "The Assyrians responded to the challenge of disaster and chaos by becoming the most ruthlessly efficient conquerors the world has ever seen. They were undoubtedly the 'fittest', and according to the Darwinian principle they should have survived. Yet, for some reason, human history contradicts the Darwinian principle – not once, but again and again." (Wilson 1984, p.141) From the era of the Assyrians, to the Romans, the excesses of colonialism, to the twentieth century, the Nazis, and onto our twenty-first century with the rise of serial killers and suicide bombers, "history has been full of ruthlessly efficient men who ended in failure" (p.141). How can this be? The answer Wilson provides is a very important one. The essence of crime is that of an individual who sees no reason why he/she should not get what he/she wants by any means. Confronted with a difficult knot, the first impulse is to cut it. This can be successful in the short term, but soon things begin to go wrong. And it is the same for criminal individuals as it is for criminal societies. So although the objection to criminal violence is that it inflicts harm on society, the *real* objection is that it inevitably fails to fulfill the criminal's objective. "For crime is essentially a *left-brain* way of achieving objectives. It refuses to recognize any value but the achievement of the objective. And somehow, the objective gets lost in the process." (p.141) Every individual criminal case in the book illustrates this, as does the development of certain societies. The Assyrians are a good example, the Spartans a perfect one. Both were fixed in a rigid militaristic conservatism; the historian Arnold Toynbee compared the latter to soldiers permanently on parade with arms presented. Wilson sees them as suffering from a spiritual arthritis as cobwebs grew over them. The Spartans' obsessive and paranoid need to guard against attack meant they never really developed any lasting culture, and they had no equivalent of the Greek drama, an invention to which Wilson attaches particular importance. Because with the invention of the drama, the gamble of 'double consciousness' was starting to bear fruit— the ability to live in two worlds at once, the physical world and the world of the imagination. No amount of precise, calculated aggression, no matter how forceful, could produce as much change as the spectacle of a few actors in masks indulging in 'fantasy'. With the development of the drama and eventually the invention of the novel, human consciousness and attitudes would be changed even further.

To say that a book—and a fiction book at that—can somehow be able to alleviate serious problems like crime sounds absurd, yet Wilson is well aware of the charge. "I am inclined to believe that man is on the brink of a new 'evolutionary leap', and that it will come about through the *deliberate investigation and control of the power of the imagination*. This may not seem to offer much comfort in our crime-ridden world. But nevertheless I suspect that it will prove to be the answer." (Wilson 1989, p.118) Wilson suggests that the effects of Samuel Richardson's *Pamela* (1740) and Jean Jacques Rousseau's *Julie, or the New Heloise* (1760) were extremely far-reaching. It is of course true that there were many novels before these. In fact, two of the most influential were written by characters with criminal tendencies themselves; The *Morte d' Arthur* may have influenced Europe with its *fictional* ideals of knightly chivalry, yet its author was a rapist and cattle rustler. And *Robinson Crusoe*—which Wilson regards as the most important artwork since the invention of the Greek drama itself—was actually written by a man of borderline criminal tendencies. Yet despite this irony, their "dubious personal morality died" whilst their "artistic integrity went marching on." (Wilson 1984, p.420) The reason for this being that unlike these earlier novels, Richardson and Rousseau's modern

'Romantic' works relied on an interior monologue. The tone is personal and reflective. "To grasp what happened, you only have to turn to Pepys's Diary, written a hundred years earlier. Pepys is always describing what he *does*—a trip to the river, a visit to the theatre—but never what he thinks or feels." (Wilson 1975, p. 37) You could say that earlier fictions were still 'unicameral' in that there isn't much self awareness, just endless descriptions, and this tone would be pretty much heard until the publication of *Pamela*.

Wilson does not accept Q. D. Leavis's notion that this 'senti-mentality' was a change for the worse. Quite the opposite: he has suggested the novel, with its ability to introduce extreme states of absorption, was responsible for the cessation of the witch trials, and the inspiration for the French and Industrial Revolutions.[9] McLuhan makes similarly convincing claims regarding the development of the printing press, the book and technology and its effects on the individual and society. "Imagination is that ratio among the perceptions and faculties which exist when they are not embedded or outered in material technologies." (McLuhan 1962, p.265) So, what Wilson seems to be suggesting in this particular 'criminal history', and indeed in all of his work, is that whereas the development of the drama, the novel and their contemporary extensions (films, television, interactive media) has been a partial outering of the imagination, the full development of this imaginative process will create a new faculty which Wilson labels 'Faculty X' [10]. This is one of his most important concepts and in my opinion one of the defining aesthetic and philosophical concepts of our age. The criminal mentality, with its superficial strength and materialistic triviality is no use in our development, despite serial killers' persistent abuse of the imaginative faculty. [11]

McLuhan quotes Blake's lines from *Jerusalem* to demonstrate his concept of technology and perceptual or imaginative change: "The Spectre is the Reasoning Power in Man, & when separated from Imagination and closing itself in steel..." (McLuhan 1962, p.265). Wilson sums up his book with a similar image. "But if this history of human evolution has taught us anything, it is that 'criminal man' has no real, independent existence. He is a kind of shadow, a Spectre of the Brocken, an illusion." (Wilson 1984, p. 670) The *Brockengespenst* is a phenomena observed by mountaineers; an optical illusion which projects the observer's shadow high onto the mist with huge magnification and distorted perspective. If the Spectre is man's rationality which throws out distorted and superficially frightening shadows such as 'criminal man', as Wilson suggests in his book, then the terrors of history which disturbed H. G. Wells's pragmatism do not seem so frightening after all.

References:

McLuhan, Marshall (1962) *The Gutenberg Galaxy*, R.K.P.

Nietzsche, Friedrich (2001) *The Gay Science*, Cambridge University Press

Wilson, Colin (1966) *Introduction to the New Existentialism*, Hutchinson

Wilson, Colin (1969) *A Casebook of Murder*, Leslie Frewin.

Wilson, Colin (1978) *Mysteries*, Hodder & Stoughton.

Wilson, Colin (1984) *A Criminal History of Mankind*, Granada Publishing

Wilson, Colin (1989) 'Sex, Crime and the Occult' in *Rapid Eye*, R. E. Publishing.

Notes:

1   *The Encyclopedia of Murder* [Arthur Barker, 1961], *A Casebook of Murder* [Leslie Frewin, 1969] and *Order of Assassins* [Hart-Davis,1972].

2   Wilson opens his *The Strength to Dream* (1962) by drawing a

parallel between horror fiction's own Bard, H. P. Lovecraft, and the notorious serial killer Peter Kürten.

3   *Religion and the Rebel* [Gollancz, 1957], *The Age of Defeat* [Gollancz, 1959], *The Strength to Dream* [Gollancz, 1962], *Origins of the Sexual Impulse* [Arthur Barker, 1963], and *Beyond The Outsider* [Arthur Barker, 1965].

4   In *Criminal History* [p. 153], Wilson has timely suggestions that this mental underdevelopment is the basis of most modern comedy and satire. This is supported by Maslow's observations on humour and Wilson's remarks on the insecurity of authority-rebellion. See *New Pathways in Psychology* [Gollancz, 1972] p. 170.

5   See the anecdote about Lord Russell's unthinking colonial superiority [p. 150] and newspaper headlines reporting domestic violence [p. 56] for examples.

6   Alan Travis, *The Guardian*, April 22nd, 2010.

7   Sartre meant self-deception [*mauvaise foi*] which means more when thinking of his own criticisms of Husserl. See Wilson's *Below the Iceberg* [The Borgo Press 1998]

8   See Wilson's *Frankenstein's Castle* [Ashgrove Press, 1980] for more on 'bicameralism'.

9   See: Colin Wilson, *The Occult* [Hodder & Stoughton, 1971] p. 432 and *Mysteries*, p. 259

10 For a fuller discussion of this term, see *The Occult*.

11 The murderer Dennis Rader claimed that his crimes were the result of "Factor X" - which he could have got from the back cover of Wilson's *Mammoth Book of the Supernatural* (1991) which misspelled the concept. See the Links page at www.colinwilsononline.com.

Beyond the Occult [1] (1988)

In my Father's house are many mansions. John, 14:2.

George C. Poulos

Colin Wilson's Outsider cycle, began with *The Outsider* (1956), and concluded in 1966, with *Beyond the Outsider*. Wilson's longer Occult cycle, began with an invitation by *Random House* in 1969 to write a book about *The Occult*, which was published in 1971. The etymology of the word *occult* derives from the 1540s, and means 'incapable of being apprehended by the mind', and 'beyond the range of understanding'.[2] Originally Wilson was skeptical about occult phenomena. As he deepened his research, he discovered, however, that the evidence in favour of the paranormal was both consistent and overwhelming. The occult cycle, including 10 major books, and 6 other edited, co-authored, or compendium editions, on the subject, concluded with the publication of *Beyond the Occult* in 1988. *Beyond the Occult* was "an attempt to summarise everything I had learnt about the paranormal in the past twenty years." Wilson describes it as 'probably my best book',[3] because it is here that the two great streams of his work, existentialism and occultism, came together, the two strands being of equal importance.

What Wilson calls 'occult', most researchers refer to as psi (ψ), paranormal, supernatural, or extrasensory phenomenon. These include telepathy: consciousness-to-consciousness communication, where a percipient shows knowledge of information in the consciousness of an agent or sender. Clairvoyance: knowledge of things without recourse to the senses. Precognition: perception of a random, inherently unpredictable future event. Psychokinesis: direct influence of consciousness on a state of matter. Psychic healing: direct influence of consciousness on biological matter. Psychometry: the ability to discern the history of objects by touch or sight. Poltergeist: literally 'noisy ghost or spirit', physical manifestations attributed to 'disembodied consciousness'. Out-of-body experience (OBE or sometimes OOBE): experiencing consciousness in a place outside/beyond the body. These interests merge with phenomenon from the domain of psychology and psychiatry, including, hypnagogic experience: the transitional state between wakefulness and sleep. Multiple personality, and dissociative experience, either as a result of stress, or in states such as hypnosis.

Those who are not well versed with Wilson's work often 'fret and fume', to use Kenneth Allsop's phrase,[4] in response to the breadth of his writing interests, and the seeming disconnection between them. What has existential philosophy got to do with the occult, for example? How can there possibly be a connection? Those who have taken the time to read Wilson closely and empathetically understand that all his work is informed by one big central idea.

Colin Wilson's "one big thing central idea" – transcendent states of consciousness

In 1953 Isaiah Berlin published a long essay called *The Hedgehog and the Fox*.[5] Berlin took the title from a fragment of verse by the 7th century (B.C.) Greek poet Archiolus: "The fox knows many things, but the hedgehog knows one big thing". Wilson is a self-confessed hedgehog. He knows one big thing and he knows it exceedingly well. And that one big thing, the organizing principle of all his work, from philosophy, to criminology, the occult, sexology, literary criticism, sociology, biography, through novel writing and drama is, *transcendent states of consciousness*.

Wilson's first book, *The Outsider* (1956), seemed to be an in-depth analysis of individuals who feel alienated from society. He admits however that "...*The Outsider* could have been entitled

Moments of Vision, for this is what it was essentially about." [6]

Semantic multiplicity....so many ways to designate transcendence.

Wilson has never settled on one word by which to designate transcendent states of consciousness. He uses variously, moments of vision, Maslow's peak experiences, Chesterton's absurd good news, amongst many others. The word transcendence is not included in the indexes of the major books in the occult series. *The Occult, Mysteries* (1978), or *Beyond the Occult*, or in *Super Consciousness* (published 2009, but sketched out in detail in 1995). He often slips into using the word. In *Beyond the Occult*, for example, he talks about 'the Romantics and their moods of "transcendent consciousness"'.[7]

Transcendent appeals because it is generic, all-encompassing and inclusive. *Un*, and *sub* when used in reference to consciousness indicate inferior. *Altered* indicates fake, and *alternate*, unreal. William Braud argues that *trans* not only means above and beyond, also carries two additional meanings: *across* and *through*.[8] *Trans* is also helpful with respect to defining developments in psychology. Abraham H. Maslow chose transpersonal psychology (1969)[9] to designate the fourth force in psychology, and we speak of transformative experience and transpersonal growth.

In 1959 Wilson received a letter from Maslow, enclosing some of his papers. Despite expressing themselves very differently, they recognised a concordance of ideas, and maintained a correspondence until Maslow's untimely death in 1970. Maslow saw Wilson as a key participant in a philosophical revolution that was under way. "A comprehensive system is swiftly developing, like a tree beginning to bear fruit on every branch at the same time." He described a group he thought of as transcenders, who we will call from this point onwards, **transcendists**, 'advance scouts for the race', individuals who "far exceeded the traditional criteria for psychological health."[10] He compiled a list of around three hundred creative, intelligent individuals and groups of individuals whose lives were marked by frequent 'peak experiences'. In *Farther Reaches of Human Nature*, in a neglected section of the work, Maslow set out 24 characteristics of his transcendists. The first of these was that "...peak experiences and plateau experiences become the most important things in their lives, the high spots, the validators of life, the most precious aspect of life".[11] Wilson's outsiders are transcendists first, and outsiders 'collaterally'.

Transcendists and transcendent states of consciousness.

One of the features of Wilson's work is his access to a vast repository of transcendent states of consciousness experiences. Wilson heaps a great number of these experiences together in *Beyond the Occult*, as he does in most of his books.[12] He utilises very skilfully other transcendists' descriptions of transcendent states of consciousness. What characterises these states?

On the basis of the work of F.W.H. Myers, Richard Bucke, William James, Evelyn Underhill, Walter T Stace, amongst others, the following key features emerge:

1. A powerful sense of the unity of all life. A sense that 'all is one'. Individual consciousness and external reality are sensed as co-extensive. A balancing of the subjective and the objective. Insight and outlook.

2. A noetic quality. The ability to apprehend reality directly. An "inner knowing," intuitive consciousness—direct and immediate access to knowledge beyond what is available to the senses, the average state of consciousness, and to logical reason. The transcendist feels *directly* aware of the purpose of human life, and the purpose of evolution.

3. A sense that beyond, below, and above the average sense of

self, is a powerful transcendent self that forms the core of both the individual self, and the entire cosmos. This transcendent self is inherent in, and accessible by all other selves in the world. In profound transcendent states, the transcendist feels god-like, or imbued by a sense of godliness. In perennial philosophy this is the basis of the concept of God.

4. Transcendence of time and space. In Wilsonian terms, 'Faculty X'.

5. Powerfully optimistic mood. Deep emotion of a positive kind. A sense of being in touch with the sacred. Often leading to a sense of universal love – a love of all things – unconditionally. Embracing a transcendent ethics and morality system. A feeling of being able to overcome all obstacles. A sense of flow. Being in tune with the world, and with life.

6. In profound transcendent states, the ability to maintain, paradoxicality, complementarity and Janusian thinking. This has been described as the *coincidentia oppositorium* – the unity of opposites. Coupled with this an enhanced ability to generate internal images that are as powerful as those existing externally.

7. Transcendence of sexuality. Both in the sense of fusing Jung's *anima* and *animus*, and in Powys sense of "...rousing a peculiar exultation in yourself ... which is really a cosmic eroticism ...".[13] Ultimately this may lead to transcending the need for physical sexuality. Not of concern to us here, but Wilson has developed a theory of transcendent sexology, over a number of works.

8. What is 'learnt' in the transcendent state is applied to 'real life.' Persisting positive shifts in attitude, behaviour, and lifestyle, and life pathway. A deep ecological conviction grows. A strengthening of the self ensures, with an enhancement of resilience, and the ability to endure 'aloneness'. Some transcendists are content to seek out transcendist states of consciousness intermittently. Others, like Wilson, make it the primary purpose of their life. They are obsessed with the quest,

and reorient their lives in pursuit of the transcendent. Transcendence becomes a daily ritual and pursuit.

Wilson does not use these philosophical terms, but any profound transcendent state of consciousness causes a radical shift in *ontology* and *epistemology*. Ontology relates to how man perceives and conceives the core being of his self and external nature, and epistemology is the framework or belief system, by which we conceive, comprehend, and believe in, the nature of reality.

Two other features that are often mentioned in transcendist literature are ineffability, and transiency. Ineffability, the inability to convey in words the nature of transcendence, certainly doesn't hold in Wilson's case. He has written millions of words to prove it. And hundreds of thousands of transcendists around the world can understand perfectly well what he is trying to convey. Particularly over the last 150 years, a vast body of knowledge has grown around the subject of transcendence that is easy to comprehend.

James and Maslow, amongst others, have also asserted that the transcendent state of consciousness is inevitably and inherently transient. Wilson's advance in the philosophy of transcendence is to argue that this is not necessarily so.

Wilson's central idea. Man's ultimate purpose.

Wilson asks the question, if the transcendent state of consciousness is sought by the transcendist so much, why are they allowed to dissipate so quickly? Why not make an intense effort of concentration to maintain the state of consciousness? His answer is that despite possessing the 'muscles for compressing consciousnesses and achieving these states, we use them so rarely, that we are hardly aware of their existence'. An effort of will and concentration needs to be exercised continuously. In 'Glimpses', the final chapter of *The Occult*, Wilson provides two examples from his own experience of such moments of absolute and total control over consciousness and time.[14] For Wilson the ultimate purpose of mankind, which is also the purpose of consciousness, life, and evolution, is to move from occasional and temporary transcendent states of consciousness, to a permanent state. Wilson's central concern in philosophy is to explain how this can be achieved.

A faculty for transcendence – 'Faculty X'

In *Poetry and Mysticism* (1969) Wilson introduced his notion of 'duo-consciousness,' the curious capacity of human consciousness to exist in two 'states' simultaneously. In *The Occult*, an encyclopedic history of 'lunar knowledge,' 'duo-consciousness,' is expanded further, becoming what Wilson labels, 'Faculty X'.

Witchcraft and magic depend upon transcendent consciousness, a wider grasp of reality than man normally possesses. In this they are closely related to mysticism. In a superb introductory chapter to *The Occult*, Wilson calls magic – *the science of the future.*

Man is driven by impersonal or transpersonal impulses. Wilson alerts us to a scene in Johnson's *Rasselas, Prince of Abyssinia*, in which the hero looks at the peaceful pastoral scenery of the Happy Valley where he lives, and wonders why he cannot be happy like the sheep and cows. He reflects gloomily: "I can discover within me no power of perception that is not glutted with its proper pleasure, yet I do not feel myself delighted. *Man has surely some latent sense for which this place affords no gratification,* or he has some desires distinct from sense which must be satisfied before he can be happy."[15]

Man also has a profound desire to transcend the triviality of everydayness. He spends most of his life bogged down in the present, attending to inconsequential concerns. 'Faculty X' allows man to transcend boredom – to overcome what Wilson calls the 'robot'. The 'robot' comprises all those functions which we learn to perform unconsciously and automatically. It has a habit of taking over 'our lives' – causing 'life failure'.

Man also possesses natural animalistic and instinctual powers. With the growth of civilization these powers are subsumed by intellectual powers. Wilson argues that man can strive to develop his instinctive powers, in the same way that he strives to develop his intellect. "The poet, the mystic, and the magician, (in fact all transcendists), have this in common: the desire to develop their powers 'downward' rather than 'upward'. To reconnect with their deepest nature. In this way 'Faculty X' also unites the two halves of man's mind, conscious and subconscious." [16] This is what Carl Jung, defines as the *transcendent function*[17] – making the subconscious, conscious.

Wilson emphasises that 'Faculty X' is not a 'sixth sense', but an ordinary potentiality of consciousness. Ultimately it is the key 'not only to uncover man's hidden powers, and the occult experience, but to the evolution of the human race'.[18]

Various levels of consciousness. The Ladder of Selves.

Wilson has never outlined a theory of how the average state of consciousness develops. But he does regard it as a deficient and subnormal 'state'. All transcendists know that the sense of *self* in the average state of consciousness, and transcendent states of consciousness, is very different. They experience self-consciousness as anything from the average, to the God-like. Inevitably they draw up 'mind maps' or 'cartographies of consciousness', in an endeavour to define various levels of consciousness. Most serious transcendists have drawn up 'maps' of this kind. Wilson is no exception. He begins with the basic state of non-consciousness that we experience in very deep sleep, and calls this Level 0.

The next level, Level 1 is the level we experience as we dream, and which persists in hypnagogic experiences.

Level 2 is the most basic level of waking consciousness: that is *mere awareness*. Consciousness is merely a mirror reflecting the outside world.

At Level 3 consciousness has become self-aware but it is still dull and heavy — so heavy that we are only aware of one thing at a time.

Level 4 is the normal consciousness we experience every day. It is no longer too heavy to move or to cope with existence but life still seems a grim battle. Consequently it tends to sink back easily towards Level 3. The characteristic that Levels 1-4 have in common is a *passive* attitude towards life and experience.

At Level 5 this ceases to be the case. This level Wilson calls 'spring morning consciousness' or 'holiday consciousness'. Life becomes *self-evidently* fascinating and delightful.

Level 6 he calls the 'magical level'. In such states we feel a total reconciliation with our lives. 'For moments together my heart stood still between delight and sorrow to find how rich was the gallery of my life', says Hesse's Steppenwolf. Problems seem trivial; we see that the one real virtue is courage. Consciousness has become a continuous 'plateau' peak experience.

Level 7 is 'Faculty X' — as already discussed, this provides a sense of *mastery over time and space and consciousness.*

In *Beyond the Occult*, Wilson explores Level 8, through profound transcendent experiences of Peter Ouspensky, and experiments with lysergic acid, (1954-1957), by R. H Ward. Elsewhere Wilson has also reviewed Aldous Huxley's mescaline experiences, in the *Doors of Perception*, and *Heaven and Hell*.[19] Wilson's cartography of consciousness is relatively simple compared to maps such as Timothy Leary's 8-circuit model of consciousness [20], and those of John Lilly, Stanislav Grof, Stanley Krippner, and Ken Wilber, amongst numerous other 20th century transcendists.

Level 8 consciousness seems to "*contradict* the evidence of our senses and of everyday consciousness. The inner becomes the outer, the outer becomes the inner, man is the whole universe and a mere atom, space and time are seen to be illusions". [21]

Average Self and Transcendent Self.

Much of human development is unconscious. You could argue that we all possess an evolutionary, physiological, sociological, cognitive, psychological and neurological unconscious. Very little consciousness goes into the average state of consciousness. The average sense of Self is underpinned by a vast network of unconscious processes. To put it another way, what we understand by the Self, is a very small sub-unit of a much greater self. As we progress up the levels of consciousness, we also expand the sense of Self, until at level 8, the Self becomes the equivalent of God.

Wilson has a number of nineteenth-century authors whose work he admires, and returns to frequently. In the Occult series, these include Thomson Jay Hudson, Frederic Myers and William James. They were heavily influenced by researchers in Europe, including Jean-Martin Charcot, Sigmund Freud, and Pierre Janet. All were prominent in the period when dynamic psychiatry, with its focus on the unconscious, self-identity, and dissociation, rose to become a dominant force in medicine, psychiatry and world culture (1880-1914).

On the basis of experiments in hypnosis in particular, Hudson came to the conclusion that man has two minds, a 'practical' mind which engages in everyday external concerns, and a 'non-practical' mind which orchestrates the inner workings of consciousness. Hudson called these the *objective* and *subjective* minds. The highest function of the objective mind was reason, and of the subjective, intuition. The subjective could draw on a vast store of power and energy, had limitless memory, and was like a 'hidden self' working constantly in the transliminal margins of consciousness. The objective mind suppressed the workings of the subjective. Average men had little or no access to it. It could, however, be accessed by transcendists.

In England, over the course of his lifetime, Frederic Myers developed a similar theory. After co-founding the *Society for Psychical Research* (*SPR*), London, in 1882, he authored some books, and numerous papers on parapsychology. His monumental work *Human Personality*, was published posthumously in 1903. Myers investigated a range of experiences including normal (e.g., sleep), abnormal (e.g., hysteria, insanity), creative, and supernormal (e.g., paranormal). His efforts led William James (1903) to state that Myers "made a sort of objective continuum of what, before him, had appeared so pure a disconnectedness that the ordinary scientific mind had either disdained to look at it, or pronounced it mostly fictitious".[22]

At the centre of his theory lay notions of subliminal perception, and out of this grew his concept of a subliminal self. Myers construed this as the 'real self', a vast powerful substratum of the average self.

Hidden in the depths of our being Myers discerned not just a rubbish-heap, but also a treasure-house. The subliminal self was concerned with the "supernormal, or … phenomenon which goes beyond the level of ordinary experience, in the direction of evolution, or as pertaining to a transcendental world".[23] Myers subliminal Self was also, according to Wilson, 'a *superconscious* mind…an attic'[24], or more correctly, a transcendent self. John C. Lilly, concluded *The Centre of the Cyclone* with, "…the miracle is that the universe created a part of itself to study the rest of it, that this part, in studying itself, finds the rest of the universe in its own natural inner realities".[25] Lilly, Myers, Wilson and many other transcendists have all arrived at the same conclusion. That at the centre of the self lies a transcendent self which, under the requisite conditions, can not only transcend time and space, but which controls the workings of the individual body and consciousness, and has access to ALL 'knowledge' in the universe

In 2006, Edward F Kelly and other co-authors, published a monumental work, reassessing the ground-breaking theories of F.W.H. Myers, and William James, called, *Irreducible Mind: Toward a Psychology for the 21st Century.*[26] Kelly and associates argued that Myers and James had created a viable model of consciousness and of the self, by the early 1900s, and that most of philosophy, neuropsychology, psychology, and parapsychology in the twentieth century had missed the point of their discoveries. A well directed psychology of the 21st century, would do well to go back, reappropriate their theories, and utilise them as a new point of departure.

There is an interesting parallel between the rise of dynamic psychiatry in the 1880s, and the preoccupations that began to dominate the psychological sciences in the 1980s. This was fuelled by research in transcendent states of consciousness, cognitive processes, epistemological enquiries in physics and biology, cybernetics, hypnosis, in particular Ernest Hilgard's neo-dissociation theory, *Dissociative Identity Disorder* (DID), and the parallel rise in childhood abuse/repressed memory cases. The result has been that consciousness studies, in a multidisciplinary manner, have assumed centre place in scientific enquiry, for the first time in human history. Particularly since the first *Tuscon Conference on Consciousness* (1994). Cognition journals have proliferated. Even a journal focused *solely* on *Dissociation* appeared in 1988. Interestingly enough, the same year that *Beyond the Occult* was published. Wilson's philosophical pursuits anticipated the rise in consciousness studies in the second half of the 20th century.

The information universe, *Mind At Large, the Transcendent Self.*

At the end of Part One of *Beyond the Occult* Wilson asserts that what was missing amongst the early parapsychologists was a comprehensive theory of the paranormal, "...although Myers made a very creditable attempt." It is easy to argue that Wilson's occult cycle is in fact both a reiteration and an expansion of Myers theory. Throughout the Occult cycle, Wilson is very sympathetic to the transcendent self theory.

In *Beyond the Occult*, he reviews favourably the theories laid down in *The Soul of Things* (1863) by William Denton regarding psychometry, that every object in the world carries its own history inside it, and that most people can develop the ability to read this history, simply by holding it in their hands. "Denton believed that this information includes every event that has ever occurred in the history of the universe, and that everyone can gain access to it..." Wilson calls this the *information universe*. Note that psychometry can also be interpreted through Myers *transcendent self* theory.

Other notions consistent with this theory that Wilson acknowledges include William Blake's the 'eternal reflected in nature' in the *Descriptive Catalogue*, Eileen Garrett's description of entering a superconscious state during her mediumship, and Upton Sinclair's theory of telepathy, including the notion of a universal mind-stuff.

Whitehead's *theory of organism* also receives Wilson's approval. "He argued that *everything* in the universe is, in some sense, capable of 'feeling'. Both Whitehead and Bergson insisted that the universe is characterised by an *underlying web of consciousness*. But in order to survive human beings have to focus on one thing at a time, so we have to 'screen out' the connections." [27]

Following on theories expounded by C. D. Broad, Aldous Huxley, declared himself an advocate of a similar theory in *The*

Doors of Perception. "Each person is at each moment capable of remembering all that has ever happened to him and of perceiving everything that is happening everywhere in the universe. The function of the brain and nervous system is to protect us from being overwhelmed and confused by this mass of largely useless and irrelevant knowledge, by shutting out most of what we should otherwise perceive or remember at any moment, and leaving only that very small and special selection which is likely to be practically useful. According to such a theory, each one of us is potentially *Mind at Large.*"[28] A transcendent self.

Elements that detract from Beyond the Occult:

Adopting a spirit 'hypothesis' to explain poltergeists.

Beyond the Occult is constructed in two parts. In Part Two Wilson undertakes to explore more fully a number of paranormal phenomena that he believes do not 'fit' with theories he enunciated in *The Occult* and *Mysteries,* and do not comply with the *information universe* theory, or the transcendent self theory. One of these is the disturbed (un)consciousness theory as an explanation for poltergeists. After discussions with Guy Playfair, and after re-examining various poltergeist cases, Wilson becomes convinced that poltergeists are actually *spirits.* This spirit theory was initially enunciated in *Poltergeist* (1981).

Beyond the Occult begins with an in-depth analysis of Lawrence LeShan's *The Medium, The Mystic, and the Physicist.* LeShan is unconvinced by spirit explanations. 'It is perfectly useless from a scientific viewpoint to try to "explain" this paradox by saying "spirits do it." Spirits (or "discarnate entities," "people who have passed beyond this plane of existence," or what have you) may or may not exist; that is not the question. Suppose that they do exist: the problem

remains....We must still ask—if we accept "spirits" as a factor—
How do the spirits do it? How do they violate the laws of the
cosmos and produce impossibilities like clairvoyance and
precognition? We can complicate the question all we wish by
adding hypothetical factors like spirits, but the problem and the
paradox remain.' [29]

Occam's razor is the philosophical principle that 'entities
must not be multiplied beyond necessity'. In the case of the
spirit hypothesis, we could add that 'entities must not be introduced beyond necessity'. The transcendent self theory is based
on a viable theory of consciousness. It is sufficient to explain the
phenomenon. Wilson's argument for spirits is one of the least
compelling ideas in *Beyond the Occult*.

Split brain research.

Laterally the brain is divided into two hemispheres, which are
connected by a network of 300 million nerve fibres, called the
corpus callosum. Put simplistically, in right-handers, the left
brain controls events on the right side of the body, and the right
brain, events on the left. The left brain processes sequential and
logical data, and the right brain relational and holistic data.
Many neuroscientists and philosophers have defined the
different ways by which the left and right brain process reality.
Propositional-appositional; lineal-non-lineal; abstract-concrete,
etc.

In the early 1960's operations were performed on humans to
sever the corpus callosum, effectively 'splitting the brain'.
Whilst undertaking average tasks the patients displayed few
deficits. They maintained a unity of consciousness. However
when information was delivered to each side of the brain
separately, patients were incapable of processing the information in a unified manner. What was presented to the left brain
was 'unconscious' to the right, and vice versa. Two separate

fields of consciousness had been created – two minds in one brain. The left brain did not know what the right brain was doing. The results were dramatic, and generated a neuropsychological revolution, and a neurophilosophical controversy which raged for a generation.

Wilson derived his knowledge about 'split brain' or 'double brain' research from two sources. Various works of Robert Ornstein, including *The Psychology of Consciousness* [30] (1972), and Julian Jayne's, *The Origin of Consciousness in the Breakdown of the Bicameral Mind* [31] (1979). He admits, that what he did next, was "proceed to extrapolate, and to spin interesting and totally unproven theories." [32] This can be dangerous.

Soon after being introduced to Jayne's work in 1979, Wilson plunged headlong into the neurophilosophical controversy. The comedians, Stan Laurel and Oliver Hardy were 'contracted' to 'star' in his right brain-left brain theory of neurosis, the self, and creativity – *the Laurel and Hardy Theory of Consciousness*.[33] Not all Wilson's neologisms, analogies and metaphor's are effective. Firstly, developing an analogy between two comedians, Laurel and Hardy, and the profound and awe-inspiring nature of consciousness, and *acts of creation*, doesn't 'come off'.

More importantly, some of the conclusions that Wilson reached about the function of 'left brain' and 'right brain', contradict neurophilosophical findings. The key neurophilosophical questions are: do the results of 'split brain' experiments mean that the left brain is the repository of the conscious mind, and the right brain, of the unconscious mind? And even more perplexing, does that mean that man possesses two fields of consciousness, or two selves – one in each hemisphere?

Neuropsychological confusion is dispelled if you construe the architectonics of the brain as a multi-modular 'system'. Various circuits, at various levels of the brain contribute to creating a global 'stream of consciousness'. In each circuit, and at each level, some processes are allowed to enter into consciousness, and others remain, unconscious. The notion that *the unconscious* can be found in the right hemisphere, as Wilson claims, or the cerebellum, as Stan Gooch[34] asserts, or in *any* particular localized structure of the brain, is naïve. Extrapolations go awry with the assertions that the right brain IS the unconscious, that the left brain, IS the 'real me' and that the right brain IS the transcendent self.

The hemispheres contribute to consciousness by processing 'reality' in two different ways. But, the self cannot be ascribed to the right hemisphere or the left hemisphere, or to any localized brain structure. The self transcends the processing style of both hemispheres. The average state of consciousness self, lies beyond, behind, above – it is difficult to localise – the workings of either hemisphere. And the transcendent self also lies 'beyond' either hemisphere in the same way. Theories of consciousness, the unconscious, the self, and the transcendent self break down if they are made to fit this right brain – left brain straightjacket.

The Laurel and Hardy theory of consciousness.

During the course of writing the second chapter of his book on Wilhelm Reich, it struck Wilson that that his theory of neurosis works just as well 'if you substitute the right and left brain for Stan and Ollie'.[35] Wilson's right-left-brain theory of neurosis unfolds like this. Ollie — consciousness — is construed as the boss. "Stan takes his cues from Ollie. If Ollie looks miserable, Stan is sunk in gloom. If Ollie looks cheerful, Stan is positively ecstatic. *Stan always over-reacts*".[36] If we take a gloomy attitude into our day, the unconscious mind begins to feel depressed. An hour later, we feel miserable and exhausted — *because the unconscious mind controls our vital energies.* This confirms our feeling that this is 'one of those days', so Stan becomes more depressed than ever. The depression becomes self-sustaining.

Assuming an optimistic attitude has the reverse effect. The unconscious releases more energy, which gives Stan the feeling that this is how life should be. Ollie believes life is wonderful, Stan releases even more energy, and one of those perfect days where everything just 'goes right' transpires. We can all recognize the mechanism in ourselves — how pleasant anticipation revitalizes us; how self-pity and boredom deprive us of our natural powers.

For Wilson, 'this interplay between Ollie and Stan explains the aetiology of neurosis far more convincingly than Freud's explanations about sexual disturbances festering in the unconscious'.[37] This may be true. Equally true is the notion that ideas and preconceptions can have a profound effect on emotion, mood, and well-being – our level of optimism. However, it is neurophilosophically impossible to justify the assertion that the right brain is the *sole*, or *primary* brain structure involved in this process.

Easier to justify is the relationship between the processing styles of the two hemispheres, and creativity. As a prolific writer, Wilson is very conversant with this interplay:

"My instrument of communication is words — a left brain function. But what I write *about* are patterns, insights, intuitions — a right brain function. When I started to write, in my early teens, I used to find it hard and depressing work. The words were always killing the intuitions...analysis is the enemy of insight. But as the years went by, I persevered, and gained a certain command over words. Sometimes... insights would defy me, and refuse to be turned into words. But then I learned to keep on trying — sometimes for months or years —until I saw how it could be done.

When I am writing well, there is an interesting balance between the intuitions and the words. And *'I' seem to somehow straddle the two*, gently encouraging the intuitions, gently translating them into language and allowing them to flow on to the paper. If I get tired or frustrated, this balance is upset. I try *too* hard, the intuitions dwindle, and the words become clumsy and inappropriate. But some days, I am positively brilliant. I turn the intuitions into words so neatly that the right brain gets excited to see itself expressed so well; it shouts 'Yes, yes, that's it!', and sends up more intuitions. And my left brain, pleased to be praised, makes an even greater effort, and catches the intuitions as they come pouring out. And suddenly, the tennis match is worthy of Wimbledon, both sides playing with unaccustomed brilliance. This is the state called 'inspiration'.

All this makes it clear that our basic problem as human beings is, in effect, to get both players into a mood of warm cooperation. It would seem that our two aspects have two quite different functions. The left brain is the 'front man'; its job is to cope with practical problems, to stand on guard, prepared for emergencies. Its chief instrument is crude willpower. It always seems to be in a hurry. And if we allow it to get too dominant, we end in a state of permanent tension."[38]

Wilson now has the metapsychology of consciousness and the self correct when he observes that "'*I*' *seem to somehow straddle the two*". The self utilises, but transcends, the processing 'styles' of the two hemispheres. He repeats this more neurophilosophically correct double-brain theory of creativity in *Super Consciousness*, whilst discussing Alfred North Whitehead's book, *Symbolism, Its Meaning and Effect*, and Whitehead's use of two modes of perception, 'presentational immediacy' and 'causal efficacy'.[39]

The solution to recruiting Ollie and Stan, and the right-left brain to carry the burden of being the conscious and unconscious, the 'real' self and the average self, and the transcendent self, as well as the basis for neurosis is simple. You terminate their contract. That is edit them out of the script. Wilson's theories, derived from the two modes of consciousness, work equally well *without* being *directly* linked to the 'double-brain theory'.

Summing up.

Is *Beyond the Occult* Wilson's best book? The detracting elements above would lead me to say definitely not. Nor does it possess the driven inspiration of *The Outsider*, *The Occult* or *Mysteries*. It has the feel of a mopping up operation, a farewell to the subject of the occult. You gain the impression that after almost 20 years 'in the cycle', Wilson has said enough about the occult, and is 'fed up' with it. Moreover, many of the occult phenomenon are trivial. Who cares if on very rare occasions poltergeists 'get noisy'? Is there any real purpose or need for *cultivating* out of body experiences? Creatively and philosophically, Wilson had already moved *beyond the occult*, at the time he wrote the book.

After reading all the books in Wilson's occult cycle, you become aware that there is not much knowledge that is left "occluded". Looking at the occult through the lens of what Wilson calls 'Faculty X', most, if not all of the mysteries of the occult are resolved. To refer back to the original definition of *occult*, the phenomena are now 'capable of being apprehended by the mind', and 'within the range of understanding'. Wilson has applied Jung's transcendent function, and moved *beyond the occult*.

Most importantly many of the occult *powers* are an adjunct to Wilson's central idea, and man's key purpose. This is the development of the ability to sustain transcendent states of consciousness at will, and for prolonged periods of time. Ideally

– indefinitely. The ultimate purpose of life is to turn the transcendist into THE TRANSCENDIST – a ˙ *permanent* transcendist. This is the most profound sense of what Wilson means when he says we need to move *beyond the occult*. Achieve the central purpose, and all the other 'occult' powers follow.

From the publication of *The Outsider* in 1956, Wilson's importance and pre-eminence has derived from his ability to cut through various superficial and academic problems in philosophy, and engage with the core issues of human existence. He consistently endeavours to answer the questions – what is the nature of the self and consciousness, and what is the purpose of life? Taking into account Wilson's work as a whole, we need to stop pretending that we no longer know where we are going, or how to get there.

In the year 2050, men will look back and ask themselves, why did it take so long for us to place the study of not just consciousness, but transcendent states of consciousness, to the centre of philosophical and scientific enquiry? Those of us celebrating Colin Wilson's eightieth birthday with this festschrift will know which philosopher was at the forefront of this transcendent revolution, and was most able to discuss the matter in a way which would lead man to an ultimate solution.

Looking back from the year 3000, he will be acknowledged as the philosopher to have most influenced events in the 21st century. He will also have contributed to the greatest shift in the 21st century – from the transcendist to THE TRANSCENDIST, the shift he describes repeatedly as heralding the next stage of human evolution.

Notes:

1   Colin. Wilson. *Beyond the Occult*. 1988. Bantam Press. London. New York. This edition has been used for references.

2   *Online Etymology Dictionary.*
    http://www.etymonline.com/index.php?term=occult
3   Quoted in, Dossor, Howard F. *Colin Wilson : the man and his mind.* 1990. Element Books. Shaftesbury, Dorset. Howard Dossor shared/s Colin Wilson's opinion.
4   Kenneth Allsop. *The Angry Decade, A Survey of the Cultural Revolt of the Nineteen Fifties.* 1964. Peter Owen Ltd. London. Third edition.
5   Isaiah Berlin. *The Hedgehog and the Fox.* 1953. Simon & Schuster. New York.
6   Howard Dossor. 1990. *op cit.*
7   Colin Wilson. *Beyond the Occult. op cit.*
8   William Braud. *Nonordinary and Transcendent Experiences: Transpersonal Aspects of Consciousness.* 2003. *Journal of the American Society for Psychical Research* 97 (1):1-26.
9   Anthony Sutich. 1969. *Statement of Purpose. Journal of Transpersonal Psychology,* Vol. 1. No. 1. pp. 5–6.
    Anthony Sutich. *The founding of humanistic and transpersonal psychology: A personal account.* 1976. Unpublished doctoral dissertation, Saybrook Graduate School, San Francisco.
10 Abraham Maslow. *Farther Reaches of Human Nature.* 1971. Viking Press. New York. See in particular, Part VII. *Transcendence and the Psychology of Being,* Chapter 21. *Various Meanings of Transcendence* p. 259-269, and Chapter 22. *Theory Z* p. 270-286.
11 Abraham Maslow. 1971. *ibid.*
    See also, Abraham Maslow. *The Farther Reaches of Human Nature. Journal of Transpersonal Psychology.* 1969. Vol 1. No 1. p.1-9.
    Abraham Maslow. *Various Meanings of Transcendence. Journal of Transpersonal Psychology.* Vol 1. No. 1. pp. 56-66.
12 Colin Wilson. *Beyond The Occult.* 1988. *op cit.* See pages 36-44.
13 John Cowper Powys. *Autobiography.* 1934. The Bodley Head, John Lane, London.

14 *The Occult.* 1971. *op cit.*

15 Quoted in, *The Occult.* 1971. *op cit.* Chapter 2.

16 *The Occult.* 1971. *op cit.*

17 Carl G Jung. *The Structure and Function of the Psyche.* Volume
    8 of the *Collected Works of Carl G Jung.* 1960. Bollingen Series
    XX. Pantheon, New York.
    See also, Jeffrey C Miller. *The transcendent function: Jung's
    model of psychological growth through dialogue with the uncon-
    scious.* 2004. State University of New York Press. Albany,
    New York.

18 *The Occult.* 1971. *op cit.*

19 Peter D. Ouspensky. *A New Model of the Universe.* 1931.
    Rouledge & Kegan Paul. London.
    R. H. Ward. *A Drug Taker's Notes.* 1957. Gollancz, London.
    Aldous Huxley's mescaline experience discussed in, Colin
    Wilson. *Frankenstein's Castle. The Double Brain, Door to
    Wisdom.* 1980. Ashgrove Press.Sevenoaks, Kent.

20 Timothy Leary. *Exo-Psychology.* 1977. Starseed/Peace Press,
    Culver City, CA. USA.
    Timothy Leary. *Info-Psychology. A Manual on the Use of the
    Human Nervous System According to the Instructions of the
    Manufacturers.* 1989. Falcon Press. Tempe, AZ. USA.
    Wilson's eight-levels of consciousness theory and Leary's 8-
    Circuit Model of Consciousness, are similar. In both, the
    'lower' four levels deal with the 'average' state of
    consciousness. Leary calls the upper four levels, *stellar
    circuits.* These deal with 'psychic', 'mystical', and
    'enlightened' states of consciousness, and with psychedelics.
    Wilson, as we know, does not share Leary's enthusiasm for
    psychedelics.

21 *The Occult.* 1971. *op cit.*

22 William James. *Review of Human Personality and Its Survival of
    Bodily Death. Proceedings of the Society for Psychical Research.*
    1903. 18, 22-33.

23 Frederic W.H. Myers. *Human Personality and Its Survival of Bodily Death*. 1903. Longmans Green and Co. London. Vol. 1, p. xxii.

24 *The Occult*. 1971. *op cit*.

25 John C Lilly. *The Centre of the Cyclone. An Autobiography of Inner Space*. 1972. Julian Press. New York.

26 Edward F. Kelly, Emily Williams Kelly, Adam Crabtree, Alan Gauld, Michael Grosso, & Bruce Greyson. *Irreducible Mind. Toward a Psychology for the 21st century*. 2007. Rowman and Littlefield Publishers Inc. Maryland, USA.

27 *The Occult*. 1971. *op cit*.

28 Aldous Huxley. *The doors of perception*. 1954. Harper. New York.

29 Lawrence LeShan. *The Medium, the Mystic, and the Physicist*. 1974. Viking Press. An Esalen book. New York.

30 Robert Ornstein. *The Psychology of Consciousness*. 1972. W. H. Freeman. New York.

31 Julian Jaynes. *The Origin of Consciousness in the Breakdown of the Bicameral Mind*. 1979. Houghton Mifflin. Boston.

32 Colin Wilson. *The Laurel and Hardy Theory of Consciousness. Second Look* (Magazine), October 1979. Reprinted in *The Essential Colin Wilson*. Grafton Books. A Division of Collins Publishing. London. 1987.
The double-brain theory was first outlined at length in *Frankenstein's Castle*.1980. *op cit*.

33 Colin Wilson. *The Laurel and Hardy Theory of Consciousness*. 1979. *op cit*.

34 Stan Gooch. *Total Man. An Evolutionary Theory of Personality*. 1972. Allen Lane/Penguin Press. London.
Chris McManus has recently taken Stan Gooch to task for poor double-brain neurophilosophy. See, *Right Hand, Left Hand: The Origins of Asymmetry in Brains, Bodies, Atoms and Cultures*. 2004. Harvard University Press. Cambridge.

35 Colin Wilson. *The Laurel and Hardy Theory of Consciousness*.

1979. op.cit.

See also, Colin Wilson. *The Quest for Wilhelm Reich*. 1981. Granada. St. Albans.

The Laurel and Hardy and double-brain theory of Consciousness was outlined in the 1979-1981 period.

36 *Beyond the Occult*. 1988. *op.cit.*
37 *Beyond the Occult*. 1988. *ibid*.
38 *Beyond the Occult*. 1988. *ibid*.
39 Colin Wilson. *Super-Consciousness: the Quest for the Peak Experience*. 2009. Watkins Publishing.

The Books in My Life (1998)

Colin Wilson's *The Books in My Life*

Antoni Diller

Wilson's friend, the science-fiction writer A. E. van Vogt, coined the term 'fixup' to describe a novel which, rather than having been written from scratch, was put together using several previously published short stories. Usually, some changes would be made and some newly written linking material added to make the final book appear unified and coherent. The term has no pejorative connotation; it is purely descriptive and is used as such throughout, for example, the excellent *Encyclopedia of Science Fiction*, edited by John Clute and Peter Nicholls. Some famous novels are fixups, including Issac Asimov's *Foundation* (1951), Frank Herbert's *Dune* (1965) and J. G. Ballard's *The Crystal World* (1966). Although *The Books in My Life* is a work of non-fiction, its manner of composition is that of such a fixup. The chapter on Sherlock Holmes was first published in the anthology *Beyond Baker Street* (1976), which Michael Harrison edited. The chapter on Huysmans was written to introduce a selection of Huysmans's writings that Brian Banks was editing. Unfortunately, this project never saw the light of day. Most, if not all, of the remaining chapters were originally written as articles for the Japanese magazine *Litteraire*, which also published Wilson's important essay "Below the Iceberg". Paul Newman intended to include the *Litteraire* articles in successive issues of *Abraxas*, but realising it would take years for them all to appear, decided to publish groups of them as supplements to the magazine. The first of these appeared towards the end of 1997. This contained the first twelve chapters of *The Books in My Life*, as finally published, except for the chapter on Sherlock Holmes. No further supplements appeared, because Frank DeMarco

242

published *The Books in My Life* in October 1998. Before I say more about the book itself, I think it is worth recounting how its publication came about.

DeMarco came across Wilson's writings by accident in February 1970 when he was twenty-three years old. Waiting to be served in a drugstore, he noticed a paperback copy of *The Mind Parasites*. Reading that changed his life. Up to then he had aspired to a career in politics; he was well on the way to getting a chance to run for Congress. Wilson's book made him aware that human beings possess latent powers and abilities that could transform their lives if developed. He began to investigate methods of developing these abilities and his book *Muddy Tracks* is a record of what he has learnt. He became especially interested in the work of Robert Monroe who believed that playing different sounds to each of a person's ears increased the chances of that person having an out-of-the-body experience. When DeMarco heard that Wilson would be visiting New York in March 1995, he got himself invited to a party being given in Wilson's honour by the paranormal researcher Alexander Imich. He wanted to persuade Wilson to visit the Monroe Institute and try out some of the techniques on offer there. Sadly, Monroe died on the day the party took place and that cast a shadow over it. Some years earlier, DeMarco had set up the Hampton Roads Publishing Company with Bob Friedman and, as well as talking about Monroe at the party, he asked Wilson if he could publish one of Wilson's future books. In due course, Wilson offered him *The Books in My Life*. In some ways this was a strange choice as Hampton Roads mainly publishes books on metaphysical subjects: 'books for the evolving human spirit', as their publicity material puts it. There is no extended discussion of anything occult or paranormal in *The Books in My Life*; in no way could it be described as a New Age book.

Ostensibly, *The Books in My Life* is about some of the books that have influenced Wilson. He does indeed discuss quite a few of the books that made him think, and a number that did not, but it also contains much more than this. There is a lot of autobiographical information as well as reflections on keeping a diary and his views on sex, crime, the history of philosophy and of literature, the meaning of life and the nature of consciousness. Although Wilson mentions almost two hundred books in *The Books in My Life*, most of which are novels, he devotes far more space to providing information about his early life and to expounding his views on how consciousness can be expanded than to discussing any one of these or their authors. In virtually every chapter Wilson has something to say about heightened consciousness and the final chapter is entirely devoted to this topic. Most of the books referred to are ones that Wilson encountered in the first thirty or so years of his life; we learn practically nothing of what influenced him later. A large number of these books should be familiar to students of Wilson's work as he has written at length about them in several of his other books. In any case, there are too many of them to list here. There are, however, a few surprises. We learn that he thinks highly of the Sherlock Holmes stories and rereads them every two years and that he considers Bram Stoker's *Dracula* to be a masterpiece. We discover his admiration for Ernst Cassirer's *Essay on Man* (1944). Indeed, Wilson considers this philosopher to have been 'one of the cleverest men of the [twentieth] century'. We also find out that Wilson loved reading literary criticism in his teens. In fact, many people may well be surprised, as I was myself, by the large number of such works included in *The Books in My Life*. Amongst these are F. O. Matthiessen's studies of T. S. Eliot and Henry James, the accounts by Julius Meier-Graefe and Nicholas Berdyaev of the work of Dostoevsky, Marc Slonim's *Russian Literature: 1900–1917* and E. M. Forster's *Aspects of the Novel*.

Because of the number of topics covered in it, it is possible to write about *The Books in My Life* in a variety of ways. Robertson (1999), for example, sees it as an exercise in existential literary criticism. (This evaluates works of fiction by looking at the vision of life they present and considering what they have to say about the purpose and meaning of life.) Robertson's approach is not surprising given that he wrote his doctoral dissertation on this very aspect of Wilson's philosophy. My interest in Wilson is different. One aspect of his writings that I find fascinating concerns the various techniques he has developed to increase the pressure of consciousness. (One day I hope to write a study of all the disciplines Wilson has devised.) Such methods are very important to him. Although Wilson has written about a large number of topics, all his diverse interests relate in one way or another to such techniques. In the introduction to *The Essential Colin Wilson* (1985, p. 7) he says that 'a single thread runs through all' his work, namely 'the question of how man can achieve these curious moments of inner freedom, the sensation of sheer delight that G. K. Chesterton called "absurd good news." ' It is true that various methods have been developed in Eastern religions to do this. However, apart from a brief flirtation with meditation in his youth, Wilson prefers techniques that he himself has developed using ideas forged in the Western philosophical tradition. He has, indeed, become very critical of Buddhism. In *Dreaming to Some Purpose* (2004, pp. 336–337) he sees it as being fundamentally negative and considers the goal it sets for its adherents, namely that of complete detachment from all their desires, as being radically mistaken.

In *The Books in My Life* Wilson discusses one technique of intensifying consciousness in more detail than he does anywhere else in his published writings. The elaboration of this method is, in fact, one of the main themes of the book. This is the 'St Neot Margin trick', as he calls it in *Dreaming to Some Purpose* (2004, p. 339), and it is on this that I intend to focus. Before doing so, however, I need to place it in the context of Wilson's general philosophy.

245

I think it is worth distinguishing between two main types of technique that Wilson has written about even though he does not differentiate between them. These disciplines produce two different kinds of heightened consciousness. In *Alien Dawn* (1998, p. 308) and *The Devil's Party* (2000, p. 286), Wilson mentions that he has had around a handful of experiences of non-leaking consciousness. The one he writes about most often occurred on New Year's Day 1979 when he was driving through deep snow along a narrow country lane in Devon and concentrating for dear life to avoid landing in one or other of the ditches on either side of the road. The state of intensity he had induced heightened his perception. Everything around him seemed interesting and more real than it usually appears. He could easily have stopped to examine at his leisure something as straightforward as a country cottage because it looked so fascinating and full of meaning.

These intense experiences he regards as very important and, interestingly, they have all occurred while he was engaged in activities that were outside his normal routine. Indeed, he has written that he has been unable to produce such states while living and working as he usually does. It is not easy to say why this should be the case with any degree of certainty. It is possible, however, to make a number of observations. All these significant experiences of non-leaking consciousness were preceded by an extended period of intense concentration. Furthermore, in all cases, Wilson found himself in circumstances where his options as to what to do were seriously limited. When he has greater choice over his activities, he prefers to spend his days reading and writing. States of heightened consciousness are extremely important and significant, but Wilson does not think they should be an end in themselves. We would not achieve very much if we spent our days in a state of euphoria, marvelling at the beauty and complexity of the world. As he says in *Poetry and Mysticism* (1986, p. 55), such states show us what to do, but are not conducive to hard work; that needs to be carried out in states of ordinary consciousness.

In this paper I am not concerned with methods of achieving intense states of heightened consciousness. I am concerned, rather, with techniques that can be used on a daily basis, even by busy people, in order to remind themselves of the world of meaning. Wilson has admitted that he is something of a workaholic. He spends most of his days reading and writing, yet he has built certain techniques for reconnecting himself to the world of meaning into his daily routine. One of these is the 'St Neot Margin trick'. In the unpublished *The Search for Power-consciousness* (1994, p. 78), he says that he uses this quite frequently in the middle of the afternoon when he feels tired after working hard all day. He seems to use it as a pick-me-up in order to enable him to carry on working; it does not produce an intense experience of non-leaking consciousness.

For Wilson, the world is an endlessly fascinating place and a fundamental assumption of his metaphysics is that the universe is meaningful. This meaning, moreover, is objective; it is really out there. It is not created by the mind, as Sartre thought. When we look at a beautiful landscape the beauty of it is really out there in the world. We do not add the beauty to an aesthetically neutral region of the earth's surface. The beauty is not created by our consciousness. The beauty remains when we leave and, more importantly, the beauty is still there when, looking at the landscape, it fails to move us. The beauty has not disappeared; something has gone wrong with our ability to grasp it. Natural beauty is not the only example of objective meaning that Wilson considers; he also sees certain human artistic creations, like the paintings of Van Gogh and the music of Beethoven, as being intrinsically meaningful.

Unfortunately, the nature of modern life and the mechanisms that we have developed to cope with its complexity make it easy for us to lose sight of the meanings that surround us. In our modern, complex civilisation it is easy to enter into what Wilson calls 'robotic consciousness'. The 'robot' is Wilson's name for that part of us that learns how to do certain activities automatically. It takes a lot of effort, for example, to learn to ride a bicycle, but once learnt controlling the bicycle becomes automatic. We no longer have to pay conscious attention to the task of staying upright. Our 'robot' does that for us. In our complex world having a 'robot' makes it possible for us to cope as the 'robot' deals with many mundane tasks. The 'robot' is a wonderful, labour-saving device, but it needs to know its place. Unfortunately, as well as taking much of the drudgery out of life, it has the potential to take much of the joy out of it as well. By allowing us to do many tasks without much conscious awareness, it frees the conscious mind to think about other things. But without challenge, the conscious mind can easily become bored and passive. As many of the tasks we perform have been made automatic, we make fewer efforts and life appears to us as boring and meaningless. If this continues for some time, we are in danger of entering that state that Wilson calls 'life failure'.

Crises shake us awake and we take over control from the 'robot'. These crises force us to concentrate and focus our attention and such effort raises the pressure of consciousness. The reality of death, or even its possibility, can shake us awake and Wilson likes to quote several examples of how the prospect of death has transformed people's consciousness. Samuel Johnson was already aware of this. When he learnt that Dr Dodd was to be executed, he remarked, 'Depend upon it, Sir, when a man knows he is to be hanged in a fortnight, it concentrates his mind wonderfully.' In *The Books in My Life* Wilson quotes or refers to this comment no less than six times (on pp. 178, 195, 240, 258, 277 and 304).

An example of the transformative power of the imminence of death that made a tremendous impact on Wilson when he read about it in his teens is provided by an incident in the life of Dostoevsky. Wilson mentions this in many of his books and at least six times in *The Books in My Life* (on pp. 75, 169, 195, 231, 272 and 301). Dostoevsky was reprieved from execution by firing squad at the last minute and the experience completely altered his outlook on life and turned him into a great writer. Joseph Frank, in his book *Dostoevsky: The Years of Ordeal* (1983, p. 62), expresses the character of this transformation thus: 'Dostoevsky was never to forget the wave of renewal that swept over him at this moment; nor would he ever abandon the hope that he could communicate to others the same conviction of infinite possibility that had thrilled through every fiber of his own being.'

Wilson observes that it does not take something as drastic as the prospect of death to increase the pressure of consciousness. Any sort of averted threat can have a similar, if less intense, effect. The incident that gave the 'St Neot Margin trick' its name is a case in point. In the summer of 1954 Wilson and his girlfriend Joy Stewart were hitch-hiking from London to Peterborough in order to see Joy's parents who wanted to know why they were not making plans to get married. Wilson had not yet told them that he was already married to another woman. He was in a state of fatigue and life-devaluation; he was not looking forward to the meeting and he was not keen to return to London where he was working in a dreary plastics factory. Wilson's accounts of what happened next differ slightly. The following is largely based on the version found in *New Pathways in Psychology* (1972, p. 27).

Wilson and Joy eventually found a lift, but after a few minutes the lorry's gearbox started to make a strange noise and it looked as if the lorry might break down. The driver tried various things to stop the noise and found that he could do so by driving at about twenty miles an hour. As they passed through St Neots, he said, 'Well, I think if we stay at this speed, we should make it.' Although the situation was very far from being satisfactory, Wilson experienced a surge of joy: his boredom and indifference vanished. He had been threatened with a great inconvenience and then the threat had been withdrawn. The 'St Neot Margin' is the idea that 'there is a borderland or threshold of the mind that can be stimulated by pain or inconvenience, but not pleasure.'

A sudden crisis shows us that futility and pessimism are wrong and that its absence would be wonderful (pp. 80 and 127; all page references that follow are to *The Books in My Life*). However, it is not always possible to engineer a crisis in order to snap out of robotic consciousness. Wilson suggests either using the memory of a past emergency to do this or using the imagination to conjure up a possible crisis in order to wake up. He does not go into any detail about how remembering a past crisis can be used to improve your psychological state. He just mentions that it can help (pp. 75 and 178–179). He goes into a lot more detail about the use of the imagination to do this (pp. 81, 83, 115 and 178–179). He discusses two examples in considerable detail; these illustrate the way in which the 'St Neot Margin trick' operates. In the first he envisages a person suffering from life failure who suddenly remembers that he has left a saucepan full of potatoes on the stove and this is on the verge of boiling dry. Such a person may well feel that life is meaningless, but he will still rush to the kitchen to prevent it from filling up with black smoke. He may feel that nothing is worth the effort, but the reality of the potatoes burning shows him his lethargy is self-induced and illusory. Preventing the potatoes boiling dry enables him to reconnect to the worth of meaning and value; life appears self-evidently wonderful (pp. 80–81). It is open to anyone to put themselves into the position of this person and to reap the same benefits just by imagining a potential disaster which is then averted. It is easier to write about this technique, however, than to put it into practice!

In the second extended example Wilson reflects on his use of the old-fashioned word processor on which he wrote some of the essays that became *The Books in My Life*. He recounts his feelings when he thought he had inadvertently deleted a file containing many hours' work. His first reaction is shock and alarm and then his heart sinks as he realises that he will have to spend many hours retyping several days' work. He dwells on how inconvenient this will be and all the effort that will be needed to recreate the file. However, on learning that the file has not been deleted after all he experiences relief and his spirits rise.

Putting the 'St Neot Margin trick' into practice is far more difficult than you might think. Give it a go and see how successful you are! The problem is that our imagination is very feeble; our ability to conjure up an alternative reality is very weak. This is one of the reasons Wilson puts so much emphasis on what he calls 'Faculty X'. This is the ability to imagine a situation so vividly that you feel it is as real as the actual world it briefly replaces. The experience is far more intense than that of simply getting absorbed in the fictional world of a novel you are reading. Wilson's favourite examples of 'Faculty X' are Proust's experience of eating a madeleine dipped in herb tea and Toynbee's experiences of witnessing a number of historical events as if he was actually present when they took place (p. 128). Although Proust's account is found in *Swann's Way*, the first volume of *Remembrance of Things Past*, it is based on his own experience of being transported to his childhood when, on summer mornings, he visited his grandfather Nathé Weil in his bedroom and sipped some of the old man's tea. (In the novel, Proust's grandfather is replaced by the narrator's aunt Léonie.)

On a number of occasions Toynbee was transformed from being a remote spectator of certain historical events to being an immediate participant in them. In each case he had either been reading about the event in question or he was physically present in the place where it took place. He compares these experiences to what happens when an aeroplane encounters an air-pocket and loses height suddenly; he felt he had entered a time-pocket. One experience related to the suicide of Mutilus in Teanum in 80 BC during the war between the Roman Republic and the Italian Confederacy. Reading about this Toynbee saw Mutilus plunge his sword into himself, and the events leading up to this, as if he, Toynbee, was just a few feet away.

Wilson believes that the cultivation of 'Faculty X' is of paramount importance. It would have many advantages. One of these would be the ability to easily employ the 'St Neot Margin trick' to heighten consciousness. Unfortunately, he does not say how we might go about developing 'Faculty X'.

In this short paper I have only been able to look briefly at one of the themes of *The Books in My Life*. As already mentioned, the book contains discussions of a wide variety of topics that interest Wilson. I would urge anyone to read it carefully for themselves especially if, like myself, they are more interested in Wilson's views on philosophy, psychology and literature than in his work on true crime, the occult and ancient civilisations.

Acknowledgements:

I am grateful to Frank DeMarco for replying to my request for further information about the origins of *The Books in My Life* and I would like to thank Debra Barton and Colin Stanley for reading through an earlier version of this paper and making several helpful comments about how it could be improved.

References:

Clute, J. and Nicholls, P. (eds) (1993). *The Encyclopedia of Science Fiction*, Orbit, London.
DeMarco, F. (2001). *Muddy Tracks: Exploring an Unsuspected*

Reality, Hampton Roads, Charlottesville (VA).

Frank, J. (1983). *Dostoevsky: The Years of Ordeal: 1850–1859*, Robson Books, London.

Harrison, M. (ed.) (1976). *Beyond Baker Street: A Sherlockian Anthology*, Bobbs-Merrill, Indianapolis.

Robertson, D. V. (1995). *Colin Wilson: His Existential Literary Criticism and his Novels*, PhD thesis, University of Auckland.

Robertson, V. (1999). 'Wilson returns to ELC!!!', *Abraxas* 15: 36–37.

Wilson, C. (1970). *Poetry and Mysticism*, Hutchinson, London.

Wilson, C. (1972). *New Pathways in Psychology: Maslow and the Post-Freudian Revolution*, Gollancz, London.

Wilson, C. (1985). *The Essential Colin Wilson*, Harrap, London.

Wilson, C. (1998). *Alien Dawn: An Investigation into the Contact Experience*, Virgin Publishing, London.

Wilson, C. (1998). *The Books in My Life*, Hampton Roads Publishing Company, Charlottesville (VA).

Wilson, C. (2000). *The Devil's Party: A History of Charlatan Messiahs*, Virgin, London.

Wilson, C. (2004). *Dreaming to Some Purpose*, Century, London.

Dreaming to Some Purpose (2004)

Colin Wilson & 'The Joyous Overplus'

Paul Newman

Writing autobiography suits Colin Wilson who likes to lean on his own authority. The role of author-perceiver suits him – he uses the singular form freely and without awkwardness. His autobiography *Dreaming to Some Purpose* is streaked with animating instances of epiphany or physical revelation, even if only recording a shift of mood after digging away snow or the seeping away of mental tension and the replacement of it by spiritual uplift. It is almost as if he is the figurehead of his own ship cruising into the golden sunset of self-realisation, laying down guidelines and assertions, even on tenuous issues, such as what is it we do when we grasp at meaning or to what extent it is anchored by our own intentions rather than, say, an aesthetic impulse when the phenomenon itself overwhelms the observer.

His preferred vantage is the objective middle-distance focus. There are many lively impressionistic sketches of those who pass through his life. It is not a religious document like St Augustine's *Confessions* but it does explain how the author arrived at a set of beliefs. It is therefore thematic in intention – if not as narrow and intense, say, as *Mein Kampf*. The opening chapter and conclusion drive home his shibboleth or rallying cry: to find the purpose for our life on earth and live in a more heightened, fulfilled way.

Far from being self-conscious literary prose, *DTSP* is less self-analytical than, say, Graham Greene's *A Sort of Life*, but more broadly entertaining, boisterous and familiar in tone. Generally Wilson does not sink too deeply into textures, sensations and Proustian moments – save when set off by the noisy alarm of the sexual impulse. He is no Laurie Lee who, on the opening page of *Cider with Rosie*, trumpets his arrival into the "daylight nightmare" with a luscious fruit-burst of evocative prose, but then he was born amidst the gold and green uplands of the Cotswolds whereas Colin Wilson's homeland was Leicester, the ancient dwelling-place of Black Annis, a blue-faced witch with iron claws and a taste for child flesh.

Not surprisingly, Laurie, whose sway over women was considerable, adopts a tone of sustained lyricism, his sisters placing the baby boy down amid a nest of grass, "each blade tattooed with tiger-skins of sunlight", while Colin's opening is less enraptured:

"When I was sixteen, I decided to commit suicide?"
(Wilson 2004, p.1)

Which of the two is the natural optimist?

This question is relevant. For Colin Wilson states that his optimism arose from 'logic' rather than temperament. Vigorously he opposes boredom or any suggestion of life being meaningless. In contrast with the low-key, natural acceptance of sporadic bouts of gloom that millions have to make, he enlarges these murky patches into looming Brocken Spectres. This is reminiscent of G.K. Chesterton making life more heroic by portraying the jammed drawer he's struggling with as a fearsome mythical monster. Such a standpoint serves his prose well, marking out the highs and lows, heightening and relaxing tension as a blaze of assertion dispels the ashes: "Pushkin compared the poet's heart to a coal that glows red when the wind of inspiration blows on it, but turns into a black cinder when it dies away."

To read such perfection of phrasing is uplifting. Many such examples are streamed into *DTSP*, elevating the tone and gritting the texture.

Voyage to a Beginning

His early years mingle intellectual curiosity, frustration and drab intensity – there is much brooding, searching, filtering. Like a young man pursuing the philosopher's stone, a cloud is on his mind and he is in a hurry. Skilfully he moves from physical sketch to character assessment and triggering anecdote, using the technique of the efficient journalist, framing the subjects and nailing them by an illustrative episode.

If so inclined, he is capable of that specific style of presentation critics used to automatically admire. The early pages of his first attempt at autobiography, *Voyage to a Beginning*, demonstrate that on a purely literary level he is an outstanding communicator:

> As a child, my father had once joined a group of boys who entered a big store, probably Woolworth's, through the roof; I believe some of them were caught. I often daydreamed about my father's story, and spent hours imagining in detail exactly what I would take if I could get into Woolworth's by night. Chocolate, fountain pens, magnifying glasses, penknives, devices for looking behind you without turning round (called 'Seebackroscopes') and sheets of metal that made a noise like smashing glass when you dropped them. I was also particularly proud of some small red books I stole called 'Inquire Within for Everything' or some such title, giving all sorts of statistics and information: 'Do you know the seven highest building in the world?' 'Do you know the longest tunnel in the world?' (Wilson 1969, p.16)

To me, this vividly recalls the detailed inanity of the objects I craved as a child: lighters, tiny pipes – one dreadfully called 'A Wee Lady's Pipette' – Jetex motors, itching powder and grey pills that, if ignited, unfurled as acrid-smelling worms of ash called 'magic serpents'. I also recall the fabled 'Seebackroscope', finding its pointlessness strangely depressing, for it was impossible to see a thing through its meagre reflector.

More limited in scope than *DTSP*, *Voyage to a Beginning* (1969) is a concise, compelling account of Colin Wilson's early years and rise to fame, taking him up to the age of 35. Because it did not aim at epic inclusiveness, he was able to linger over key episodes, especially his early life in Leicester and the brief period in the RAF. But it is also less frank than its sexually rampageous successor; that was how the publisher, Cecil Woolf, preferred it. In some respects this was an advantage as the salacious bits in *DTSP*, although well handled, distract somewhat (the 'peek' experience overshadowing the 'peak' experience). They failed to hold my attention in the way that the literary and social observation did – although I dearly would have liked to meet that attractive yet sublimely bored German girl who lay down in the middle of the road, seemingly preferring a truck to run over her body rather than a man's hand. Quite a number of seduction scenes are summarised in a brisk, mechanic way, coloured by decorative phrases that hold a slight whiff of the Bible, "a tingling in my loins." These read straightforwardly yet some of them create an atmosphere of solemn, hangdog pointlessness, as if the author is pursuing a hedonism that leaves him ill at ease.

Most writers' autobiographies are static – simply because practising their trade means putting writing before living. This is not true of Colin Wilson whose regime had many breaks. Though of a stay-at-home disposition, he travelled, lectured and promoted his work in places like Russia, America, Japan, Norway, France and Germany. Hence he was projected into incidents and intrigues that draw in the reader, especially his clandestine meeting with the secretive Graham Greene at the Algonquin Hotel in New York who provided an insight into his shadow life, describing a souvenir shop that traded ghastly relics, like the hand of a dead airman, and showing no interest in the critical comments passed on his work in *The Strength to Dream* (1962).

There is also the bizarre story Kenneth Rexroth related about a woman he came across on a train from Oxford to London. Beneath her jet-black hair her face was dead-white; she had on a filthy black dress, greasily shiny and stained with food and sperm. Her breasts flopped, and she appeared not to be wearing pants either. Lying out full length on a carriage seat, she proceeded to read *Phaedo* in the Greek edition. When a respectable woman got on the train and expressed concern for her bedraggled aspect, enquiring, "Are you feeling well?" she received the reply, "Bugger off, bitch!" Two days later in London, an MP introduced the same girl to Rexroth, now looking attractive and elegantly dressed. "I want you to meet the most intelligent girl in London," he said (Wilson 2004, p.252).

Away from it all.

Through succeeding decades, Colin Wilson's presence on the literary horizon dimmed and flared up bearing a slightly different placard. The first wave of interest was based on *The Outsider* (1956), the second on crime and sex, the third on *The Occult* (1971) and the fourth on the ancient wisdom industry, all of which he loosely integrated by applying theories historicising consciousness and left-brain-versus-right-brain usage. Because each phase brought travel, meeting people, betrayal and adventure, a plethora of anecdotes scramble out of the pages of *DTSP* and jostle for attention. If it's lingerie glimpses you're after, there are plenty, verging from saucy to scandalous. If it's brainy stuff – lasering your thoughts into needlepoint beams and being rewarded with knockout insights – there's a lot of that, too. If it's character stuff, there's a Balzacian cast, many fitted out with interesting kinks and theories. In fact *DTSP* brims with curiosity and energy and stands as one of the liveliest autobiographies of the decade. It took quite a few knocks from reviewers who seemed incapable of settling down and enjoying an engrossing, intellectually stimulating work. God knows why – dozens of shriekingly dull memoirs receive polite plaudits every week and yet a highly entertaining, very readable book, was treated in an irritated, desultory tone, save by reviewers like Gary Lachman who got the point (Lachman 2004, p.28-29).

What is enjoyable is the stripped honesty of candid recall that at times takes on a nostalgic buoyancy. Ireland in the 1950s is recreated delightfully. There is an account of Colin and Joy escaping to the countryside and Dublin after the horsewhipping scene and the ensuing adverse publicity. In the capital they meet a friend of Samuel Beckett, Con Leventhal and his wife. "I got the feeling," he remarked, "that Con and Eithne regarded us as incredibly lucky, rather like Scott and Zelda Fitzgerald, and there in Dublin surrounded by happy drinkers, I must admit I felt incredibly lucky. In a pub on the quays we ate magnificent ham sandwiches and drank Guinness, and had salmon in Jammet's restaurant, in the days when salmon was still an expensive rarity. I found it hard to remember that, only the previous year, I had been struggling to raise money for the rent."

Certainly a magic wand had been waved over his life, a fairytale affirmation of his talent. And yet the full scope of Wilson's promise was largely untested. Frenzied publicity ensured that newspapers and magazines would ask him to comment on both trivial and important questions. Frequently he was invited to provide in excess what he actually had to offer which resulted in some edgy, over-opinionated pieces. Hence one article by him, in *The Daily Express*, was alleged to reveal the sombre, despairing soul of a young writer unable to discern a gleam of hope for the future of humankind.

This brooding young intellectual is not prominent in *DTSP*

which is often very funny. For instance, there is the account of the man whose writing was so manically and consistently porno-graphic that even Colin Wilson, usually dauntless about such matters, had to give up – after sampling it for half an hour, he felt he had been rolling around in his own dung like a pig. There is an amusing exchange when John Fowles tells him that *The Magus* was the worst film ever made, but Wilson argues that 'The Space Vampires' exceeded it in sheer gratuitous, monot-onous inanity (Wilson 2004, p.332). And then there is his first impression of W.H. Auden: "Auden really did look like something from *Famous Monsters of Film-land.*"(p.245)

In the Gothic vein

After the success of *The Outsider*, his subsequent books were coolly, often patronisingly received. The majority of reviewers of *DTSP* did not appear to have the slightest knowledge of the 1950s and even less of what Colin Wilson had been writing for the past fifty years. None had the faintest idea how to appraise his work or fit it into a recognisable milieu.

For Colin Wilson, far from being marginal, belongs to a discernible British tradition. Not the academically canned, claus-trophobically restricted 'Great Tradition' of F.R. Leavis, but something older and more culturally hospitable. Like William Blake, he occupies the slot of backstreet visionary or seer with considerable recondite expertise, exploring philosophy, crime and occultism for the insights they supply. Like Daniel Defoe, he is an author and journalist, not averse to mixing the high and low, religion, sex and skullduggery. There are other Englishmen to whom he may be peripherally related, the prophet, mystic, reformer and historian of ancient Egypt, Gerald Massey, possibly Havelock Ellis, the poet Percy Bysshe Shelley, with his chemistry set and obsession with probing nature's mysteries, Bernard Shaw in his *Übermensch* phase and Aldous Huxley who diagnosed Western man's loss of a spiritual dimension and envisioned a hallucinogenic utopia in his novel *Island*.

In his search for an elixir of existence, Wilson is as doughty as Professor Challenger who penetrated the hinterlands of Spiritualism in *The Land of Mist*. These areas of enquiry are indigenous rather than exotic to the British temperament as a perusal of the works of Peter Ackroyd will confirm. It is strange that John Bull – a pugnacious beef-eating stalwart – has become so emblematic of the race, together with the notion of England's "green and pleasant land", when the island supports a heterogeneous population of immigrants, dreamers, misfits, tradesmen, public school boys and red-faced farmers. But these are little more than agreeable stock characters rolled out for the literary tourist. So much else is going on. For instance, there is our fascination with ghosts and omens: Black Shuck the demon dog who roams the Norfolk, Suffolk and Essex coast, the startling apparitions of Borley Rectory, the shaggy-horned, monstrous Herne the Hunter who stalks Windsor Park, and Tutankhamen's curse that blighted the life of Lord Carnarvon. Underlying the Anglo-Saxon psyche are subterranean currents throwing up a miasmic spray of deranged luminaries like Christopher Marlowe, Dr John Dee, Lord Rochester, Thomas De Quincey, Lord Byron, Sir Richard Burton and Aleister Crowley. The world's greatest vampire story was generated by an Irishman residing in London, Bram Stoker, who conjured a fanged, cannibalistic, red-eyed monster, from whom the world of media has never recovered, and then there is history's most notorious slasher, Jack the Ripper – a personage lodged in the national psyche like an axe sunk in an oak.

And then there are remarkable oddities, like the supernatural archaeology pioneered by T.C. Lethbridge, whose ideas about ghosts, ghouls and spectral tape-recordings pervade that hefty paranormal compendium *Mysteries* (1978), and the evocative, startling visions of Neo-Romantic artists like Graham

Sutherland and Michael Ayrton. Colin Wilson's interest in perversion and female clothing is mirrored by the paintings of Stanley Spencer who similarly fetishised while composing massive, resurrection-themed oils of his beloved Cookham, showing it as a paradise on earth where, on Judgement Day, the living and the dead are restored and united in love and sexual fellowship.

There is also the tragic, suicidal strain in English music embodied in composers like Peter Warlock, who veered between rollicking drinking ditties and pieces like *The Curlew*, noted for its mournful, frozen bleakness. And then, opposed to such seductive strains, are the mad, violent creatures of legend and folklore, part solid, part imaginary, beings like Sweeney Todd the Demon Barber, Sawney Beane the Cannibal and Springheel Jack whose eyes sparked fire as he took tremendous leaps from street to rooftop. These nightmare creations are akin to gleeful escapees, leaping out of the fastness of repressed, workhouse minds into the open arena of expression. In addition, there are the burning idols of horror films like *The Wicker Man* as well as gloomy unsolved crimes like the 'Walton Murder' and 'Bella and the Wych Elm' that leave bloodstains on the smiling countryside. Such images and themes are liable to tumble out of any book by Colin Wilson, resulting in an exhilarating, intoxicating variousness that has the power to ensnare and overwhelm. In his long, trailing cloak of ideas, amid the gold dust of spiritual rejuvenation, there is so much extra ideological and speculative bric-a-brac. Above all, there is the unfailing pull of the sexual urge that promises more than it delivers:

> Like Georges Simenon, I have always been fascinated by the psychology of the people I've met. And it has always seemed to me that the most important key to the psychology of an individual has been how far he or she has achieved sexual fulfilment. I had noticed as a child

that my mother was fascinated by film stars like Clark Gable and Ronald Coleman, and it was obvious that, as far as she was concerned, they were a kind of masculine ideal, and the same applied to a great many working-class women friends of my mother. On the other hand, my father's favourite film star was Loretta Young – she obviously somehow embodied his ideal of the 'eternal feminine'. When I met Marilyn Monroe, I could see immediately why she represented the 'eternal feminine' for millions of males all over the world. She had that yielding, rather helpless look, as if saying to every male in the world: 'If you wanted to carry me off to bed, how could I resist?' (extracted from the manuscript of *Dreaming to Some Purpose*, not in the published version.)

As Jung pointed out, a curiosity about pornography, sexual desire, violent crime and scandal is a natural enough tendency. A healthy layering of rich, black, mental sludge makes a useful compost for the imagination, especially in a writer. It is helpful to early come to terms with such things in order that they should sink or ascend to their appropriate levels. Colin Wilson is curious about sex – for it strikes to the root of the personality. Just as a geologist is compelled to take an interest in cracks and fault-lines in layers of rock – the junctures where a strata may shear or become displaced – so must a student of psychology study the snapping-points of the personality. Sex often proves to be the point of psychosis or trauma, where character is liable to bare itself, either in breakdown or breakout.

Ritual in the Dark

Warped sexual desire running amok was a theme of Wilson's major novel *Ritual in the Dark* (1960). He was shrewd in choosing a thriller format, taking the tip from writers like Patrick

Hamilton, Graham Greene and Friedrich Dürrenmatt. It was the genre that hoarded the most possibilities for development. The quiet, family-centred novel of the pre-war years, revolving around events like an unexpected divorce disrupting middle-class harmony, died an inconspicuous death, as did the stream of consciousness epics of the 1940s. The thriller demanded something vital should be at stake, a man's life, a country's security, a statesman's honour – notions forcing the author towards crucial scenes and climaxes, and also, while suspending revelation, allowing space for speculation and discussion on more profound matters.

Not temperamentally a literary novelist, Wilson became a highbrow writer of pulp thrillers and science fiction with titles like *The World of Violence* and *The Mind Parasites*. This was in keeping, for spiritualism, gangster stories and reports of sex crimes in the *News of the World* had made up his early reading, deepened somewhat by astronomy textbooks and the formidably droll *Practical Knowledge for All*. It was only to be expected that, on attaining maturity, he would use a popular form for his own purposes as had G.K. Chesterton – a youthful idol of his – in the *The Man Who was Thursday*. Nowadays most promising novelists use the thriller form at some point in their careers. Martin Amis has produced pastiche American pulp and Sebastian Faulks taken up the assignment of 'James Bond' as well as turning out tense, psychology-laden chillers such as *Engleby*. William Boyd also writes strong, plot-driven fictions that explore fascinating psychological areas.

I remember asking my teacher at college if he had read *Ritual in the Dark*. He frowned and slowly asked, "Is that the book where this chap keeps taking his cycle clips on and off?" Obviously he did not know what to make of a story that concerned a bloodthirsty homosexual killer who, unusually, picked out female rather than male victims. Because of its bohemian milieu and relaxed sexual morals, reviewers adopted a tight-lipped, slightly hoity-toity tone, as though the very text steamed an aroma of carnal stains and burnt offerings from the gas-ring. The mix of ideas, the colliding dispositions of the characters, in which savage pessimism rubbed against arrested sexuality and soul-searching analysis, created a metaphysical tapestry in which mortuary philosophy mingled with something more upbeat and bracing. Back in 1960, it was damned as an upshot of the Angries, a kitchen sink drama in a London portrayed with greasy realism, but nearer the mark was *Daily Express*: "Never, since the time of Dickens, has murder been treated in a book of such size and seriousness." Reading it today, I would tend to class it not as kitchen sink so much as Post Empire Gothic, the product of an essentially romantic, yearning imagination, thrilled by the negative charge of violence, melodrama and perverted sexuality and yet seeks a charge of equivalent potency at the positive pole.

This voyaging for spiritual shores and hinterlands was evident in *Eagle and Earwig* (1965) and *The Craft of the Novel* (1975). Wilson formulated the idea of 'existential criticism', meaning a novelist should possess a life manifesto – a notion of how his story might creditably grapple with the metaphysical and social problems of the age. If this sounds over-prescriptive, for some young people growing up in the 1960s, it provided an inspirational spearhead, spotlighting an eccentric yet stimulating range of titles, from Russian classics to the notes of a drug-taker and obscure Zen fables that confounded as much as they illuminated. Where other critics obfuscated, Wilson *communicated*.

Instead of the traditional standbys of the Bronte sisters, Jane Austen, George Eliot, Thomas Hardy and Charles Dickens, he chose an exotic curriculum, overturning the apple barrel of world literature and spilling out titles like *L'Enfer* (*The Inferno*) by Henri Barbusse, the *Diary of Vaslav Nijinsky, Steppenwolf* by Herman Hesse, *A Glastonbury Romance* by John Cowper Powys,

A Voyage to Arcturus by David Lindsay and many another weirdly appealing masterwork. With his analysis of anti-life novels in *The Craft of the Novel* comes an appraisal of *The Unbearable Bassington* by Saki that leaves one eager to obtain the work. This openness rendered him an exhilarating, jackdaw critic, unpredictable but accessible, adopting the wide-ranging style of George Orwell who at random dealt with *King Lear*, children's comics and the confessions of Salvador Dali.

The brimming goblet

Modifying Wilson's romantic imagination is an Anglo-Saxon heritage of common sense and stoicism detectable in Augustan figures like Samuel Johnson, Tobias Smollet and Henry Fielding. Wilson often cites Wordsworth's undiluted joy in nature, but he was strongly touched by the Edwardian era, in which G.K. Chesterton wrote about the feeling of receiving "absurd good news". Another author of that period, in whom the germ of this message can be found, is the novelist and essayist Ernest Raymond who brought out a book of essays *Through Literature To Life* (1928), the last two chapters of which contain two alternating viewpoints, that of tragedy 'Lacrimæ Rerum' (The Tears of Things) and that of celebration 'The Joyous Overplus'.

Ernest Raymond's style flows. There is a brimming-goblet quality to his prose as he baritones his supreme love of existence, taking a breath to jam in quotes from identically delighted or mystic scribes, including Richard Jefferies, John Masefield and, quite naturally, himself – for he was a novelist of distinction. Essentially Raymond claims that optimism and joy is life's natural outlook. Whatever tragedy may be lying in wait, the human personality is prone to disperse it like warm air does a cloud. "Something instinctive and elemental," he wrote,

rises up in me to resist and rebut such doctrines; and as I

shall strive to show you, I believe that indignant force to be life itself, by the very instantaneousness of its demurrer, more good than bad. I can hearken to the whole argument for despair and admit its cogency, and yet – how do you answer this? – I *enjoy* the argument, I declare the talk to have been magnificent, I beg my opponent to continue it for it is too early to go to bed yet, I point out that he is as thrilled and delighted as I am, I say that there is no pleasanter way of spending the night than this: "Let us on with the tale," I say, "for what a joy there is in cudgelling our brains for words and what a keen relish when we have shaped them well!" (Raymond, 1928, p.213)

Herein lies a response which Wilson does not dwell on unduly: people's propensity to read gloomy, tragic tales and feel uplifted, like the manner in which, for instance, they might discuss a fresh presentation of Shakespeare's *Macbeth*, deriving pleasure in the acting and production rather than being oppressed by the contents. John Ballard regarded *The Naked Lunch* as a hilarious shocker, an innovative masterpiece, despite what many would see as the revolting nature of its contents; also William Golding concluded that, as so many eagerly devoured his grim fables, with their implacable, ruthless endings, they must possess impregnably cheerful dispositions. If they were truly open to the message he was sending out to the world, they would have long ago killed themselves.

(Of course, reading a tragedy like *Tess of the d'Urbervilles* is not 'tragic' in itself. The novel is aesthetically organised so as to metamorphose into a haunting portrayal of how cruel fate can be. It is 'beautiful' in the sense a Pre-Raphaelite or Victorian painting of Ophelia floating in her death-throes is. This is very much a question of relative sensitivities. Some are profoundly affected by the miseries and privations of others: Simone Weil, hearing of the fate of her fellow citizens in Nazi-occupied

France, felt such empathy that she adopted their diet, literally starving herself, living through what most would 'distance' or objectify.)

In summary Ernest Raymond declares:

> In all living things there is a boundless excess of life over the needs of living: that is the fundamental fact. And this ebullient excess, in trees and hedgerows, bursts into flower; in larks and nightingales into a cataract of song; in children into romping and shrieking and laughter...and though in a few men it would seem to be totally perverted, and though in all of us it is occasionally misused, yet a thousand times more often than not it is bearing us on waves of happiness so soothing and serene that we mark them no more than we mark the hours they fill, and thus in the last audit of our lives we credit them with immeasurably less than their due. (*ibid*, p.215)

Like Wilson again, Raymond emphasises a sense of purpose is necessary to human happiness:

> That we are happy when we are making something – that we are near to complete bliss when we are in the throes of creation – is shown to us by a baby making a mud-pie in the garden, a schoolboy bowed over his fretwork tools, or Gibbon writing the last words of his "History." (*ibid*, p.248)

Despite the markedly pastoral Edwardian context, this is broadly Wilsonian in flavour, but nobody would class it as philosophy. It is very much a playful essay, a surge of verbal foam, the type of thing that Chesterton or Belloc might throw off to enliven the pages of some middlebrow weekly.

Colin Wilson's optimism taps a different source, arriving at a parallel insight through the back door of French existentialism. Added to the philosophical discipline are observations from the behavioural sciences and Abraham Maslow on the hierarchies of need and, more significantly, the 'peak experience', creating a metaphysics that challenges Sartre's sense of absurdity with an affirmation – a universe irradiated by values and meanings that man imposes through achieving his own freedom. Colin Wilson does not say each individual should politically commit himself but rather raise his consciousness in order to make the right decisions. This is a striking proposition and genuine English offshoot of continental existentialism.

Mystical existentialism

Linguistic insights tend to be tautological in nature. 'I think therefore I am' requires only the first two words to fulfil its implication. Thousands of novels and textbooks are published that, when analysed, tirelessly elaborate pithy observations like "most men lead lives of quiet desperation" because it is the nature of language to dig deeper into itself, endlessly elaborating, finding equivalencies of sensation and metaphor as opposed to its more important function of getting round whatever new phenomenon appears to be entering the domain of knowledge, especially when a scientific or perceptual breakthrough is extending the boundary lines.

Basically arguments amount to claiming 'things are like this' as opposed to 'things are like that'. So when Colin Wilson proposes reality – whatever that is – to be more radiantly alluring than the manner in which we, through our bad habits, happen to view it, we may legitimately argue, though both his and our viewpoints, lacking full possession of the facts, will be open to doubt.

The key reference is on p.173 of *DTSP* when, in conversation with Albert Camus, Colin Wilson states the answer to the absurdity of existence lies in the mystical affirmation the former expressed in a story in *Exile and the Kingdom*. Surely, he told Camus, here is a rejoinder to human contingency or insignificance? But far from agreeing, Camus merely gestured towards a teddy boy in the street, saying, "No, what is good for him must be good for me also."

Wilson protested, saying the teddy boy was a false analogy. If Einstein had adopted that criterion, there would have been no Theory of Relativity.

The argument goes deeper than a teddy boy's indifference. Ignoring the political dimension, Wilson believes a more authentic, clearer-sighted engagement with daily life may be obtained through a healthy, self-realizing attitude. But Camus appears to think that, while the mind may impose fascinating constructions on the phenomenal world, nothing tangible supports them. So far as he's concerned, each thinker is confined to a solipsistic bubble – whatever's out there is an enigma. Wilson rejects this, holding man is a creator of meanings. Each day he may discover a new validation or affirmation whereas Camus denies there's a universal solution here, only a euphoric delusion conferring a temporary sense of well-being. "He who despairs over an event is a coward," he once wrote, "but he who holds hope for the human condition is a fool."

It is easy to take Wilson's side – for Camus did let slip a hint of parsimonious optimism. He might have cold-shouldered Wilson's suggestion because he viewed his story as artistic prose rather than philosophy – a discipline isolating the thinking person from the average citizen. He might even have extended the domain of renunciation, asserting man cannot truly understand himself anymore than fish a can step out of the water and become a student of marine biology. And yet, if we are to believe Darwin, that is exactly what fish did, evolve into another species, leaving evidence of its other selves in fossil form. When Shaw pointed out in *Back to Methuselah*, natural selection appears to have the ability to "turn a pond full of amoebas into the French academy", he was not merely being witty but providing an epigrammatic précis of the theory's implications. Hence, from a futurologist's standpoint, many a fabulous potential awaits manifestation.

Poisoning the cultural wells

Theoretical cures for the ills of the world have never been in short supply. The gargantuan problem has always been creating a political structure by which any one of them could be *implemented*. Being impervious to regimes and borderlines, Colin Wilson believes the peak experience capable of solving most or all of human ills. It is all a question of improving oneself from within and then making manifest the inner transformation.

Lack of a positive outlook, he believes, stunted the outlooks of both Camus and Sartre. To that may be added the accusation that writers like Samuel Beckett and Graham Greene "poison the cultural wells" by their plays and novels which lack optimism. But is optimism in need of promoting? Surely it is already implicit in the genetic code. Nature is heedlessly positive, blindly ebullient and forward-rushing, expressing the joyous irresponsibility of maggots boiling in a carcass. In *The World as Will and Idea*, Schopenhauer found himself drawing back from its ruthless fertility. Those humans who feel endemically miserable about their lot commit suicide early or, alternatively, opt for a regime of medication.

In several of his stories, Anton Chekov gave voice to the joy of existence, while retaining a pessimistic outlook because he saw people *en masse* behaving destructively and insensitively. Yet he continued to fight his corner and suggest how things might be better handled. Compare his salutary forethought with the blind optimism of Hitler and Stalin who managed to sweep their policies through unopposed, as do present-day business magnates who opt for growth whatever the cost, plundering the world's dwindling resources under the impression that no human price will be exacted for such random ransacking. Beside such massive infiltrations, the minor glooms of the literary sty are negligible.

Interpreted rationally, to justify such implicit faith, the optimism Colin Wilson promotes has to be of an adroitly discriminative 'superman' brand rather than the agent of chaos I have depicted in the foregoing, presumably stressing the literary angle because the written word remains a primary conveyor of culture and reform.

Beyond the small print of causal accountability, his message shows people how to direct and raise the quality of their lives, using the imagination as a tool that can be honed and adapted to overcome obstacles and achieve practical goals. Every major scientific and social breakthrough has its origin in a thought process. In such a sense, peak experiences and surges of spiritual replenishment have been fuelling and inspiring social and political changes in healthy minds for centuries, sometimes winning through and sometimes, possibly, cancelling each other out. It says a great deal for the achievement of a single writer, hardly born in the most propitious of circumstances, that not only has he produced an enormous, distinguished literary oeuvre, he has devised a *raison d'etre* for the continued advancement and progress of humanity. In an age of science and of scepticism, he has flung open the dawn portals, revealing the magical potential of human kind and declaring that it is not the personal 'I' that matters but the moments when we lose the personal and take forward our freedom in the cause of the species, creating more contexts in which we may develop and refine our capabilities, so that humans will eventually achieve the legendary stature attributed to the occupants of Atlantis.

References:

Lachman, Gary (2004) 'More Life, Not Less' *Independent on Sunday ABC Section* (June 6, 2004).

Raymond, Ernest (1928) *Through Literature to Life*. London: Cassell & Company.

Wilson, Colin (1969) *Voyage to a Beginning*. London: Cecil & Amelia Woolf.

Wilson, Colin (2004) *Dreaming to Some Purpose*. London: Century.

Super Consciousness: the Quest for the Peak Experience (2009)

Super Consciousness: the literary crux

Geoff Ward

In Chapter 13 of *Super Consciousness*, Colin Wilson describes how in 1947, at the age of 16, he discovered the *Bhagavad Gita* and meditated every morning 'focusing my mind intently on the identity of Atman with Brahman'. To his delight, the meditative practices worked and, as he walked to his work as a laboratory assistant at the school where, not long before, he had been a pupil, he felt 'curiously buoyant and optimistic'.

> Walking through the slum streets where my father had grown up, I would pause to look with fascination at a cracked windowsill or a battered front door. (Wilson, 2009, p. 182)

Compare the following passage from *Backwater* (1915), the second of the 13 chapter-volumes that make up Dorothy Richardson's monumental novel *Pilgrimage*.

> What was life? Either playing a part all the time in order to be amongst people in the warm, or standing alone with the strange real true feeling – alone with a sort of edge of reality on everything; even on quite ugly common things – cheap boarding houses, face-towels and blistered window frames. (Richardson, 1967, p. 320)

Richardson is acutely aware of the importance of such revealing moments. In *Pilgrimage*, the narrative often contrasts the apparent futility and negativity of existence with the uplifting power of transcendent ecstasies which make the central character, Miriam Henderson, feel truly alive. That 'edge of reality on everything' is just what the teenage Wilson had discovered, too, as he walked through the back-streets of Leicester – early intimations of that gateway to 'super-consciousness': the 'peak experience' or 'epiphany', the elusive mechanisms of which he has sought to identify in a lifelong endeavour to confirm humankind's evolutionary potential; in *Super Consciousness*, key elements from this endeavour are drawn together from his writings over five decades.

In the 1960s, the American psychologist Abraham Maslow took up the study of transcendent or intensity experiences, introducing the term 'peak experience' and, in subsequent decades, Wilson built on Maslow's work to establish a theory for the attainment of an intensified or higher consciousness, and its inducement.

The question of how people can achieve these strange ecstatic moments of inner freedom, of sheer delight, when we feel our energies are more than adequate to cope with any challenge – those moments of 'wonderful optimism about the future, the feeling that life is infinitely complex and infinitely exciting' (Wilson, 2009, p. 4) – is central in Wilson's vast body of work. Such brief occasions of intense well-being are in stark contrast to normal consciousness, in which we seem to sense our energies are never quite up to the mark, or feel ourselves to be in the grip of impersonal forces which are much stronger than ourselves.

Peak experiences, or epiphanies, have the potential to alter a person's values and outlook on existence. Their purpose seems to be to reveal something that everyday consciousness and the worldly dimension cannot, to bring about an affir-mation of life, to 'move more closely to a perfect identity' (Maslow, 1974, p. 66), and create a sense of "fulfilled purpose" (Wilson, 1990, p. 149). They are enhancing and enriching to life:

'they point forward; they are positive; they are benign' (Maxwell and Tschudin, 1990, p. 40).

I must say at the outset that I believe epiphany and the peak experience – along with transcendent ecstasy, mystical experience, cosmic consciousness, awakening experience or breakthrough or power consciousness, to give some of the other terms used – merely to be different names for what is essentially the same phenomenon undergone by individuals at varying degrees of intensity. Even if the 'oneness with the universe' feeling of the mystical experience may be absent from the secular epiphany, it still provides the subject with a moment of profound insight or revelation and, in my view, the respective experiences are intimately related.

Throughout the history of literature, art and philosophy there are references to and examples of the value of this experience which, to me, seems linked closely to the attainment of selfhood, that quality that constitutes one's individuality. William Wordsworth spoke of 'spots of time', Thomas Hardy of 'moments of vision', James Joyce of 'epiphanies', and Virginia Woolf and Dorothy Richardson of 'moments of being'.

Glance through the index of *Super Consciousness* and you will find the names of no fewer than sixty novelists and poets – from Auden to Joyce, from Kafka to Yeats. Although there is a chapter headed 'Philosophy' there is not one headed 'Literature' because Wilson's text is so infused with literary references (up to the mid-twentieth century) illustrative of his theme; he has done us a service by identifying and bringing together in this and previous books an important group of writers connected with the implications of 'breakthrough consciousness'.

I want to consider, in Wilson's terms, first the significance of the peak experience, or epiphany, in the novel during the 'modernist' period of the early twentieth century, because this saw the climax of its increasing consequence in literature during the previous century, and then how it relates to the moral sense as I detect it within existential criticism – and what this ought to mean for literature in the 21st century: what I term the literary crux.

For Wilson, the evolution of the novel since the eighteenth century has been bound up with the evolution of consciousness. He quotes George Bernard Shaw who, in *Back to Methuselah*, describes art as a 'magic mirror' which reflects the soul, but Wilson adds that this mirror has an even more useful function: to reveal the direction of human evolution. The literary epiphany is indispensable to this idea, and the great works of modernism turn on it, their task being to 'redeem, essentially or existentially, the formless universe of contingency' (Bradbury and MacFarlane, 1987, p. 50). Epiphany is thus an important aspect of the novel's potential for indicating the future trajectory of human consciousness, of our 'becoming'.

Marghanita Laski, in her investigation of the ecstatic experience (Laski, 1961, p. 1), pre-echoed Wilson when she asked: 'Was ecstasy perhaps a foretaste of a next development of man when knowledge would be wordless and greater?' Interestingly, Laski, in reference to the 'capital letter device', the use of initial capitals for hypostasised nouns, gives Wilson's *The Outsider* (1956) as an example of how 'in English writing today among literate people this practice seems to be almost confined to those who are writing to prove that ecstatic experiences prove the existence of a Supernatural Reality, and to meet with this device is to know with reasonable assurance what kind of book it is one has encountered' (Laski, 1961, p. 240).

From the Romantics at the turn of the eighteenth century, one can trace the path of epiphanic revelation and the concomitant elevation of consciousness through the poetry of Emily Bronte, Tennyson, Browning, Gerard Manley Hopkins, Dante Gabriel Rossetti, Hardy, Yeats, Eliot and to Ezra Pound and the other Imagists. It takes various forms – Coleridge's 'flashes', Browning's 'infinite moments', Hopkins' 'inscape' or Eliot's 'still point' – the strong similarities between them far outweighing any differences, and indicating a common attempt to define and unify the self with a similar centre, or to gain access to the type of values and state of being which super-consciousness embraces.

Epiphany is an important factor in the continuation of the prophetic strand in Romantic poetry which refers to a future paradise; both Wordsworth and Coleridge follow such a chiliastic quest. Existence, in their vision, tends to 'evolve and ascend [...] up to a point in time where it fuses entirely with a transcendent, ideal state' (Roppen, 1956, p. 174).

In the novel before 1900, instances of epiphany are isolated, but they can be found in *Tristram Shandy* by Laurence Sterne, *Shirley* by Charlotte Bronte, *Daniel Deronda* by George Eliot, *Born in Exile* by George Gissing, and *Jude the Obscure* by Thomas Hardy.

The principal writer to extend the meaning of the word was James Joyce in *Stephen Hero*, the forerunner to *A Portrait of the Artist as a Young Man* (1916). When Stephen witnesses a 'trivial incident' in Eccles Street, Dublin, involving a snatch of conversation between a young couple on the steps of a house, it makes him think of collecting such moments in a 'book of epiphanies'.

By an epiphany he meant a sudden spiritual manifestation, whether in the vulgarity of speech or of gesture or in a memorable phase of the mind itself. He believed that it was for the man of letters to record these epiphanies with extreme care, seeing that they themselves are the most delicate and evanescent of moments. (Joyce, 1966, pp. 215-216)

Morris Beja modified this into his own 'working definition'.

A sudden spiritual manifestation, whether from some object, scene, event, or memorable phase of the mind – the manifestation being out of proportion to the significance or strictly logical relevance of whatever produces it. (Beja, 1971, p. 18)

Beja distinguishes modern epiphany from the traditional visionary mode, and the 'classical scene of recognition' (anagnorisis), by offering two criteria: the Criterion of Incongruity, in that the epiphany is not strictly relevant to what produces it, and the Criterion of Insignificance, whereby the epiphany can be triggered by a trivial incident or object (Beja, p. 16).

While one of the reasons why the epiphanic experience became secularised may well have been the decline in the observance of conventional religion taking place at the time, it could still be said to represent a species-wide need for an alternative form of spiritual expression, not in the sense of belief in any religion, but in terms of an effect on the human spirit as opposed to physical or material things.

The fact that certain novelists from 1900 decided to integrate transcendent experiences into their narratives is therefore significant in terms of the times in which they were writing. The seeds of the kinds of changes they were witnessing, involving social and cultural rupture, had been sown in the last decades of the nineteenth century, and the secular epiphany was to act as a bulwark against encroaching pessimism, disorientation and a growing sense of meaninglessness in a rapidly changing world. Appropriately, as Wilson says, the peak experience is 'a sudden surge of meaning' (1972, p.5).

Joyce, Dorothy Richardson and Virginia Woolf all recognised the 'destructive element' in life posited by their contemporary Joseph Conrad (who preferred not to consider the implications of epiphany) and so pursued the luminous image for an answer to the problems posed by a world seemingly without order, meaning or belief. All four writers imply a super-consciousness acquired during moments of enlightenment, those 'gleams like the flashing of a shield', as Wordsworth wrote.

At this time, epiphany was an important presence also in the works of a number of American, European and other British authors, for example, Henry James, Edith Wharton, E. M. Forster, D. H. Lawrence, Thomas Wolfe, William Faulkner, Anton Chekhov, Marcel Proust and Hermann Hesse, as well as the New Zealander Katherine Mansfield.

Conrad's attitude to the moment of vision, that 'pulsation of the artery', to use Blake's phrase, which occurs frequently for Conrad's characters, especially his surrogate narrator Marlow, reflects but peculiarly reverses the thought of Nietzsche, the general movement of which was towards the affirmation of life because what Nietzsche regarded as a contradictory force – perhaps what Conrad pessimistically saw as a 'remorseless process' – demonstrated its capacity for, and its constant need of, the rapt vision for its redemption (Nietzsche, 1993, p. 25). Wilson asserts that literary pessimism is 'quite simply a mistake, a logical error that leaves something important out of account' (2009, p. 115), that it poisons our cultural heritage and impedes human evolution; no writer is justified in declaring that human existence is meaningless, he states (1998, p. 298-99).

In the project of selfhood, epiphany stands in contrast to efforts in modernist literature to 'deconstruct the self'. Both modernist and postmodernist texts, paradoxically, contain simultaneously a will to strong selfhood and an anarchistic urge to dissolve the self. Modernist epiphany gains its significance within a larger struggle for the very meaning of the self in which an allegiance to traditional notions of the soul conflict with a vision of a dispersed, transient emotional life that has no unifying centre (MacGowan, 1990).

It is my view that the ideas of Wilson and Maslow serve to elevate the importance of epiphany in literature to a role which demonstrates the potential for the further evolution of human consciousness and the strengthening of the identity of the individual. The final chapter of *The Outsider* (1956) and the Autobiographical Introduction and first chapter of Wilson's next book, *Religion and the Rebel* (1957), herald his detailed consideration of the peak experience from 1969 when he was asked to write a biography of Maslow.

Maslow says the peak experience is felt as a self-validating, self-justifying moment which carries its own intrinsic value with it: 'There seems to be a kind of dynamic parallelism or isomorphism between the inner and the outer [...] as the essential Being of the world is perceived by the person, so also does he concurrently come closer to his own Being (to his own perfection, or being more perfectly himself)' (Maslow, 1968, p. 95). Maslow argues that precisely those persons who have the clearest and strongest identity arising out of the peak experience are the ones most able to transcend the ego or the self and to become selfless, or who are at least relatively selfless and egoless.

For Maslow, the peak experience was essentially a passive experience, of being overwhelmed by ecstasy, and he thought that it could not be induced, but Wilson is sure it can. He has posited a 'ladder of selves', a concept to which he returns in *Super Consciousness*; assisted by the peak experience and the recognition of potential that it brings, consciousness can climb this ladder towards states of pure delight and 'Faculty X', when the mind seems so energised that other times and places become as real as the here and now.

Wilson says his life has been given an inner consistency by the search for the formula of the intensity experience, which can be sustained by 'sheer perception of meaning' (2009, p. 208), and for which the human capacity is greater than we realise: 'We are misusing ourselves out of ignorance of our capacities.' The process of creation is a matter of driving oneself, of *creating* oneself, but the 'passive fallacy' means that a person feels somehow permanent and unchangeable; he or she should not accept this low condition as normal. The 'trick' of mystical consciousness, the mental act that needs to be mastered, is to make consciousness *stand still* by an act of attention (1970, pp. 224-27).

Clearly, Wilson rejects Derridean attacks on the 'metaphysics of presence' in favour of a humanistic criticism of literature which elucidates an original meaning, or centre, of a novel which can be approached, and sometimes reached, through perceptive reading; narrative enacts a meaning to which epiphany is crucial. Wilson, of course, is the founder of the optimistic 'new existentialism', an offshoot of which is the existential criticism of which he has been a proponent for half a century, and which requires both close reading of a literary text and insight into the psychology of the author. The standard of value of existential criticism is existence, the opposite of the limiting personality.

It is ironic, to say the least, that Wilson, who was probably the first critic in the twentieth century to spell out a literary theory of any kind, should have been swamped by the multi-faceted explosion in literary theorists from the 1970s who, to their shame, failed utterly to acknowledge his work. The general turn to theory in academia was the revolution, and not the techniques of existential thinking which Wilson hoped would become commonplace in England and America when he wrote his seminal essay on existential criticism for the *Chicago Review* in 1959 (reprinted, with slight amendments, in his 1965 book, *Eagle and Earwig* – in fact, Wilson's first reference to existential criticism came in an article on Aldous Huxley in *The London Magazine* in 1958).

As an ideas-led critic, rather than a text-led one, Wilson stands in the illustrious line of Sidney, Wordsworth, Coleridge, George Eliot and Henry James, all of whom tackled the big general issues affecting literature which later also came to be among the concerns of critical theorists in the late decades of the twentieth century.

Wilson has said he believes existentialism to be the key to the creative development of literature. While his existentialist criticism embraces humanistic formalism, it takes it up another notch – to evaluate literature by assessing it in terms of its capacity to satisfy the depths of human need, to clarify the image of 'what we are yet to become' on the evolutionary spiral. Wilson wants to know what, fundamentally, an artist is saying, what concepts of human purpose lie in the basic assumptions of the work, and how far the work succeeds in revealing existence as potentiality. Indeed, a deeply demanding form of criticism, but one which is just as relevant in today's world as when it was originally conceived, if not more so.

In the 1920s, Rudolph Otto, the German historian of religion, wrote about his view of overpowering mystical experience as a non-rational paradigm, similar to the effect in extreme cases of music or the erotic, and inexpressible in language, but as able to induce a sense of mystery and awe capable of overthrowing human hubris – the arrogant, amoral sense that we and our technology represent the pinnacle of existence. Otto used the term 'numinous' to describe this transcendent reality which could break down the everyday sense of reality, and which could be both terrifying and fascinating.

Steve Taylor, in his Wilsonian study of the 'awakening experience', to which he brings a new moral imperative, lists a series of 'wake-up' calls for the vexed times in which we are living (Taylor, 2010, pp. 229-30): we need to wake up so that we can free ourselves from social chaos and conflict, stop abusing the Earth's life-support systems, and participate in a 'universal consciousness'. Taylor seems to accept that consciousness has a spiritual function, evidenced crucially in the peak experience, through which, he believes, evolution is impelling us to wake up – but he warns that if we do not do so collectively, we may not survive as a species.

If one agrees that super-consciousness, in this way, points to the possibility of a step forward in human evolution (thereby revealing its relevance to existential criticism), then that entails a moral position because of the presumption that the change would be for the better, the *summun bonum*. Like all great philosophers and artists, Wilson 'takes us into the world of our values' (Dossor, 1990, p. 8); in other words, Wilson expands our moral imagination, and the idea that our evolving consciousness fosters the good is implicit in his critique. To proceed otherwise, of course, would be to take a pessimistic route – anathema to the new existentialism. Wilson, following Gratiano's advice to Antonio, ever urges us to 'fish not with this melancholy bait'.

An intensified and more comprehensible awareness of values can be attained through the ability of the arts to qualitatively increase human vitality by providing a keener perception of the world. Art can expand the range of individual freedom by increasing awareness of possibilities for action and modes of human relationships beyond those that present themselves in the quotidian, something of which Wilson is acutely aware in his statement that the novelist's task is to use a 'wide-angle lens' to make readers aware of their freedom (Wilson, 1990, p. 222).

Of course, art can also be seen as morally questionable or deleterious, even as curbing freedom, by pessimistically presenting debased visions of human nature, for example, and cynically perpetuating stereotypes or mere fashions of the moment, or pursuing image over substance. But my interest here is to reflect on the positive potential for art, and literature in particular, to direct us to morally serious and sagacious consideration of the 'human condition'. This, of course, goes beyond the common connotation of morality, as referring to standards of behaviour and conduct which change as society changes, to the question of the *moral value* of literature: how it justifies our readership, and what it can and ought to be.

Mark William Roche, in his magisterial and timely discussion of this very issue (Roche, 2004), is concerned with literature as a teacher of virtue. The arts and humanities involve themselves with the prospects and fate of the human race, which are now increasingly influenced by technology; in a technological age, literature gains in importance precisely to the extent that our sense of intrinsic value is lost.

Roche traces the current crisis in the humanities back to the separation of art and morality when, a century ago, modernity was losing its belief in a religious or moral frame – significantly, just when Joyce and others were using epiphany as a central artifice and an organising narrative principle, attempting not simply to record the experience but to produce and reproduce it. Dorothy Richardson goes furthest on the scale of evolving consciousness by enacting, through her protagonist Miriam Henderson, the Wilsonian ideal of being able to induce and sustain the peak experience.

As an analogue of the human person, a literary work interests us, says Roche, because it 'provides a vision, a critique, an epiphany, a mood, something of value to a broader consciousness' (p. 24), and he laments the loss from literary criticism (due to the rise of theory) of artwork aesthetics, of intelligibility, and of the 'existential interest' (pp. 73-74). He makes a plea for the return to literary criticism of the aesthetic experience – the 'psychological mechanisms' of which are identical to the mystical experience, says Wilson (1970, p. 16) – and the urgent reinstatement of the integrative or 'existential moment' which penetrates to the essence of literature, arousing in the reader 'a moment of pleasure, enthusiasm, excitement, elation or ecstasy' (Roche, p. 84); in other words, a moment of super-consciousness. This suggests to me a possible new direction in reception theory whereby we can envisage a relationship between narrator and reader where the former passes on the qualities of the epiphanic experience to the latter, whose consciousness is raised to the potentialities therein.

We can see how Wilson's existential criticism which, as I have suggested, stems from a deeply moral standpoint as it advocates positive human potential, complements Roche's position on the existential worth of literature, 'not only the value of the existential relationship to literature but also appreciation of literature as an end in itself and recognition of those virtues elicited in aesthetic experience but neglected in modernity' (p. 257).

Like Wilson's, Roche's existentialism is optimistic, standing out against the endemic pessimism and defeatism of our times, and the tendency to reject substance and meaning in favour of image and ephemera. For Wilson, meaning – which shines through powerfully in the peak experience – is the antidote to pessimism and to the sense of the absurdity and pointlessness of existence.

Consciousness was barred from serious scientific research for most of the last century, but today it is a swiftly growing area of study for psychologists, philosophers and neuroscientists, although their studies are far from conclusive about the nature of it, and consciousness is frequently referred to as 'the last great mystery of science'.

One recent approach has been to argue that throughout evolution there have been emergent properties in the brain and in consciousness, with underlying biochemical explanations (Watson, 2006, p. 1014). It may be that such novel properties, leading to the formation of an evolutionary substrate, develop in the brain at a certain stage of complexity, and that the incidence of the peak experience over the past two centuries is a demonstration of one such faculty, with the purpose of taking brain functions to a higher level. Evolution, after all, is cleverer than us; if, as under quantum physics, consciousness can be taken as a gestalt, as being a universal field in which humans participate rather than a discrete property of individual minds, then it could be that the 'book of nature' is preparing us for a new role in its next chapter on our species.

The theoretical neurobiologist Bernard Baars seems to be

thinking of epiphany when he argues that one reason for the split in the twentieth century between the sciences and the humanities was that the sciences simply ignored 'all the wonderful things that the humanities were saying about consciousness, James Joyce being an example of that' (Blackmore, 2005, p. 22).

Only now, a hundred years after Joyce, does that rift show signs of being bridged, a bridge which, I would say, Wilson has been building in his own work, fiction and non-fiction, for fifty years with his view that our personal development depends very much on experiences of heightened perception.

For Wilson, the German philosopher Edmund Husserl (1859-1938), the founder of phenomenology who had a huge influence on European thought, is 'the greatest of modern thinkers'. Wilson's positive existentialism is based on Husserl's method which recognised that consciousness is intentional, that it is active not passive, that when we see something we fire our attention (*noēsis*) at the object (*noēma*) like an arrow, indicating that there must be an 'archer', a 'real me', who shoots the arrow. Read Shelley's *Ode to the West Wind* and you will be stirred by the 'phenomenological vision', says Wilson. But Heidegger and Sartre undid Husserl's good work and dragged philosophy back into confused pessimism (Wilson, 2009, p. 169-75).

Wilson wants us to see the novel, in particular, as an instrument of intentionality with the capacity, through that heightened perception, to extend us in the direction of selfhood, the true purpose of the novelist being 'to liberate the human imagination and to give man a glimpse of what he could become' (1990, p. 241).

Under this idea, the literary epiphany reveals itself as a vital experiment into future consciousness. Wilson consistently draws our attention to this; in so doing, he highlights the connection between literature and the values desperately needed in a time of moral crisis, and marks out a crucial role for literature in the 21st century.

References:

Beja, Morris, *Epiphany in the Modern Novel: Revelation as Art* (London: Peter Owen, 1971)

Blackmore, Susan, *Conversations on Consciousness* (Oxford: Oxford University Press, 2005)

Bradbury, Malcolm, and James MacFarlane, eds., *Modernism: 1890-1930* (London: Penguin, 1987)

Dossor, Howard F., *Colin Wilson: The Man and his Mind* (Shaftesbury: Element Books, 1990)

Joyce, James, *Stephen Hero*, ed. by Theodore Spencer (London: Four Square, 1966)

Laski, Marghanita, *Ecstasy: A Study of Some Secular and Religious Experiences* (London: The Cresset Press, 1961)

MacGowan, John, 'From Pater to Wilde to Joyce: Modernist Epiphany and the Soulful Self' in *Texas Studies in Literature and Language*, 32.3 (1990), 418

Maslow, Abraham H., *Toward a Psychology of Being*, 2nd. edition (New York: D. Van Nostrand Company, 1968)

Maslow, Abraham H., *Religions, Values and Peak Experiences* (New York: The Viking Press, 1974)

Maxwell, Meg, and Verena Tschudin, *Seeing the Invisible: Modern Religious and Other Transcendent Experiences* (Harmondsworth: Arkana, 1990)

Nietzsche, Friedrich, *The Birth of Tragedy* (Harmondsworth: Penguin, 1993)

Richardson, Dorothy M., *Pilgrimage I, Pointed Roofs, Backwater, Honeycomb* (London: J. M. Dent & Sons, 1967)

Roche, Mark William, *Why Literature Matters in the 21st Century* (New Haven and London: Yale University Press, 2004)

Roppen, Georg, *Evolution and Poetic Belief: A Study in Some Victorian and Modern Writers* (Oslo: Oslo University Press,

1956)

Taylor, Steve, *Waking from Sleep: Why Awakening Experiences Occur and How to Make them Permanent* (London: Hay House, 2010)

Watson, Peter, *Ideas: A History from Fire to Freud* (London: Phoenix, 2006)

Wilson, Colin, *Poetry and Mysticism* (London: Hutchinson, 1970)

Wilson, Colin, *New Pathways in Psychology: Maslow and the post-Freudian Revolution* (London: Victor Gollancz, 1972)

Wilson, Colin, *The Craft of the Novel* (Bath: Ashgrove Press, 1990)

Wilson, Colin, *The Books in my Life* (Charlottesville, VA: Hampton Roads 1998)

Wilson, Colin, *Super Consciousness: The Quest for the Peak Experience* (London: Watkins Publishing, 2009)

Bibliography:

Dossor, Howard F., *The Philosophy of Colin Wilson: Three Perspectives* (Nottingham: Paupers' Press, 1996)

Husserl, Edmund, *Ideas: General Introduction to Pure Phenomenology*, trans. by W. R. B. Gibson (London: HarperCollins, 1931)

Otto, Rudolph, *The Idea of the Holy* (London: Penguin, 1959)

Stanley, Colin, *Colin Wilson's Outsider Cycle: A Guide for Students* (Nottingham: Paupers' Press, 2009)

Wilson, Colin, *The Outsider* (London: Phoenix, 2001)

Wilson, Colin, *Religion and the Rebel* (Bath: Ashgrove Press, 1984)

Wilson, Colin, *The Age of Defeat* (Nottingham: Paupers' Press, 2001)

Wilson, Colin, *Introduction to the New Existentialism* (London: Hutchinson, 1966)

Wilson, Colin, ed., *The Essential Colin Wilson* (London: Grafton Books, 1987)

Wilson, Colin, *Dreaming to Some Purpose* (London: Century, 2004)

Appendix One

The Man Who Saw the Future, Colin Wilson and
T. C. Lethbridge: A Personal Appreciation

Terry Welbourn

Described by its curator as, "Three Dementianal (sic) Nights of Barbarian Rock 'n' Roll", Julian Cope's *Rome Wasn't Burned in A Day*, held at the Hammersmith Lyric in the autumn of 2003, culminated on 1st November with an event dedicated to the archaeologist and psychic investigator T.C. Lethbridge. As a guest of the musical collective known as 'The Sons of TC-Lethbridge', Colin Wilson delivered an entertaining lecture citing Lethbridge as, *"One of the most wide-ranging and original minds in modern parapsychology."* (Wilson 1978, p.46).

During his presentation, Wilson described how Lethbridge demonstrated his own potential for greatness that was akin to his own belief that man was at the centre of his own destiny. He described parallels between his own life and that of Lethbridge. In 1957, Routledge and Kegan Paul published Lethbridge's *Gogmagog - The Buried Gods*. The book documented Lethbridge's controversial discovery of chalk hill figures on the slopes of Wandlebury Camp, Cambridgeshire. The publication was to prove to be his most controversial work to-date and was destined to change the course of his life. The previous year had seen Wilson make his own headlines when *The Outsider* – published by Victor Gollancz – appeared in bookshops across the country and propelled him too into the media spotlight. The two writers had independently ignited contentious careers that would ultimately lead to their names being inextricably linked.

As a result of the storm in academia caused by the publication of *Gogmagog*, Lethbridge felt compelled to leave his home in Cambridge and move to Hole House in the Devonshire village of Branscombe. It is likely that Wilson perceived Lethbridge as a 'like-mind', for he too had found the need to move to the West Country to 'escape' the hostile glare of the media that misguidedly labelled him as one of the 'Angry Young Men' alongside the likes of John Osborne, John Braine and Kingsley Amis in the late 1950s. As Wilson pointed out in his lecture: this label was absurd as he was not angry at all, but when offered £500 for an interview on the subject he found it quite easy to think of something to be angry about! (Wilson 2003).

Wilson's lecture at the Hammersmith Lyric commemorated the release of *A Giant: The Definitive T.C. Lethbridge* – a double CD long-box set that included a 36-page booklet containing a new Lethbridge essay by Wilson and my own anthological review of Lethbridge's entire published works. The first CD contained rock music inspired by Lethbridge featuring, amongst others: Cope, Doggen Foster and Kevin Bales from the rock band Spiritualized. The second disc consisted of spoken-word contributions from Wilson set against sonically challenging backing tracks. Wilson had become a reluctant associate of rock 'n' roll, despite openly admitting he knew, or cared little about the musical genre! But how did this unlikely union come into being?

Discovering T.C. Lethbridge

On 24 September 1992, I was leafing through a copy of *The Independent* newspaper when I encountered a photograph of the rock musician Julian Cope leaning against the megalithic tomb known as The Devil's Den near Marlborough, Wiltshire. In the corresponding article, Cope discussed his recent interest in megalithic culture and his discovery of T.C. Lethbridge through the writings of Colin Wilson. The article struck a chord with me, for I too had discovered Lethbridge through Wilson's writings. By the end of the decade I had become acquainted with both

Cope and Wilson and it was this association that had culminated in the production of *A Giant* and the performance at the Hammersmith Lyric in 2003.

The planning and recording of *A Giant* was also an eventful affair. On 11 September 2001, as the twin towers burned in New York City, Cope and I proceeded to Gorran Haven to record Wilson's spoken word contributions for the Lethbridge project. It was an extraordinary day for everyone involved, not just because of the backdrop of the atrocities on the other side of the Atlantic, but to see two remarkable characters like Cope and Wilson thrown together in unusual circumstances. The day included a crash course, delivered by Cope, on rock terminology: phrases such as power-trio, axe-victim and speed-metal were added to Wilson's vocabulary!

My own interest in Wilson began on the morning of Thursday 19 November 1987, when I found myself on Newark station about to board an Inter City train destined for London King's Cross. The journey would have been typical of any grey, autumnal commute had it not been for an unfolding drama at the scene of my destination. The previous evening, a fire had swept through the underground section of King's Cross Station, causing massive devastation and resulting in the death of 31 passengers.

The experience of that fateful morning, if not significant enough already, had further implications in store. I had taken the opportunity of the journey to begin reading Colin Wilson's *Mysteries*, a weighty, intriguing tome that had been recommended to me by my friend the writer Simon Brighton. During my journey I had become engrossed with Wilson's masterwork and on arrival at King's Cross, I carefully bookmarked my page and closed the volume. I was unaware that the previous two hours of reading were destined to change my life. My train of thought was briefly interrupted by the mundane nature of my working day, but the return journey home to Lincoln provided me with another opportunity to continue my literary indulgence.

Published by Hodder and Stoughton in 1978, *Mysteries* is a tantalising sequel to Wilson's previous study *The Occult* in which he attempts to provide the *Principia* of psychic science by exploring a whole variety of occult phenomena including hauntings, demonic possession and precognition. However, the underlying theme focuses on mankind's own ability to utilise and harness its own untapped and neglected potential. *Mysteries* is split into three parts, but it was the first section that had intrigued me, for it was almost entirely dedicated to the ideas and investigations of a remarkable man called Thomas Charles Lethbridge.

Perhaps it would be an overstatement to say that *Mysteries* changed my life, but it did provide for me a portal into another world – a parallel universe. The following year I would stumble upon the magnificent stone circle of Avebury, a chance visitation that would lead to an ongoing preoccupation with prehistoric culture. As I progressed around the megalithic sites of Britain, both Wilson's and Lethbridge's mind-expanding theories became pertinent to my own undertakings.

I acquired my first T.C. Lethbridge book from a secondhand bookshop in Winchester whilst visiting the West Country over the August Bank Holiday weekend of 1988. *The Essential T.C. Lethbridge* edited by Tom Graves and Janet Hoult, is an assemblage of Lethbridge's investigations into occult phenomenon. The foreword to the book was written by Wilson who remarked upon Lethbridge's prevalent sense of humour and his, *"Good natured pragmatism that made his early books on archaeology so delightful."* (Lethbridge 1980, p.*xiv*) Wilson's words had placed a seed in my mind and as I progressed on my own megalithic crusade around Britain I felt it was pertinent to discover more about T.C. Lethbridge.

T.C. Who?

Lethbridge held the honorary position of Keeper of Anglo-Saxon Antiquities in the University Museum of Archaeology and Ethnology, Cambridge for over 30 years. A somewhat unremarkable career to the layman, yet Wilson is quoted as describing him as was one of the most remarkable and overlooked men of the 20th century. But why was this?

Initially, Lethbridge wrote a number of well-received books based on his passion and understanding of ancient British culture and maritime history: *Merlin's Island: Essays on Britain in the Dark Ages* (Methuen & Co., 1948), *Herdsmen & Hermits: Celtic Seafarers in the Northern Sea* (Bowes and Bowes, 1950), *Coastwise Craft* (Methuen & Co., 1952), *Boats and Boatmen* (Thames & Hudson, 1952) and *The Painted Men: A History of the Picts* (Andrew Melrose, 1954). Wilson believes that he demonstrated two key qualities that made him a good historian: a lively imagination and a consuming curiosity (*Ibid, p.vii*). However there were many strings to his bow: he was also an Arctic explorer, a talented artist and an experienced offshore sailor. It would therefore be remiss to state that Lethbridge was simply an archaeologist. In fact Wilson reminds us that Lethbridge complained that, *"Archaeologists never use their imagination; they only want to know what date something took place, or where the artefacts originated."*(Ibid, p.vii)

However, his wide-ranging pursuits progressed far beyond the remits of his vocation into areas that challenge our very understanding of the universe. Mention his name today and it is likely that you will draw only blank expressions. Occasionally however, you may hear the retort, *"Isn't he the pendulum man?"* It is sadly ironic that Lethbridge, like many great writers, should solely be remembered for single, specific aspects of their illustrious careers. Wilson too will sympathise here: continually being assimilated with *The Outsider, The Occult* and *Mysteries,* whilst being the author of well over 130 titles, many of equal standing, including the insightful and often overlooked *A Criminal History of Mankind* (Granada, 1984).

Lethbridge had a natural enquiring mind and initially, he had no interest in the paranormal: he simply wished to find things out. This prompted Wilson to describe him as, *"A kind of Sherlock Holmes."* (*Ibid* p.*xiv*) He believed that magic and the paranormal were simply powers of the mind that had yet to be explained by science. This was a view that appealed to Wilson's own scientific approach: Lethbridge was emphatically no 'occultist' (Wilson 1978, p.49).

"The more I read Lethbridge, the more I become convinced that he is the only investigator of the twentieth century that has produced a comprehensive and convincing theory of the paranormal." (*Ibid*, p.46)

It would be foolish then to simply divide Lethbridge's published work into two camps the 'historical' and the 'occult', for to do so would conceal the subtle, but profound evolution that occurred throughout his writing. What we witness in his work, as Wilson describes, is the development of an astonishing and original mind.

These enquiries were documented in eight remarkable books – published by Routledge and Kegan Paul – written during the last decade of his life: *Ghost and Ghoul* (1961), *Witches: Investigating an Ancient Religion* (1962), *Ghost and Divining Rod* (1963), *ESP: Beyond Time and Distance* (1965), *A Step in the Dark* (1967), *The Monkey's Tail* (1969), *The Legend of the Sons of God* (published posthumously, 1972) and *The Power of the Pendulum* (published posthumously, 1976). These publications, described by Wilson as, "marvellously readable" (Wilson 2003(2), p.6) document his investigations into occult matters, including ghosts, extra-sensory perception, divination, dreams and precognition.

Lethbridge believed that every inanimate object had the ability to store information: to somehow capture its history within itself. By using the pendulum as an instrument of detection, and by compiling tables of 'rates' he believed he could unlock information 'recorded' within any given object. Wilson stated that: *"Lethbridge was convinced that he had discovered a fundamental secret of nature – that everything has its own 'rate'"* (Wilson 1988, p.118)

Lethbridge's explanation of ghosts and ghouls was based on a similar theory; in that rooms, places or atmospheres, could, in the right given conditions, somehow 'record' themselves onto the ether. For these 'recordings' to be replayed, it would of course, require the right person and appropriate conditions to be present. It is a theory central to Nigel Neale and Peter Sasdy's cult film *The Stone Tape* – commissioned by the BBC as a Christmas ghost story in 1972.

Mysteries

Immediately after his death in a West Country nursing home in 1971, it seemed likely that Lethbridge's lifetime's achievements might be forgotten. Fortunately, this injustice was avoided by virtue of a number of coincidences that would lead to him being recognised as a crucial figure not just in the world of archaeology, but also in the field of psychical research.

In Cornwall during the 1960's, Wilson's wife Joy had been indulging herself in Lethbridge's ongoing research into psychic and occult matters. After the publication of Wilson's own book, *The Occult* in 1971, he was commissioned by his American publisher Random House to write a sequel. At the time, he had little idea what it was actually going to be about.

"It was Joy who solved the problem. I had picked up a second-

hand copy of a book by T.C. Lethbridge called Witches, written in a casual, personal style by a man who was obviously a scholar as well as an archaeologist and a dowser." (Wilson 2004, p.294)

Wilson immediately purchased all of Lethbridge's books, and after reading them he realised that his omission from *The Occult* was a major oversight. He simply had to champion the work of this extraordinary writer. He made a decision to pay gratitude to Lethbridge's original ideas by devoting the first four chapters of his new book to him.

Brooding over the sequel to *The Occult*, he sent a copy care of Lethbridge's publishers. Two weeks later, he received a reply from Lethbridge's wife Mina, explaining that her husband had recently died, and asking if she should return the book. Naturally, he told her to keep it, and invited her to come and stay at her convenience. When Mina, along with her friend Jo Erskine Collins, eventually drove to Cornwall from her home in South Devon, he was able to show her the opening chapters of the book that was eventually to become *Mysteries*.

Mina's association with Wilson also resulted in him contributing the foreword to Lethbridge's final, posthumous work that existed in typescript form. Lethbridge's working title for his final publication was *The Dream Book*, but was eventually published by Routledge and Kegan Paul as *The Power of the Pendulum*. Credit is therefore due to Wilson, for acknowledging Lethbridge as, *"One of the most remarkable and original minds in parapsychology."* (Lethbridge 1976, p. *ix-x*)

The Superconscious

Lethbridge believed that 'mind' was distinct from brain and that intellectual consciousness was a faculty that we had developed in our own development. He had problems with both the

Darwinian vision of evolution and the view expressed by the theologians. He believed that a middle way was the more likely solution to the conundrums of human development and the growth of consciousness. In his Foreword to *The Essential T.C. Lethbridge,* Wilson timely reminds us that, *"The mind does not study nature; it is intimately involved with it and cannot escape this involvement, except when engaged in the crudest form of measurement."* (Lethbridge 1980, p. *xiv*)

In *The Occult,* Wilson had discussed the work of J.W. Dunne and his extraordinary book *An Experiment with Time* (A. & C. Black Ltd, 1927). It would have come as no surprise to him on discovering that Lethbridge too had also cited Dunne as a major influence. He had come to accept, that on the next vibrational level, that he had discovered through the use of his pendulum, time and sequence were irrelevances and pertinent only for earth level existence. Dunne had identified a superconscious mind that lay beyond sleep and death. Lethbridge understood that mind was distinct from brain, which was simply an organ that acted as a censor for earth-level thinking. He described this realm as a 'country' where nothing could be quantified, or proved to the satisfaction of the earth-bound scientist. He astutely realised that the experimenter had to develop his own faith to satisfy himself. Experiments with the pendulum had led him to discover this and other dimensions, but he understood that it was our dreams that provided a glimpse into this 'other' world.

Wilson once remarked how Lethbridge's breezy willingness to admit that he might be quite wrong always remained basically reassuring to him. Many have criticised his work for being repetitive and inconclusive, but Wilson believed that this was necessarily so, stating: *"This seems to me to be one of the most exciting things about Lethbridge."* (Lethbridge 1976, p.*xv*) His ideas were constantly changing and he often felt the necessity to revisit topics in the advent of new evidence. By reading Lethbridge we are privy to a developing and evolving mind, which Wilson suggests is akin to the working journals of Leonardo, or any important discoverer.

"None of his books attempts to present a complete 'system' of ideas; a theme that is only mentioned in one may be developed in another. The final impression is of a brilliant, intuitive intelligence that never ceases to develop." (Ibid, p.xiv)

Only today, four decades after his death, science is finally beginning to acknowledge that he was one of the most remarkable investigators of his time. His understanding of dimensions operating on different vibrational rates is akin to String Theory, an ongoing branch of science instigated in the late 1960s by the theoretical physicist Gabriele Veneziano.

Wilson believes that his publishers Routledge and Kegan Paul are to be congratulated for their vision and foresight. Collectively, his later works build into a remarkable and unique study and demonstrate an enquiring mind unshackled by dogma and convention. Wilson goes as far as suggesting that Lethbridge be recognised as, "...*a classic: not just of parapsychology, but of English Literature." (Ibid, p. xx)*

Lethbridge, like Wilson, did not set out to be controversial, he viewed his approach as being simply 'common-sense', something that he believed was lacking not just in his own vocation, but in the wider field of academia. He perceived this inability to see beyond the literal as an affliction that he termed 'the block'. It was an obstacle that inhibited not only his profession, but also one that transcended all aspects of comprehension. He believed that mankind's true potential could only be released once we had rid ourselves of preconceived ideas and agendas. It was a philosophy close to Wilson's own heart.

Since the release of *A Giant* and the launch of an associated website dedicated to Lethbridge (www.tc-lethbridge.com), there now appears to be a growing audience who find his ideas even more pertinent and relevant in this new millennium. Lethbridge, like Wilson, revealed to me that there is more to the world than we are led to believe. The odd and the extraordinary are there to be disentangled and deciphered, not hidden away, or swept under the carpet.

The significance of events on that November day in 1987 when I first discovered Wilson's work become even more pertinent when I explain how I had missed the train down to King's Cross the previous evening due to a sudden and inexplicable change of heart. It was a journey that would have seen me entering the King's Cross underground system at the time of the fire. My possibly life-saving decision is an occurrence that happens to someone, somewhere everyday of the week, but it is during these moments of intense significance when we feel glad to be alive. It is these crucial moments, or 'glimpses' as Wilson refers to them, that enable us to readjust our focus away from everydayness onto the fundamentals of existence and maximise our potential. It is this train of thought that motivated Lethbridge to challenge the frontiers of his own existence.

References:

Lethbridge, T. C. (1976) *The Power of the Pendulum*, Routledge & Kegan Paul. *Foreword* by Colin Wilson.

Lethbridge, T. C. (1980) *The Essential T. C. Lethbridge*, Routledge & Kegan Paul. *Foreword* by Colin Wilson.

Wilson, Colin (1978) *Mysteries*, Hodder & Stoughton.

Wilson, Colin (1988) *Beyond the Occult*. Bantam Press.

Wilson, Colin (2003) 'Rome Wasn't Burned in a Day' Lecture at Hammersmith Lyric 1/11/03.

Wilson, Colin (2003(2)) *A Giant: the definitive T. C. Lethbridge*. Aegir Recording Company.

Wilson, Colin (2004) *Dreaming to Some Purpose*. Century.

Appendix Two

Dawn—Young—Heaven

Laura Del Rivo

The squalor of the café was peaceful. It gave absolution.

Colin was 21 when he first appeared in the café. He was lanky, bespectacled, practical in maintenance skills, everyouth except that he was a genius. He rode a bicycle for which he wore trouser clips. Sometimes the ladder that he used for speaking in Hyde Park was fastened to the crossbar. Although like Sorme he was the hero of his own intellectual *bildungsroman*, he was already a lecturer. He carried a leather satchel which contained spare food and the manuscript: literally handwritten: of his work in progress, the Sormebook, *Ritual in the Dark*.

Ritual is about a man who suspects that his friend is a serial killer. There was a juvenile prototype in which Sorme himself may or may not be the murderer. The draft in the satchel is still traceable in the final, published version. The triangle was in place whose points are intellect, physicality and emotion; in the novel, Sorme, Nunne and Glasp. Other early pieces include the old man episode followed by climbing out onto a roof, and the nightclub scene where Sorme vomits into a bluepatterned lavatory pan and later hallucinates Nunne as the *Spectre of the Rose*. These episodes and others which express loathing and alienation followed by exultation belong to the satchel draft. The oddly named Miss Quincey existed. Missing is a disturbing incident about drowning a mouse which in the satchel version had equality within the script.

The style is most experimental in the juvenile version and least in the published version. The version in the satchel was between. There was the blossom of chaos from order; and also small things e.g. "the" instead of "his" makes an object exist more heavily and obtrusively and "Sorme said:" works better for serious dialogue than "said Sorme". Style was less intrinsic than the angles and lighting of a noir film. When Colin read aloud I felt inspired as part of a new writing generation. He influenced many in the café whose student ageband made it an arena of intellectual, as well as social and sexual, adventure.

Rereading the published version, I experienced the same excitement. The prose has a rhythm, formed by its use of punctuation and cutting, like Prokofiev or modern jazz. Descriptions such as that of the subsidence of sexual desire: "He felt an ache across his chest and back, as if someone had beaten him with some padded objects" and revulsion: "He stood, holding the receiver, contemplating with distaste the moisture that had condensed round the mouthpiece from a previous user" are analytical. The author stands outside his pleasure or pain with a notebook.

At the time of the satchel draft, Colin had not yet met Bill Hopkins or Carol Ann who would appear in the final version as Bill Payne and Caroline. It was in fact Bill who suggested that the novel should open with the Diaghilev exhibition.

There is a line in Bill Hopkins' *The Divine and the Decay* which describes Plowart "shearing" through the water. I do not suppose that "shearing" was the original verb. I suspect that there was a lesser word and that "shearing" appeared in a visitation enabling Bill to *xxxx*-out and type in. The inevitability of "shearing" is of course in its double workload. It references overarm swimming and the ruthless character of Plowart.

The character of Bill Hopkins, like that of his prose, seemed the result of an act of will. He was the most charismatic man in the cafés, a verbal duelist using provocation, outrage and wit. I was ineptly in love with him.

When Colin lent his bundle of manuscript to Bill, it was returned with a note: "You are a man of genius. Welcome to our ranks" showing Bill's heroic style. However the hero externalizes

302

whereas Colin internalized. His genius was in his use of a writing style, which he deliberately discontinued, and in intellectual passion, which defined him. When I lived at home in Cheam, Colin hiked through Nonsuch Park, weak eyed against the wind, enthusiastically: literally possessed by a god: but also compulsively expounding. Intelligence is accompanied by an adrenalin rush. There was something obsessive compulsive about his need to communicate insight even to someone not good at understanding.

His susceptibility to women showed in paternalistic (potentially not actually perverted) kindliness and indulgence. This is clear in the treatment of the two women in *Ritual* and was a sexual form of his active tolerance of people in general.

An episode in *Ritual* describes a rich, befurred couple emerging from the lift of some mansion flats. Colin was born into the Leicester working class but unlike contemporaries Alan Sillitoe, John Osborne and John Braine, whose mindset is class politics, class is as irrelevant to Colin's obsession as it is to physics or mathematics. Sorme feels mildly benevolent towards the rich couple because he has the innate superiority of not needing validation by encumbrances. In this sense, he is free.

In later years, Colin has provided himself with the bourgeois comforts and routine, established with Joy, that he finds necessary for mature work. The Wilsons' house and outbuildings contain his library. Books of course exist as both matter and non matter.

The young Colin appeared as among disciples and antagonists in the cafés. He was and is spontaneously generous and helpful, taking responsibility for the welfare of friends. The hostility which he has since provoked in the literary world seems inexplicable without his qualities of rightly claiming genius and of affability. Their co-existence devalues the opponent as irrelevant. Colin is socially egalitarian and considerate but sees no social reason for false modesty about the stature and importance of his work. This is probably the reason why journalists set-off for Cornwall with their malicious articles pre-determined as if interviewing Antichrist.

Psychological Types by Carl Jung (1921) describes a man who "shrinks from no danger in the world of ideas. He will not shrink from thinking a thought because it is dangerous or offensive and when he launches his work onto the world it is not in the manner of a solicitous parent. He simply dumps it there and gets extremely offended if it fails to thrive of its own account. If in his eyes a work appears correct and true then it must be so in practice and others must bow to its truth."

Jung continues that this man "usually has problems with rivals in his field because he does not understand how to curry their favour," and that "he provokes the most violent opposition."*

The dichotomy in Colin's recent *Super Consciousness: the Quest for the Peak Experience* is the same as the dichotomy in *Ritual in the Dark*; exactly that between the pit and the sublime. *Ritual* examines ideas sufficiently dangerous to an experimental student. The published version can or can not be informed by the fever of rewritings and the organic connection of being carried in a satchel in and out of cafés and lodgings. What is certain is that the evolutionary obsession of *Super Consciousness* is the same as the evolutionary obsession of the protagonist, Colin Wilson or Gerard Sorme, cycling through bomb damaged 1950s London.

---

* The abridged quotations from *Psychological Types* are from Jung's subheading 'The Introverted Thinking Type'. Jung's analysis covers 4 or 5 close pages but most is inappropriate to Colin as it deals with a socially and sexually inept academic. Colin on the other hand is cheerful, at home in the world and has the alpha male's protective instinct; i.e. chivalry.

Appendix Three

scuba-ing for colin wilson

Vaughan Robertson (aka Rapatahana)

　　　　slicing
the sluice　gates of mind
　　d
　　o
　　w
　　n
the *giddy*
existential
arroyo,

verging
bifurcate –

which
way
to slalom?

those
sybaritic
synapse -

a quick
d
　i
　　p

　　in
　　to

logjam -

red wine
bed women
dead writers –

or

Wilson's plangent
gravitas?

contrapuntal
vista,

symbiotic – yet

so
faaaaaaaar
a p a r t.

peak
snorkeling for ^ experience

I
dive
   i
     n
       t
         o
          the
             channel
                 less taken

pullulating,

drenched,

t o w a r d the light.

Notes on Contributors

Thomas F. Bertonneau

studied Comparative Literature at UCLA, where he was a
student of Eric L. Gans, the originator of "Generative
Anthropology." Bertonneau is the author of over one hundred
publications primarily in the field of literary scholarship, but
extending to religion, cultural anthropology, linguistics, music,
and history. He is the co-author with Kim Paffenroth of *The Truth
is Out There* (2006), a study of the religious thematics of science
fiction, and a contributor to the scholarly anthologies *Augustine
and Literature* (2001) and *The Originary Hypothesis* (2009).
Bertonneau is a regular contributor to *Anthropoetics, Modern Age,
Praesidium,* and *The Brussels Journal.* He has been visiting
professor at SUNY College Oswego since 2001, where he teaches
the survey of ancient literature in translation and the science
fiction course, among other courses. Bertonneau's interest in
Colin Wilson goes back to his teens in the mid-1960s when he
first read *The Mind Parasites.* He is the happy owner of an
autographed copy of the original American edition of *Necessary
Doubt.*

Simon Brighton

is a writer and musician, his latest book, co-authored with Terry
Welbourn, is 'Echoes of the Goddess' a survey of the British
Goddess and her many forms in history. In 2003 Simon and Terry
collaborated with Colin Wilson on *A Giant,* a double CD of music
and spoken word celebrating the work of archaeologist T. C.
Lethbridge. He started reading Colin Wilson while living in a
flat in Balham, London, in the early 1980s, where a copy of *The
Occult* had been left by a visitor. After reading, "the rest of the
1980s were spent in London's second hand bookshops looking
for more Wilson books." He first met Colin Wilson, with Terry
Welbourne, in the early 1990s at the Wilson home in Cornwall,

staying, coincidentally, at the campsite where Colin and Joy Wilson had stayed on their first visit to the county in the 1950s.

Stephen R. L. Clark

formerly a Fellow of All Souls College, Oxford (1968-75), Lecturer in Moral Philosophy at the University of Glasgow (1974-83), and Professor of Philosophy at the University of Liverpool (1984-2009), is now retired from paid employment. He continues to manage an international e-list for philosophers, and to serve as Associate Editor of the *British Journal for the History of Philosophy*. His books include *Aristotle's Man* (1975), *The Moral Status of Animals* (1977), *From Athens to Jerusalem* (1984), *The Mysteries of Religion* (1986), *Civil Peace and Sacred Order* (1989), *How to Live Forever* (1995), *Biology and Christian Ethics* (2000), *G.K.Chesterton: Thinking Backwards, Looking Forwards* (2006), and *Understanding Faith* (2009). A further study: *How to Reconstruct the Mind: Myth, Metaphor and Philosophical Practice in Plotinus* with Panayiota Vassilopoulou is forthcoming. He is married to Prof Gillian Clark of Bristol University, with three adult children and one grandson. His chief current interests are in the philosophy of Plotinus, the understanding and treatment of non-human animals, and in science fiction.

Philip Coulthard

was born in May 1968 in the north-east of England. Stints as a student, mail-room clerk, industrial hygienist and hospital porter were made bearable by his discovery of Colin Wilson's writings, aged 18. He now lives and works in the north-east of Scotland where he runs a Wilson website at www.colin-wilsononline.com. He lives with his wife and two cats in a flat with too many books.

Laura Del Rivo

was born in 1934 in North Cheam, Surrey and educated at Holy

Cross Convent, New Malden and later in certain Soho cafés. In 1956 she moved into a house in Notting Hill that was full of writers and painters. It was here that she wrote her first published novel *The Furnished Room* (1961). This was filmed by Michael Winner in 1963 as *West 11* and is soon to be reprinted by Five Leaves Publishers. Her next novel *Daffodil on the Pavement* appeared in 1967. *Speedy and Queen Kong*, written between 1984 and 1988, was published by Paupers' Press in 2004. She is now working on two new stories *The Confessions of Anna Rexia* and *The Undeserving Old*. Since 1964 she has worked as a market trader on Portobello Road. Her hobbies include books, going for muddy walks and being left alone.

Antoni Diller

was born in 1953 in Birmingham, England, of Polish parents who were forced to leave their homeland by the Russians during the Second World War. After studying mathematics, philosophy, theology and computation at various universities, he eventually got a job as a lecturer in computer science at the University of Birmingham in 1987. For the next ten years or so he devoted his energies to computing and wrote three books on several aspects of the subject. Then, his interests reverted to philosophy, especially the study of testimony and the ideas of the philosopher Karl Popper. He won the 2008 Sir Karl Popper Essay Prize for: "On Critical and Pancritical Rationalism". He has been interested in those Angry Young Men that Kenneth Allsop called 'The Law Givers' since reading *The Outsider* when he was about thirteen. Over the years he has sought out their writings. In the last few years he has been studying the Law Givers more seriously. In particular, he has been researching the life and times of Stuart Holroyd. The first product of this research was the article "Holroyd in London" published in *Abraxas* in 2007. Antoni Diller is also a trained counsellor specialising in Rational Emotive Behaviour Therapy.

Murray Ewing

has been running *The Violet Apple* (www.violetapple.org.uk), a website dedicated to the life and works of David Lindsay, since 1998. Like Lindsay, he is half-Scottish, half-English, and lives in the South East of England.

Stanley Krippner

is professor of psychology at Saybrook University, and has served as president of the International Association for the Study of Dreams, the Association for Humanistic Psychology, the Parapsychological Association, and two divisions of the American Psychological Association. He is the co-author of *Personal Mythology*, *The Mythic Path*, *Spiritual Dimensions of Healing*, *Dream Telepathy*, *Extraordinary Dreams and How to Work with Them*, and *Haunted by Combat: Understanding PTSD in War Veterans*. He is the editor of *Dreamtime and Dreamwork* and eight volumes of *Advances in Parapsychological Research*. In 2002 he was the recipient of the American Psychological Association's Award for Distinguished Contributions to the International Advancement of Psychology, and the Society of Psychological Hypnosis' Award for Distinguished Contributions to Professional Hypnosis. He was the 2003 recipient of the Ashley Montague Peace Award, and has received lifetime achievement awards from the International Association for the Study of Dreams and the Parapsychological Association. He is a Fellow of the American Psychological Association, the Association for Psychological Science, the Society for the Scientific Study of Religion, and the Society for the Scientific Study of Sexuality. In 1992, the Society for Humanistic Psychology presented him with the Charlotte and Carl Buhler Award for Inspired and Distinguished Leadership in Education and Research in Humanistic Psychology, and in 1998, the Association for Humanistic Society gave him the Pathfinder Award for Enduring Contributions to the Exploration and Expansion of Human Consciousness.

Gary Lachman

is the author of several books on the meeting ground between consciousness, culture, and the western esoteric tradition, including *Jung the Mystic: The Esoteric Dimensions of Carl Jung's Life and Teachings; Politics and the Occult: The Left, The Right, and the Radically Unseen; The Dedalus Book of Literary Suicides: Dead Letters;* and *A Secret History of Consciousness*. He is a frequent contributor to the *Independent on Sunday, Fortean Times,* and other journals in the UK and US. As Gary Valentine he was a founding member of the rock group Blondie and is the author of *New York Rocker: My Life in the Blank Generation,* a memoir of his years as a musician. In 2006 was inducted into the Rock and Roll Hall of Fame. Lachman lectures regularly in London and abroad on the history of the counterculture and the western inner tradition and broadcasts occasionally for Radio 3 and 4.

Chris Nelson

was born in Texas, 1967. He took an English degree from the University of Iowa and is currently a writer and musician living in Seattle. He first encountered Colin Wilson's work in his early teens when his unsuspecting brother handed him a used copy of *The Occult* at a church book fair. He read the book thinking it had been written for him; the floodgates, once opened, never closed. Has written introductions to Maurice Bassett's e-book publications of Wilson's *The Ladder of Selves* and *The Search for Power Consciousness*. He is the author of the forthcoming novel, *The Dreaming Gods*.

Paul Newman

Former editor of the literary magazine *Abraxas* – incorporating the Colin Wilson Newsletter – Paul Newman has produced books and articles covering subjects as diverse as symbolism, topography and literature. Titles include a folklore study *The Hill of the Dragon* (1979); *The Meads of Love* (1994), a life of the poet-miner, John Harris and illustrated books on Bath and Bristol. Together with the sculptor A.R. Lamb, he shared a poetry collection *In Many Ways Frogs* (1997), followed by *Lost Gods of Albion* (1998), a study of British hill-figures; *A History of Terror: Fear and Dread Down the Ages* (2000); *The Tregerthen Horror* (2006) and *The Man Who Unleashed the Birds: Frank Baker & His Circle* (2009). His Arthurian novel *Galahad* (2003) was awarded the Peninsula Prize and he was among the international scholars who contributed to Scribner's *Dictionary of Ideas*.

George C. Poulos

was born in the mid-western New South Wales, (Australia), country town of Gilgandra in 1952. He moved to Sydney at 17 years of age to attend the University of New South Wales. A nascent transcendist, he had already read works by Camus, Sartre, Dostoyevsky, Nietzsche, James and others by his late teens. In 1971, he was given a copy of *The Outsider*, by a then girlfriend. "*The Outsider*, and later, the *Outsider cycle*, was amongst the first books directly responsible for vast changes in the manner in which I lived my life. When I encountered them later in life, *The Occult* and *Mysteries* had a similarly overwhelming effect upon me. Over forty years as a devotee, I have awaited the release of each new Wilson publication with keen anticipation. He has never disappointed. I also enjoy meeting other Wilson devotees immensely. The question Wilson grapples with in all his work is – what is man's purpose on earth? I am convinced that he has taken us to the edge of discerning *the answer*. Wilson's existence, and the existence of his body of work, make an answer **imminent** and inevitable."

George lives on the coast, in Sydney's eastern suburbs, with wife Lorraine, and near his two children, Angelique and Dean.

David Power

His initial interest was rock music. In the early 1980s he played in a number of bands and appeared on the compilation album *New Belief in Old Cities*. However, he become interested in more experimental music and, in due course, he changed direction and went to study composition with Richard Steinitz, Steve Ingham and Roger Marsh. His *Three Chamber Pieces* was premiered at the 1987 Huddersfield Contemporary Music Festival and since then his work has been performed widely. He has received a number of commissions over the years. In 1995 his *Seven Songs* was broadcast on BBC Radio Three. In 1996, he was composer-in-Residence at the Go West Festival. In recent years his music has become markedly simpler and he has become particularly interested in song writing. In 2009, his music was used in two short films by Annabel McCourt –   *Spooky* and *The Identity Crisis*. These can been seen on www.cutlimited.co.uk. In 2010, his electronic composition *Invisible Sample* received a number of performances in Germany, Italy and the USA. His *Eight Miniatures* for solo piano are on the Grimsby St Hughs Festival 2009 Highlights CD. In 1995 he co-founded the Late Music Festival in York. In 2008 he formed the acclaimed Grimsby St Hughs Festival following receipt of a substantial award from the St Hughs foundation. He has had many articles and reviews published in periodicals such as *London Magazine, Abraxas, Tempo* and the *New Statesman*. He is also the author of two short books published by Paupers' Press – *David Lindsay's Vision* (preface by Colin Wilson) and *David Bowie: A Sense of Art*; the latter was republished in the USA by Maurice Bassett in 2005.

Vaughan Robertson (aka Rapatahana)

is a New Zealander (Te AtiAwa is the **iwi** or tribe.) Always been marginalized – thus an Outsider by birth. Ph.D entitled *Existential Literary Criticism and the Novels of Colin Wilson*. Author of multifarious articles and reviews on the work of Wilson e.g *Wilson as Mystic* [Paupers' Press, U.K] as well as original philosophy in own right. Poet and published extensively as such around the World. Longlisted for the Proverse Prize in Literature in 2009. Author of the poetry teaching resource series *English Through Poetry*, 2007-2009 [User Friendly Resources, N.Z, Australia, U.K]. Has lived in Australia, Republic of Nauru, PR China, Brunei Darussalam, Hong Kong, UAE and has homes in Aotearoa [New Zealand] and Pampanga, Philippines, from where his wife hails.

Colin Stanley

was born in Topsham, Devon, UK in 1952 and educated at Exmouth School. Beginning in 1970, he worked for Devon Library Services, studying for two years in London, before moving to Bovey Tracey with his wife, Gail, and thence to Nottingham where he worked for the University of Nottingham until July 2005. One of the founders and Managing Editor of Paupers' Press, he now works part-time for the Universities of Oxford and Nottingham Trent, spending the rest at the cinema and theatre, listening to music, writing, editing, reading and watching cricket. One of his current projects involves writing a series of articles about Colin Wilson's non-fiction for the online *Literary Encyclopedia* administered by the University of East Anglia (www.litencyc.com). He is the author of two experimental novels, *First Novel* and *Novel 2*; *Sense-less*: a slim volume of nonsense verse, and several books and booklets about Colin Wilson and his work. He is the editor of *Colin Wilson Studies*, a series of books and extended essays, written by Wilson scholars worldwide. His collection of Colin Wilson's work forms the basis of a Wilson archive at the University of Nottingham. He now resides with Gail by the River Trent, close to Trent Bridge cricket ground. Their two children, Andrew and Katrina-Jane, have long-since moved on.

Steve Taylor

is the author of *Out of Time; The Fall; Waking From Sleep* and his new book, *Out of the Darkness,* which was published by Hay House earlier in 2011. *The Fall* was described by Colin Wilson as 'an astonishing work', while Eckhart Tolle described *Waking From Sleep* as 'one of the best books on spiritual awakening I have come across.' Steve is a university lecturer and researcher in transpersonal psychology, based at Leeds Metropolitan and Liverpool John Moores Universities. His essays and articles have been published in over 40 magazines, journals and newspapers, including *The International Journal of Transpersonal Studies, The Journal of Transpersonal Psychology, The Journal of Consciousness Studies, Resurgence, Kindred Spirit* and *The Daily Express.* He lives in Manchester with his wife and three young children. His website is www.stevenmtaylor.com

Nicolas Tredell

His books include *Existence and Evolution: The Novels of Colin Wilson* (1982; second edn, 2004); *Uncancelled Challenge: The Work of Raymond Williams* (1990); *The Critical Decade: Culture in Crisis* (1993); *Conversations with Critics* (1994); *Caute's Confrontations: The Novels of David Caute* (1994); *Fighting Fictions: The Novels of B. S. Johnson* (2000; second edn, 2010); *Cinemas of the Mind: A Critical History of Film Theory* (2002); and *The Great Gatsby: A Continuum Reader's Guide* (2007). He was contributing editor of *PN Review* from 1983-9 and a judge of the Geoffrey Faber Memorial Prize for Poetry in 1994. Since 1999, he has been Consultant Editor of the Palgrave Macmillan Essential Criticism Guides series, which now numbers over sixty volumes, seven of which he has himself produced. He has published essays, articles, reviews and interviews in many publications and journals including *Cambridge Guide to Literature in English; Contemporary Authors; Dictionary of Literary Biography; London Review of Books; PN Review; Times Literary Supplement;* and *Wordsworth Companion to Literature in*

English. Like Colin Wilson, he comes originally from Leicester and the discovery of *Ritual in the Dark* and *The Outsider* were among the most important experiences of his early teens. His *Novels of Colin Wilson* was the first book on Wilson's fiction and he has found Wilson's example a constant inspiration during his life as a writer. His homepage is http://www.nicolastredell.co.uk

Geoff Ward

is a British journalist, media consultant, author and musician who lives in Somerset, England. For several years, he has managed the website which he created as an appreciation of Colin Wilson (www.colinwilsonworld.co.uk) and, in 2009, Geoff launched his own world mysteries website (www.mysterious-planet.net). He is the author of *Spirals: the Pattern of Existence*, published by Green Magic in 2006 with an introduction by Colin Wilson. A former newspaper editor, Geoff Ward has a Masters degree and a BA (Hons) degree in English literature; the subject of his MA dissertation was how Wilson's ideas, building on those of the American psychologist Abraham Maslow, illuminate the existential significance of the peak experience, or 'epiphany', in the modernist novel. In addition to English literature and world mysteries, Geoff's key interests are the works of Colin Wilson, existential philosophy, Jungian psychology, cosmology and holistic science, the music of Bob Dylan, visiting heritage sites and writing short stories – he's also played lead guitar in several rock bands. He is married to Angie and they have two grown-up children in their 20s.

Terry Welbourn

has recently completed a biography of the archaeologist and psychic investigator T.C. Lethbridge. Entitled *The Man Who Saw the Future*, it is to be published by O-Books in 2011. He is also the co-author, along with Simon Brighton, of *Echoes of the Goddess: A Quest for the Sacred Feminine in the British Landscape* (Ian Allen,

2010). Born in Grantham, Lincolnshire in 1958, he studied Graphic Design at Lincolnshire College of Art and has since worked as a graphic designer; initially for the NHS and most recently for his own design agency Tekh Ltd. After 32 years of living in Lincoln, he has recently moved back to his hometown where he continues to pursue his many writing projects and currently works part-time as an Art and Design Technician at a local school. In 1998, he chanced upon the stone circle of Avebury; an encounter that was to ignite a life-long fascination with prehistoric culture. To-date, he has visited over 1,000 monuments and accumulated a unique assemblage of photographs and accompanying notes. In 1996, he became acquainted with the musician and author Julian Cope and contributed photographs and notes to Cope's *The Modern Antiquarian* (Thorsons, 1998). Discovering that they shared a mutual appreciation of T.C. Lethbridge, a musical collective, known as 'The Sons of T.C.-Lethbridge' was established. The collaboration resulted in the release of *A Giant* in November 2003 and an associated website: www.tc-lethbridge.com. In 2005 Terry Welbourne produced and recorded *Mayday! Mayday! – The Stan Gooch EP*, a CD dedicated to, and featuring, the writer Stan Gooch. The recording once again features the voice of Colin Wilson.

Index

Notes:

Main entries are in **bold** type.

All book titles are listed in *italics* followed by the author's surname in brackets. (W) indicates by Wilson.

Essay titles are listed in 'single inverted commas' followed by the author's surname. (W) indicates by Wilson.

Concepts are listed in "double inverted commas"